Celebrating Honoring Healing

Celebrating Honoring Healing

Engaging the Spirit through Ritual

A Collection of Earth-based Rituals

Suzanne Reitz and
Sandy Hoyt

Cover photograph of Sacsayhuaman in Peru by Ron Rosenstock

Cover design: Carole Allen Design Studio
Interior design: Carole Allen Design Studio

The Incan imperial city of Cusco means 'navel of the earth'. It was laid out in the shape of a puma, the animal that symbolized the Inca dynasty. The belly of the puma is the main plaza of Cusco, the river Tullumayo forms the puma's spine, and the hill of Sacsayhuaman is the puma's head.

The Quechua Shamans, descendants of the Inca, have shared their spirituality with many people around the world. Several of our rituals are influenced by the practices of the Quechua shamans and their spirituality. Calling on Jaguar, or Puma, in the West to be present at a ritual is an example of this.

Today, Sacsayhuaman is a UNESCO World Heritage site.

Printed by CreateSpace, An Amazon.com Company

ISBN-10 1514237385
ISBN-13 978-1514237380

We dedicate this book to

The Reverend Ken Sawyer and the members of First Parish in Wayland

Their openness to all forms of spirituality and their unquestionable support became the foundation upon which this book was able to become a reality

Twenty one years ago, we were inspired by the course Cakes for the Queen of Heaven, led by Sandy Schwalm and Ellen Rowan and held at our Church, First Parish Wayland. Our thanks go to these two forward thinking women who led the course and started us on our way.

Drawing on our new inspirations, and the openness and support of our minister Ken Sawyer and the members of First Parish Wayland, we were able to create and offer earth-based, feminine-embracing rituals. We are deeply grateful for this heartfelt and sustaining support, even when their understanding of the world did not always match ours.

We greatly appreciate the advice and support of so many people who helped us bring this book into being. Thank you to Evelyn Wolfson, professional author, who introduced us to the world of book writing, Kate Holland Community Life Director, who introduced us to the possibility of a grant, to Chip Roth, our editor, and Carole Allen, our graphic artist.

Our gratitude goes to the invaluable assistance of Ginny Guenette for graciously allowing us to adapt her story. Many thanks to the assistance of Ginny Elsenhans who read and critiqued an early version of these rituals, Amy Meneely,who guided us through the grant application writing and Ron Rosenstock, who enthusiastically provided the cover picture.

And our Cakes group! We are grateful for your encouragement and loyal friendship over the past eighteen years. In addition, our thanks go to Deborah Kelsey and Laurel Whitehouse for their help in creating some of the rituals. To the many people who attended our rituals over the years, we are deeply appreciative that you came out in all kinds of weather so willingly and enthusiastically.

And we cannot end without giving credit to our husbands and children for their support and love. We are thrilled that our friendship has survived the trials and tribulations of the work and passion we have put into this collection of our rituals. To everyone above, we extend sincere gratitude.

Table of Contents

About the Meaning of Ritual for Us

Ritual brings a richness, depth of meaning and reverence of the sacred into our lives in a very immediate and tangible manner. We make manifest our beliefs, our gratitude, our hopes and awe through our ceremonies, some handed down through the ages, some adapted and some newly created and inspired.

Our intention is to bring ritual to people from the experiences of our mind, heart and spirit. There is a danger that ritual can become rote, mechanistic and lacking in vibrancy and meaning. It can be an empty shell. Creating and offering our rituals sourced in our own experience, a deep commitment to our beliefs and a desire to share with others through ritual has helped us avoid this problem. We strive to offer each ritual from the passion found in our own being. The companion goal, which we hold ever before us, is our desire to help each person touch the Sacred in their own way within the ritual setting. In this way, we can use our own experience and passion in ritual, balanced by a sincere desire to offer and respect the personal experience of each person present. There will most likely be as many different experiences as there are people present at the ritual, each to be honored in their own right.

For 13 years we, Suzanne and Sandy, have been on a search for ritual ideas. Some of the best ideas were found in other books. However there is a scarcity of such books that also offer suggestions on the 'how to' of ritual that facilitate the smooth flow of the ritual and enable the leader to maintain the atmosphere and intention of the ritual with ease. This book is a response to that lack. It includes suggestions on how to run and organize a successful ritual with details that may appear trivial or inconsequential. We have observed that it was often the small details that have caused us to lose our focus during a ritual. Therefore each ritual will contain instructions that help the leader create and hold sacred space. It is our sincere hope that these be seen as suggestions, practices that have worked for us, but that can be and should be adapted to fit your own style and situation. In this way, the rituals may become an expression of your own passion and a sincere offering to others.

Our paths to ritual are different but similar. We both took the first Cakes for the Queen of Heaven class that was offered at our church. Cakes for the Queen of Heaven is a Unitarian Universalist curriculum written by Rev Shirley Ranck. The class explores the history and practices of Goddess worship and the Sacred Feminine. As with many Cakes classes, after the class was over we formed a feminine spirituality group which we creatively called Cakes. From the beginning, the group has felt strongly that the feminine model of non-hierarchical leadership was an expression of our feminine spirituality and therefore an integral part of our process. We have met monthly for 20 years with each member taking a turn creating and offering ritual. This has proven to be a source of strength and connection over the years. We have all learned and grown both personally and as a group in our rituals and our spirituality.

Sharing them with the larger UU community seemed to be the next step. As it turned out, there was a ready audience. We discovered that there was a group of people, both men and women, who wanted to experience earth-based rituals that included a strong emphasis on the sacred feminine. As Lay Ministers in a church that is open to all forms of spirituality, we were excited and honored to have the chance to offer monthly earth-based rituals open to all in the congregation who wished to attend. We began offering ritual in the year 2000. Our format and practice has deepened. The attendance varies anywhere from 6 to 25 people, occasionally including 2 to 5 men. We find this small number of attendees more satisfying than the grand scale rituals we have attended with 100 participants.

At our annual church auction people bid on our house blessing, which has been a popular item over the years. Parishioners have requested that we offer ritual for them in their times of transition, such as moving, divorce, birthday celebrations and croning. The ritual for the Sunday school and a summer lay-led service for the congregation are annual events. We have also opened and closed Church services, meetings and retreats during the year. To walk in a good way in ritual is to act with integrity and impeccability both within the ritual setting and within our lives.

Suzanne says: My holistic nursing background and my training over the last 11 years in Andean shamanism have deepened my respect and joy in ceremony. For me, earth-based spirituality seeks a constant connection with the Sacred, which is found in all things. As a woman, I also have a deep desire to honor the sacred feminine and her ways. Guiding and writing meditations is an aspect of ritual that I especially enjoy and find deeply rewarding.

Sandy says: My understanding of the goddess and earth-based religions has helped me through the crises of life. I bring my skills as a Children's Librarian and storyteller to composing and leading ritual. Based on my experience conducting programs and leading groups, I bring a how-to aspect to ritual. My talent lies in organizing and planning events to flow smoothly and to meet the needs of the participants.

Walk Through a Ritual with Us

Preparation/Inspiration

When creating ritual, we find inspiration in many ways and places, but it usually means returning to our own experience, to what has been meaningful, exciting, enlivening to one of us. Working with this inspirational idea or event begins to shape the theme of the ritual. Some of the questions we might ask are: Is this a ritual to celebrate an event or a season? What is the meaning of the event or season at this particular time? What do I want to bring about with this ritual? What is the nugget of the inspiration that I have experienced and how can I bring this into ritual? As the ritual begins to take shape, sometimes the theme may change.

When creating a ritual at one of the equinoxes or solstices we ask ourselves: what is it about the summer, fall, winter, spring that moves us to look within, seek healing, celebrate or honor the sacred? Ideas can come from anywhere, books or lectures, the practices of other cultures, meditations, or events in the community that would benefit from a ritual. When we are in balance and open to the world around us, we may be inspired by Spirit and the unseen realms in many ways.

After setting the theme, we start to talk and banter around ideas, brainstorming the shape or possible details of the ritual and how it might manifest. We research other rituals in books, on the web and that we have participated in. After we develop a more concrete concept of how the ritual will look, we begin to write, passing initial write ups back and forth for ideas and editing. This works well for us because we have a strong policy with each other of honesty, speaking openly and from the heart.

The next step is revising. We speak the parts, often literally walking through the ritual as if in a dress rehearsal. This makes a huge difference. It becomes clear what sounds good, what flows smoothly together and what fits – and what does not. We never skip speaking the ritual, as writing for speaking is quite different from writing for silent reading.

Once the ritual is set, we offer these rituals at our church, and use all opportunities to advertise using several formats. We make verbal announcements, display posters and publish a brochure to be handed out. We also have an e-mail list, use word of mouth and place a notice on our church's website. It is important to use any opportunities to advertise that fit your situation. People are so bombarded with information these days that it is important to try to appeal to as many senses as you can and to have as many different forms of advertising as possible.

Setting Up

After walking through the ritual we are ready to set up. First we clear the room if it feels needed - using smudge, spray, bells, bowls, or rattles --whatever feels right at that time. It seems to us that it makes a subtle difference in the way that people approach the room and respond to the ritual. When the room feels calm and ready, we prepare the altar. Although we use the same room each time, we decide each time where in the room it feels right to place the altar. We consider lighting, people's actions, whether we are asking the participants to move around during the ritual, and whether we want the altar table higher or lower or on the floor. How many people are coming is a factor in all of these decisions.

Our basic setup is a cloth on the altar with candles for the four directions and one for the center. A snuffer, a small lighter candle with a saucer to catch drips and matches are necessities that sit on the altar. For the cloth we like all kinds of material - glitzy, quiet, or with indigenous patterns. The choice of the cloth is sometimes purely visual and at other times based on the spirit of the ritual. We prefer to have a cloth that falls close to the floor.

The direction candles may be the color of the direction, red in the south for fire; blue in the west for water; green in the north for earth; white in the east for air. This is the usual custom, but it is not necessary and sometimes we use tea lights, or no candles at all. Sometimes we decorate the directions reflecting the symbolism of their meaning, such as stones, feathers, shells, or a unique candle. Let your imagination flower and use what seems appropriate to you. One candle is used for the center, or sometimes two for the Above and Below, depending on how we are calling the directions.

The altar is then decorated with items for the ritual as listed in each ritual and with appropriate decorative elements such as leaves or stones or ribbons to set a festive mood. Sometimes we use flowers on the altar or throughout the room.

In the rest of the room, we tend to use lots of candles and cloths for other tables that might be in the space and that will hold the candles or flowers. Chairs are placed around the altar, with space between the chairs and the altar for participants to walk around, if that is part of the ritual. After everything is all set, we have a dress rehearsal and make any last minute changes that seem right.

Once the room is set up in the afternoon, we go home and have dinner. We return refreshed and calm. If you have to set up just before the ritual, it is important to keep the participants out, so that they walk into a room that looks magical and instantly sets a mood. In addition, if you smudge them outside of the room and let them all in together, a mood is created that helps separate the every day world from the magic world of the ritual.

Just prior to opening the doors, we smudge the altar and room, dim the lights and light all the candles except the directional ones on the altar. We take a deep breath and center. Music is played if it suits the ritual and the atmosphere we are establishing.

Parts of a Basic Ritual

Smudging

Smudging is a way of clearing negative energy. Native people throughout the world burn herbs such as mugwort, sage, sweetgrass or palo santo from Peru. Herbs come bundled or loose. Sage is commonly either. Sweetgrass is braided. Palo Santo is a stick. To smudge, light the herb. If you are using an herb that is loose, a small flame proof container or shell may be used to hold the herb. Then direct the smoke over the person's body from head to toe with your hands, a feather or moving the smudge stick down the body. Be sure to do both front and back.

We refer to a smudge setup in the List of Items for a ritual. This would include the smudge, matches, a candle, and a holder for the smudge and any ashes that might collect.

Before entering sacred space, we choose a smudge mistress to stand outside the room and smudge the participants and us before we enter. We often use Palo Santo from Peru or a sage stick. This encourages participants to enter in a respectful mood and discourages social talking, which can be disruptive of the ritual mood we are trying to establish. It also helps participants leave behind the cares and joys of the day and enter into a sacred space in a quieter mood.

During our first years of leading ritual, we would smudge inside the room, off to one side, or in the vestibule of the Church Parish House. In both places there are appropriately placed smoke detectors. Before one of our rituals, as we were carefully and respectfully smudging everyone in the vestibule, the smoke detector went off. Very promptly the fire department visited us, in full force and attire, and with two engines, ready to put out the fire. They were met by a group of slightly embarrassed women, the rather "odd" smell of smudge, and a room set for a ritual meal complete with wine glasses. They sniffed suspiciously, looked very confused as they gazed into the ritual room and shook their heads politely. We apologized amid a few giggles and lots of red faces, and they went on their way, but it was the last time we smudged inside the building. We have had some wonderful chuckles since, but it is an event to avoid if possible. Not only does it pull everyone out of a ritual space, it costs the community quite a sum of money and the firemen a huge inconvenience.

Calling the Directions

When calling the directions, one may invoke the archetypes, spirits, or gods and goddesses. The participants in the circle may stand or sit or turn to the direction being called. There is no correct way, only what the ritual demands. Standing or turning to face the direction that is being called is a way of grounding the group if it is needed. It also emphasizes the creating of sacred space because we ask the participants to be more actively involved.

Since there are two of us, one reads or speaks and one lights the candles. This gives a more ceremonial feeling to the ritual. We often use a "lighter candle' or a long match because constantly scratching a match can be an annoying sound and looks less than smooth. We have seen participants react to the noise of the scratching match. Such minor things can be disruptive of the mood. When using a lighter candle it is important to have a small saucer to catch drips while moving around the altar. Volunteers may be used for the lighting of the candles.

Introduction

We explain the symbolism, mythology, theme, and origins of practices, or our goal in a brief, ceremonial manner. We give the essence of the ritual but try not to rob the participants of their own personal experience and how it will unfold for them. We are the guides during this ritual. Participants need direction and content to help them navigate the ritual and have a meaningful experience, but we do not try to explain any possible outcomes or results of the ritual. We do not want to set up expectations about the kind of experience they 'should' have.

Meditation

The most common mistake that people make when reading out loud is to speak too fast and not to pause when needed. Especially when reading the meditations in this book, it is very important to read slowly with a calm and deep voice, pausing as long as you feel comfortable where the ... dots appear. If pausing makes you anxious, when you first practice this, count to 3 or 4 at each pause including commas and ends of paragraphs.

Routine breath focusing to make a gradual entry into meditation helps relax and focus your group. There are many ways to do this and you can do it for a longer or shorter time, depending on the needs of the group. We include this in all the meditations in this book. Those with more experience with meditation require less of an introduction.

At the end of the meditation give everyone a chance to come back, get comfortable and be ready for the ritual. If one person is deep in a trance, stir a bit to signal that the rest of the group is ready to move on. Do this gently.

Ritual Actions

The activity of the ritual is to actualize the ritual theme, embodying the concept. Many indigenous peoples bring spirit into concrete worldly terms through the actions of the ritual combined with the intent. As you read through the rituals, you will see the diversity of actions we use, that range from writing or drawing after the meditation to massaging hands mindfully.

Talking Stick

We use a talking stick in the Native American tradition. There are in our groups basic, agreed upon 'rules' that help to create a sense of safety and open sharing. The stick is a sacred instrument of ritual that declares who has the privilege of speaking and that all others must listen without interrupting. In addition, everything is held in the strictest confidentiality, advice is not given unless asked for, even after the ritual, and the stick is passed from speaker to speaker in a respectful manner. It reminds us to speak honestly from the heart and to listen with respect and an open heart/mind. There is great power in being heard without judgment that is ensured by the use of the talking stick. Our groups have valued this tradition dearly.

The talking stick is a symbol. Our first talking stick was one that someone in the group had found and which had significance for them. We had a ritual in which each person brought something that held significance for them or was a symbol of a quality valued by the group. Some examples of the items are feathers, stones, shells and a prayer flag. The items were attached to the talking stick as each person shared the meaning of the object with the group. This gave the stick even more power and meaning.

Occasionally we have used a candle in a bowl or a stone in the place of the talking stick. Use whatever feels comfortable to you and is appropriate to the ritual. Sometimes we use the stick to discuss what happened in the meditation or the reactions to the ritual itself. If so, we may pass the stick twice, once for the structured use of the stick and once for a more general sharing.

If your group is new or new people appear, you may need to repeat the rules of the talking stick. We offer our stick to the one who wants to start and that usually ensures a meaningful offering, but the leader may start the talking to model. If the circle is small the talking stick can make as many circuits as the group wants. The signal to stop is when most stop talking.

In our group, the rules of the talking stick are greatly honored and respected. A breech of the rule of confidentiality led to a special gather to review the suggested rules and reconfirm our dedication to the stick. It has created a safe and meaningful place in which to share our experiences. .

Ending the Ritual

We thank the directions based on how we invited those spirits, elements or archetypes into the circle. It is best to snuff the candles rather than blow them out. Some groups feel it is disrespectful to blow out the candles, but even if you do not feel that way, the presentation is more attractive and smoother when you use a snuffer. We also avoided splattering wax on the altar cloths this way.

After the directions are thanked we may sing a chant. This may be done standing up or sitting down. Standing up and remaining standing is preferable in sustaining the ritualistic feeling of the event and it tends to make people leave more quietly. We end with the simple saying of "Blessed be" and the ritual is over. Sometimes feasting is the natural ending of a ritual, but not always.

After everyone leaves, we restore the room to its original condition. We do engage all those reluctant to leave but we do discourage help with the clean up. We find that taking down the altar, the decorations and the candles around the room, is an important part of the experience for us. It is a gradual way to return to reality. We often spend a few minutes evaluating the experience as we take down the altar and usually sit for a few minutes at the end of this process. This allows us to learn more about how to do ritual, what worked and what didn't work, what 'felt' meaningful and then to return home in a quiet mood, ready for rest.

Thoughts About Earth-based Ritual

For us, ritual honors the sacredness of all life and our earth-walk together. As Unitarian Universalists, we have struggled with what to call our concept of whatever-it-is that inspires us and fills us with love and a sense of awe and reverence. Do we name it Love, Compassion, Spirit, God or Goddess? Is it Nature, or Essence, the Oneness, Consciousness, Energy or an Energetic Force? Some call it That, the Tao, and so the names are endless. The phrase from the Star Wars movie, "may the Force be with you" rings in our ears often as a phrase free from a specific religious tradition. We have settled for the Sacred or the Oneness for the book and in many of the rituals. We have also referred to the Sacred as Spirit in many places. We invite you to use whatever name works for you, so that you might always come to ritual with integrity and authenticity.

So in whatever way you name Spirit, when we can touch and see the Sacred within ourselves and in all things our relationship changes. We become connected in a profound manner to the wholeness of life and see ourselves as an integral part of the interconnected web of life. The deep river of the Sacred runs through all beings and all humans. The animals are our brothers and sisters, the trees are our cousins, the stone people our grandparents. The earth herself is alive and becomes our mother. We are all born here, grow up and struggle here, celebrate, heal and die here. This we acknowledge in ritual.

Some of the intentions and beliefs that underpin our rituals are listed here.

- All is One.
- All things are an expression of the Oneness.
- Sourcing ritual in personal experience is rich and vibrant.
- Ritual is a whole person experience.
- Each individual's experience is honored.
- We are in a constant relationship with the Sacred that is reciprocal and mutual.
- Ritual helps us to touch and see the Sacred in all things.
- Ritual connects us with the aspects of Spirit that are unseen.
- Self-cultivation is invaluable, adding depth and meaning to rituals.

Ritual provides a vehicle for this connection to spirit within others, ourselves and to all life. It provides a vehicle to offer thanks for the beauty and abundance that surrounds us and nourishes us. Through it, we create prayers and requests for peace, love and compassion for all beings; we ask for help, guidance and use divination. We ask for healing for others and ourselves. We offer these rituals to the waters, the earth, the air and the fire, to the archetypes, to the Oneness that surrounds us and lives within us.

Sourcing ritual

How can we offer meaningful ritual if we have not found meaning in it ourselves? How can we craft an experience of the Sacred through ritual from our own experience that will also offer others opportunities to engage the Sacred in a meaningful way?

Sandy and I are by no means mystics or sages. But we all have had experiences that fill us with awe, feelings of reverence and a sense of oneness with all things. Pause a minute, reflect back on those times when you were a part of an extraordinary sunrise or sunset, when you held a newborn in your arms, when you consoled another or were consoled. We have all come upon ideas that have touched our lives and added meaning or a new outlook. These are the things that Sandy and I drew upon to source our rituals. They are the heart of a ritual.

We are inviting you to use only the ideas or rituals in this book that are meaningful to you. If there is a kernel of an idea that awakens an experience or spark in you, please go with that. Use our scripts, or not, as it works best for you. Our goal is to share with you what has worked for us in a hope that it will also excite and inspire you.

Whole person experience

Ritual connects us both to the spiritual within ourselves and to the sacred that flows throughout all life. It allows us to step into the 'deep river' of universal knowing of the Oneness. Connecting in this way transcends words. We take in this knowledge through our senses and intuition. The knowing of the sacred in this deep way dwells in our body, our muscles, bones, and the very cells that are the building blocks of our physical body. So, the more we can involve all the senses in ritual, the fuller and richer is the experience for everyone.

Sandy and I have even found that creating ritual is a very organic whole person process, involving all of our senses, our intuitions, and experiences. The rituals actually began to have a life of their own as we worked in this organic, experiential way. In this way the rituals became a whole person experience for our participants.

An individual experience

Ritual that is alive encourages each person to touch what is sacred in their own way, in their own time, through their own unique experience. So there evolves a dynamic dance between guiding and shaping the group's experience and encouraging and supporting the individual's experience, so that there is a smooth and cohesive flow to the ritual.

For example, we offer verbal guidance for meditation. Often, before meditation, permission is given to allow images to appear that may be different than the ones the meditation guide suggests. During a meditation, phrases like, 'allow an image to form for you, however this appears is fine' are helpful. One person may find a peaceful place by the ocean, another in the woods, and yet another sitting at home by the fireplace. What is important is that they have found a peaceful place. When ritual has as its cornerstone the direct experience of everyone present, allowing and honoring each person's unique process within the given structure of the ritual, a kind of deep respect and love develops.

Another way in which participants are given "space" for individual experience is through silent activities and periods of reflection. For example, during one of our rituals on gratitude, herbs and other objects are set around the altar. The meditation encourages a reflection on gratitude, and silence is maintained as participants gather their herbs and objects in a bundle to offer to Spirit. They then go outside and offer them in silence in a place of their choosing.

We always pass the talking stick at some point during the ritual. Here also, some guidance on how to reap the benefits of this practice is needed to insure the flow of the ritual for the group and the ability of each person to cherish their own experience. In a group in which the rules of the talking stick are followed, its gifts of confidentiality, the freedom to speak from one's heart without interference, and the power of being heard by others who listen deeply with respect and an open heart, creates a chance for all to listen to their own inner truth.

Reciprocity and Mutuality

Another cardinal principle that flows throughout our rituals is that of reciprocity. We live 'in relationship with' the rest of life, with Mother Earth, The Sky, Sun and Moon and all of life that lives upon or within our Mother. There is a natural flow of giving and taking that is integral to seeking balance and harmony in our relationships with Spirit and all of life. We strive to create and facilitate ritual that will bring all the participants into "right relationship with all of life", to help them move towards harmony and balance.

The very breath we breathe is a model of reciprocity, a reminder of the intrinsic interweaving of life. We breathe in oxygen, which is our nutrition from the air. It is a gift from the plant world, which releases oxygen into the air as a byproduct of photosynthesis. We release carbon dioxide as a byproduct of our respiration. Our plant relations breathe this in as a gift of life that insures their survival. We are, with every breath, reminding ourselves of the principle of giving and receiving, and the inextricable interweaving of us all into the tapestry of life. There is a multitude of ways that we practice this in ritual. When we ask Spirit for help, there is an opportunity for everyone to offer a gift. We express gratitude to Mother Earth for the beauty and abundance she offers us daily through the offering of herbs, flower petals or kintos.

Self-cultivation

Sandy and I believe that it is a wonderful opportunity to offer a vehicle, such as ritual, to others with the intention of helping them connect with what is sacred in their lives. It is also a sacred responsibility to do this work with integrity and to 'walk' in ritual in a good way.

We found that in order for us to walk the talk in ritual we must hold our own growth, spiritual practices and intentions as pre-requisites for offering ritual. We have both tried to follow this precept and found that it deepens not only our rituals but also our daily lives. We have both found it helpful to have a regular practice. It may be a daily meditation, a well-savored walk in nature, or some way of stopping and tuning in to our own deeper selves and listening to our Spirit, even if only for 1 or 2 minutes. As we listen with our open heart to ourselves, we also make room to hear the Spirit of all that we are a part of.

We have grown as we created altars in our homes and also outside in nature, so that we have a special place for contemplation and offerings set aside. We have found that this place can be very important if we are careful to use it regularly. It is a place set aside to just be, without judgment or expectations. Our being is given substance by our actions, which are given depth and meaning through our being. Often, sitting in contemplation on an event or issue has given rise to a theme for a ritual.

One of the practices we have referred to before is the use of small gifts of gratitude, such as flower petals or kintos, to Mother Earth for the beauty and abundance that she offers us. We offer these at any time and to any place that has touched us. It is a practice of gratitude that adapts itself to the busy lifestyles of many of us. It is our experience that such intentional practices also bring depth, vibrancy and authenticity to ritual.

Trust in the process

As ritualists there is also the dilemma of planning a ritual around a theme or central idea, and then letting go of any expectations or hopes for specific desired outcomes. It is a supreme test of trusting the process, and trusting what is greater than any one of us. It is a gift to your participants if you can do this. And it is an incredible gift to all when you can free your participants from their own expectations, so that they too can begin to trust in the process, accepting what arises and evolves with openness and even a bit of curiosity. We cannot speak enough about this apparently simple concept. We can always look at how to improve a ritual, and we always attempt to let go of the outcomes for each individual and ourselves.

Most important

As you move through this book, remember that ritual is a process for you to engage in that is fulfilling, nurturing, and challenging. And have fun! Enjoy this process.

Change and adapt what we have shared to fit your specific styles and needs. Please invite a flow of inspiration from your heart-mind and experience that moves outward to the external, while at the same time inviting the flow from the outer realms inward to inspire you and nourish you.

And so it is that we gather. We move into sacred space. We share deeply and openly in ritual. And we are united in community and joined into the larger whole of the Great Mystery.

The Rituals

Honoring the Seasons of the Year

The wheel of the year is a pagan symbol representing the cycle of life both in the natural world and within our own lives. The medicine wheel, a Native American symbol, also reflects this close connection to nature. The wheel is a deeply feminine symbol that reflects a constant moving through cycles or changes that are never-ending. They form a pattern that repeats but is always different. Such are the seasons, a constant moving from spring to summer, then to fall and winter, only to return to spring again. The changing seasons reflect the changes of birth, life, death and rebirth. The fruits and flowers are born in the spring, flourish in the summer, reach maturity in the fall and face their death and decay in the winter to be born again in the spring. So as we travel the cycles of the wheel, we too are born, flourish, mature and die so that we can change and re-emerge again in a new form. This cycle is one of our connections to Nature and to Spirit that resides within us.

There are innumerable cycles that are evident: the three faces of the Goddess, maiden, mother, crone, are reflected in every woman's life, the cycle of day to night, the waxing and waning of the moon are all held in the circle or cycles of the turning wheel.

The equinoxes and solstices are important markers of the seasons. They are moments on the wheel that reflect the changes in the dance between light and dark, day and night, growth and reflection. The rituals to mark these changes reflect the connection of these passages to the phases of our lives and all of life.

Spring Equinox

Spring Equinox is March 21st and is called Ostara, named after Eostre, the Germanic Goddess of the Spring. The growing light and growing plants inspire a feeling of renewal and a new sense of energy that seeks expression in the outer world. It is time for our own personal seeds to peek their heads above the surface of our contemplation and bud. Eggs and seeds are fertility symbols for this holiday and our rituals reflect this wonderful time when new things may sprout in our lives. Life returns, the sun nourishes, plants blossom, new life is born throughout the animal world, and we burst forth with renewed energy and inspiration.

The equinox is also a razor's edge of equality, of the balance between day and night, light and dark. It is a moment of perfect balance, poised on the cusp of change. And so the equinox is celebrated in the spring for this moment of awareness before the wheel again turns toward spring and our lives turn toward the task of creating anew.

Yin and Yang

Theme

At the spring equinox there is a moment when the number of minutes of daylight equal the number of minutes of night. The equinox is nature's reminder to us that there is a continual ebb and flow of apparently opposite energies in a dynamic and fluid dance. Such is day and night, light and dark. At the equinox we find a momentary equilibrium in this flow of energies. We find another symbol of this dynamic dance in the Tai Chi symbol.

Sources of Inspiration

For this ritual we drew on the Taoist philosophy concerning the Tai Chi symbol. We related this symbol to the ebb and flow of light and dark between the solstices and the dynamic dance of opposites within our own lives.

Altar

- *Brightly colored cloth*
- *Candles for the directions*
- *Yin and Yang design drawn on a platter or cardboard in the center of the altar, filled with white and black beans.*
- *Four candles for each person*
- *Large bowl of water*
- *Vase of flowers*
- *Singing bowl*

Set up

The Tai Chi symbol is in the middle of the altar. We drew the design on a cardboard that was placed inside a circular tray, or in our case a black pizza pan, and filled in the design with black beans and white beans. The border around can be done with anything. We used the edge of the black pizza pan as the border.

Calling the Directions

Light each candle as you read the direction.

EAST

Leader: Goddess of the East, of beginnings and spring, of air and flight, thoughts and musings.
Be with us here tonight.
Help us to soar and see with fresh eyes the shifting dualities of our existence and the core of our wholeness.

SOUTH

Leader: Goddess of the South, of warmth, growth and summer, of nurturing and moving towards fullness, of change and passion.
Be with us here tonight. Help us to tap the strength of your vitality.

WEST

Leader: Goddess of the West, of maturity and autumn, of ripening wisdom and the pleasures of the harvest.
Be with us here tonight.
Cradle us and hold us in the richness of your bounty.

NORTH

Leader: Goddess of the North, of quiet and winter, of the deep inner stillness replenishing and nourishing our inner life.
Be with us here tonight.
Watch over us and help us to live from our inner spirit in the outer world, knowing wholeness and acceptance from within.

CENTER

Leader: Great Goddess of the Center, of above and below, of the circle that embraces and unifies our many rhythms and cycles, reminding us of our wholeness.
Be with us here tonight.
Lead us into a knowing of our true essence, our true nature.

Introduction to The Tai Chi

Leader: Tonight we celebrate the spring equinox, the momentary equality of day and night, light and dark, rest and activity. Another symbol of this dymanic, fluid dance of opposites is the Tai Chi, which is the center of our altar tonight. The dark side of the Tai Chi symbol represents the Yin, the feminine energies of the unseen, the intuitive, of darkness, shadow, and the moon. The light side of the symbol represents the Yang, the masculine energies of the seen, the cognitive, of light, action and the sun.

Within the dark Yin of the symbol there is a white dot of Yang, and within the light Yang, there is a dot of dark Yin. Yin and Yang are inseparable and exist in a dynamic relationship with each other and within each other. There is rest and reflection within activity, work and play. Within any day, there is dark or the shadow of objects. Within any night there is the light of the stars and moon. One cannot exist or flourish without the other.

And so it is with many of the forces that seem opposite. Without the feminine, there is no masculine, without the seen, there is no unseen, without rest and reflection, there is no work or growth and without work and growth, there is no rest. And so there is a constant state of flow between these seemingly opposing forces. Today is the equinox, that moment of balance or point of equality between the changing and shifting of day and night.

Meditation

Leader: With the equinox and the Tai Chi in our awareness as symbols of the dynamic movement of opposing forces, our meditation tonight will focus our awareness on how we sense this dance playing out in our own lives. We too have times of too much and times of too little, and moments of exquisite balance. So please begin to make yourself comfortable for a guided meditation.

The script for the meditation is at the end of the ritual. Remember to leave time at the end of the meditation for people to sit quietly for a moment. This provides a gentle and thoughtful transition into the next part of the ritual. It is also important for their integration of the meditation into current time.

Ceremony

Leader: We are going to light three candles each, to honor this ebb and flow of our lives. And now, one at a time as you are ready, you may light a candle to honor those times when you have had an abundance of water in your lake. I will pass the lighting candle and please share a few words about times of too much.

Because we are passing the lighting candle three times, we had the leader start the sharing to model brevity.

Now, you may light a candle to honor those times when you have not had enough water in your lake.

Pass the lighting candle

And this time I will pass the lighting candle for the moments of balance in your life. All of these times are a part of the unique dance of our lives.

Pass the lighting stick

Leader: Notice that the Tai Chi symbol on the altar is encircled; held together as a whole by a circle that embraces both the light and the dark in its ever-changing balance. Just as this symbol is encircled, we too are held and encircled. We are whole, both yin and yang, both too much water and not enough water, and we are those moments of balance. In our earthwalk we are held together physically by our skin. Our energetic being is held together by an energetic membrane and the force of our own inner gravity. We are bounded by birth and death.

I invite you now to just pause for a moment, gazing at the Tai Chi symbol, and sense your wholeness, the boundaries of your physical being, your energetic being and your earthwalk.

Pause for several moments while people reflect on the boundaries and wholeness of their lives. One or two minutes was enough for our group.

Leader: But what is it that weaves us all together, provides the surface that we dance upon, the perceived encircling of our lives? What is it that suggests that there be a dance in the first place, or that seeks a balancing and harmony in this dance? There is a belief that we are more than just this gathering of opposing forces, held together by skin, gravity and our own birth and death. There is a belief that our true nature is beyond the dualities, transcends them, and unites us with the oneness that weaves through all things, all energies and all times. We believe we are an expression of that energy that weaves and dances. We are an expression of that energy that provides the surface upon which we dance together with all of life. And in this sense we are bound-less.

Centering

Leader: Pause a moment and just breathe........Move gently beyond the boundaries of your thinking..............Sense quietly your innermost being.........Your oneness with all that is........ with the energy or force that flows through all that is........We are this energy......... manifesting out of this energy and resting within this energy.......Like drops of water in a large gently moving river of Essence..................we are Goddess....we are Buddha nature.......................... we are Love.................................

Breathe and allow the sound of the bowl to take you to who you are.....to your essence or true nature....................

Gong the Tibetan singing bowl. We left a pause at the end of the sound to give people time to rest in the moment.. You may want to gong the bowl more than once. Pause

Leader: Let us acknowledge our knowing of our true nature. Let us acknowledge our essence as sacred, the light within which offers us the vision and wisdom for our earthwalk. Stand and as we chant, each one may light a candle to honor our oneness with Goddess or Spirit, our place in the interconnected web of all life.

Stand and hold hands. The leader or a singer leads the chant. The melody is in the appendix.

Chant:

O Great Goddess, Earth Sun Sea and Sky,
You are inside, and all around me.

Leader: When you leave here tonight, pause outside, breathe in deeply and exhale slowly and sense yourself as part of all life around you. We have some flowers here if you would like to leave an offering of gratitude to Mother Earth. Please take one before you leave.

Talking Stick

Leader: We will now pass the talking stick. Please share as you are moved. Who would like to start?

Thanking and Releasing the Directions

Snuff each candle as you read each direction

EAST

Leader: Goddess of the East, of beginnings and the spring, we thank you and release you.

SOUTH

Leader: Goddess of the South, of warmth, growth and summer, we thank you and release you.

WEST

Leader: Goddess of the West, of maturity and autumn, we thank you and release you.

NORTH

Leader: Goddess of the North, of quiet and winter we thank you and release you.

CENTER

Leader: Great Goddess of the Center, of above and below, of the circle that embraces and unifies our many rhythms and cycles reminding us of our wholeness, we thank you and release you

Lake Meditation

on the Ebbs, Flows, and Balance of One's Life

Leader:

Now is the time to get comfortable in your chair...... slowly close your eyes and draw your attention to your breathing.......as you inhale... draw your breath down into your abdomen and feel the muscles relax.........And as you exhale, breathe out the tensions of the day..... the week.......this winter season............ Breathe in and let your shoulders drop slightly, breathing softly through the muscles in your neck and shoulders.....inviting them to soften........See if you can let go of all that you have been doing and just be here........here in this moment... this equinox........

And begin to let the growing light and warmth approach softly.... so that you begin to feel a gradual warming on your skin ......a little warmer with each breath...soft and invigorating......and so a clear energizing light begins to surround you.......... it is spring..... This is a time of new growth.......a bursting forth with renewed energy......a turning towards manifesting what has been incubating under the snows of winter.

Pause

And now..imagining a beautiful lake........shades of clear blue.......reflecting the clouds that float lazily above........the water is inviting... fluid....soft and just the right warmth............and so you may float in the lake....peaceful and safe....buoyant and held by the water underneath you.........As you rest in the warmth of your lake...you notice a dam at one end of the lake......

Gradually you become aware that there is you and the lake within the field of your awareness.........beginning gently to imagine that you can become one with your lake...... embraced by the shoreline...........held safely within this embrace...you are warm and fluid.........constantly changing with the ripples and currents that flow through you and around you.....the flow and current of your inner energetic....

Pause

As you are constantly ebbing and flowing.........just for now......imagine that you begin to gather water, becoming more and more full and abundant.......you are at the top edges of your shoreline.........energized by the movement and fullness of your water ....you are almost becoming too full........It is possible that the dam that keeps you contained may overflow or burst...........There is an edge of tension to your overly full state.........

Breathe.........and reflect for a moment.......Are there times when you feel like your lake.......too busy.......too pressed for time........perhaps tense and tired?.......... What is happening in your life during those times?........

Pause, perhaps about 45 seconds or until you sense a readiness to move on. Please emphasize the just for now, as it may be reassuring to the participants to know that this is a temporary state

And now, breathing deeply.........in....and out.....allowing the breath to assist you in letting go of this image as you breathe out.........

You may explore releasing some of the fullness by opening the dam of your lake........ gradually returning to a delightful level of water..........pause here and savor this delight

And now, just for now, imagine that the water keeps draining out through the dam...slowly and gently.......and you find yourself in a time of scarcity...........the banks of your shoreline are dried and caked below their optimal level............ you may sense a shrinking of your inner energetic..... as you enter a time of depletion and drought......

And pause here...... reflecting for a moment.......Are there times in your life that you feel depleted?.....over tired and a lack of energy or resources?..........Notice how this appears in your life.........How do you see this time of less energy and depletion manifesting in your life?

Pause-45 seconds or until you sense a readiness to move on.

There is a natural rhythm in your fullness....balance.....and scarcity as the lake....... in your life...............and in the larger web of life..........

Here at the equinox there is a moment of equilibrium...........a pause in the ebb and flow that signals a time of balance.......just as there is a balance between light and dark, there is also a balance within your lake.......... Pause a moment here and reflect on the times of balance.................of a gentle rising and falling of the waters of your lake that is reassuring and stable......Are there times of relative balance....a sense of all is as it should be in your life? What does this feel like? What is happening in your life? Just notice what arises.

Pause-45 seconds or until you sense a readiness to move on.

When you are ready........breathe in deeply......and exhale slowly...steadily.... inviting yourself to return gently to our circle.......perhaps noticing how you are sitting in your chair......moving or stretching if you like...........and breathe again....in.....out.....perhaps opening your eyes as you are ready.......gazing gently around our circle.......holding your experience during the meditation gently in your heart.....renewed by what you have learned.

Bringing people gently back to the circle is a gift. You may have to suggest several deep breaths, spacing them gently for the reluctant. Changing the tone and loudness of your voice as you guide them back also helps. You can think of it as returning to your everyday voice.

SR 2007

Rebirth

Theme

Spring is a time of rebirth after a long cold winter of hibernation. Trees bud, flowers bloom and the earth dons her green and colorful mantle. Now is an opportunity to reflect on what you would like to bring forth in the coming months. What has been germinating and forming through the winter that is ready to plant and bloom.

Sources of inspiration

Following the Celtic/European traditions, we used the Oestar symbol of the egg for rebirth and fertility in this ritual. We drew a connection between the bursting forth of spring and our own personal growth.

Altar

- *Green or brown cloth*
- *At each direction flowers in appropriate colors with a candle*

    East-white

    South-red or yellow

    West-blue, turquoise

    North-green

    Center-combination of all direction colors
- *Copies of the poem, The Circle is Cast, for calling the directions*
- *Divination cards of any sort*
- *Basket of hard-boiled eggs*
- *Magic markers*

You may dye the eggs red. The participants will decorate their own egg by drawing or writing their hopes on the egg.

Set up

Decorate the altar and the room with whatever seasonal decorations appeal to you. We arranged the altar in the center of the circle of chairs.

Smudge

Smudging outside the room allows each person a brief clearing and centering before walking into ritual space.

You may appoint a 'smudger', but do not forget to smudge yourself as leaders first. You may use whatever feels appropriate to you. Some suggestions are: sage, paulo santo, or mugwort.

Have participants enter the ritual room after they are finished being smudged.

Calling the Directions

Leader: Please remain standing while we call the Directions. The calling of the Directions is adapted from a poem, The Circle Is Cast, by Robert Gass.

This casting of the circle may be printed and a copy given to everyone so that everyone can recite together. We find the impact of opening sacred space is enhanced when everyone stands

NORTH

Leader: By the Earth, that is Her body,
By the Earth, mother of us all.
By the Earth, future and past,
The circle is cast
The circle is cast

EAST

Leader: By the air, that is Her breath,
By the air, sweet wind of life.
By the air, from the first to the last,
The circle is cast
The circle is cast

SOUTH

Leader: By the fire that is Her bright spirit,
By the fire, light in the darkness ,
By the fire, warmth in the chill of evening
The circle is cast
The circle is cast

WEST

Leader: By the water, that is Her blood,
By the waters, the calm and the flood.
By the living waters, running slow, running fast,
The circle is cast
The circle is cast

CENTER

Leader: By the Sacred that is Her Heart and Core
By the stars her nightly crown
By the sun of day and moon of night
The circle is cast
The circle is cast

Leader: Please be seated.

Prayer of the Egg

Leader: Please choose an egg, keeper of possibility and new beginings, and hold it gently in your palm. We will stand and repeat the lines of the poem, one at a time. The title of the poem is

This Is an Egg Found.

This is an egg found.
This is a prayer for all lost in acts of terror.
This is an egg in hand.
This is a prayer for the healing of souls in confusion and pain.

This is an egg not thrown.
This is a prayer for justice, not mindless revenge.
This is an egg never to be thrown.
This is a prayer for peace.

Meditation

The script for the meditation is at the end of the ritual.

Remember to leave time at the end of the meditation for people to sit quietly for a moment. This provides a gentle and thoughtful transition into the next part of the ritual. It is also important for their integration of the meditation into current time.

Ritual

Leader: Eggs hold the universe within them. They have all that is needed within the fragile shell to nourish and sustain growth and a coming into being, a birthing of new possibility. You have blessed your egg with whatever it is that you would like to see grow in your life. But you are also your own egg. You bring forth your hope, birthing it in its infancy. You call upon the abundance that life surrounds you with and the abundance that you carry within you to help you tend and nourish the growth of your hope or desire.

You may help yourself to pencils or crayons. You may write or draw on your egg, creating it as an expression of your inner goals. I invite you to focus on what came up for you during the meditation. What was it that you blessed your egg with? You may also reflect on how you or your wish might hatch and grow.

As you work on your egg, questions may arise. You may consult the Divination cards on the altar for insight. Please do this in silence.

Allow plenty of time for everyone to decorate their egg and use the divination cards. We found that people were happy to use the divination cards. As people finish, they may sit quietly and reflect until the group is finished. We found that a gentle reminder of soon coming to a close was helpful for some.

Talking Stick

Leader: It's time for the talking stick. On the first round, you may share with the group where you will plant the egg and what you want to grow in your life. You may then place the egg on the altar. When you leave please take it home to plant.

On the second round you may share whatever you like.

We have found that passing the talking stick more than once keeps the ritual focused on the theme of the ritual for the first round, and facilitaties sharing of other important events in people's lives for the second round.

Thanking and Releasing the Directions

Snuff each candle as you read each direction

NORTH

Leader: We thank you for being with us, the Earth, Mother of us all.

EAST

Leader: We thank you for being with us, the Air that is Her breath.

SOUTH

Leader: We thank you for being with us, the Fire of Her bright spirit.

WEST

Leader: We thank you for being with us, the Waters that are Her blood.

CENTER

Leader: To the Sacred that is Her heart and core, we thank you for being with us.

The circle is open but unbroken.

You may want to close the circle with the chant:

May the circle be open
And unbroken
May the love of the Goddess

Be ever in your heart.
Merry meet
And merry part
And merry meet again.

Sing through three times while holding hands. Music is in the appendix.

Meditation

Your Egg of Hopes and Dreams

And now we will get ready for a short meditation. Please hold your egg....gently and lovingly in your hand for the meditation......it is a symbol of your hopes and evolution...

And breathe.......filling your belly...chest......exhaling slowly and consciously ......you may close your eyes....or gaze at your egg...whichever is most comfortable for you..... and gently and surely bringing your attention more and more to your breath........feeling your breath as you inhale.....deep down into your belly........noticing if your belly expands as you inhale......and then exhaling.........noticing if or how your belly contracts as you breathe out.......

And now.....breathe deeply down through your entire body......out the soles of your feet.....and imagine a beam of energy moving skillfully down from your body deep into the earth.......past stones...pools of water.....rich moist earth and sand.....deep into the molten core of the earth......You may drink up the deeply nourishing and anchoring energy that she offers you freely..............
you may notice a warmth....or a color that begins to gently spread up your legs....your body...arms and head...... letting it ground you in Her strength and steadfastness.....
and now imagining this beam of energy moving up through the top of your head........ connecting to a beautiful....shimmering rainbow overhead.....a source of light and inspiration and connection to the loving spirit of all things.......Imagine that you may drink freely of this revitalizing and compassionate energy that is being offered to you.......... letting it gently shower down over your head....neck...blending and balancing with the earth energy.....down your arms...trunk...and legs.....offering you a sense of balance and protection........you are surrounded and held in the safety and love of the Goddess.....

Pause allowing time for them to imagine this process

And so safely and tenderly held........begin to imagine a beautiful spring garden....perhaps with tulips and snow drops beginning to peek their green heads above ground........ some may even be budding or blooming.......and perhaps forsythia....yellow as the spring sun which brings it to life.......you may pause to explore your garden.......smelling the fresh and fragrant spring air.........feasting your eyes on the greens....yellows...... reds and purples of your garden........as you do so...you notice that the sun is also shining on you.....warm and revitalizing........ a soft spring breeze caressing your skin..... heralding the awakening........ there is a deliciousness in the moment which you may pause to savor....

Pause

And finding a comfortable place in your garden to rest........gently bring your attention to your egg......holding it gently in your palm.......marveling at the potential and light living in the middle of your egg waiting for you to invest it with form and substance......

and so bringing to mind what it is that you would like to bring forth in your life this spring.......reflecting on what would support the growth and blooming of your hope or idea......and leaving room for the magic of unfolding in ways that you may not be able to imagine just now.......letting all this flow into your egg through your hands......and blowing gently onto your egg..........breathing life and form into your egg........blessing your egg with your love and hope......

Pause

And as with all potentials filled with seeds of hope........you may plant your egg...... into the earth.......watching as it sends roots deep into the mother.....peeks its head out above the earth and draws in the strength and warmth of the sun........joining the rest of the flowers and plants of your garden..... and in doing this....knowing that you also plant your hope and dream into your own rich...earthy self.......you are the earth and ground of your hopes and dreams......the light that warms and brings forth.......you are the gardener of your possibility.......aided and joined by the nourishment that surrounds you always.....freely given......

and so breathing in deeply of this knowing.......letting it find a gentle home in your awareness.....in your heart...

Pause a few minutes to explore. You may just time out 30-45 seconds, or pause until you sense a readiness to move on.

However... now it is time to leave your garden.....so pausing to thank yourself for taking this time....begin to very softly bring your attention back to your breath......taking a gentle but deep breath in.....sensing your belly and chest filling.....and exhale slowly and consciously......gradually beginning to notice sensations.....how you are sitting in your chair..... how your feet may touch the floor.....and breathing again.........in ......and out...........each breath bringing you more and more back to here and now........ returning to the circle..................and now stretching if you like.......opening your eyes as you are ready.....and taking a few
moments to look around the space...noticing colors....feeling the air of the room..... and one last big breath in..........filling your belly and chest.....and exhaling...allowing yourself to return completely and wonderfully back to the circle.....

If some people seem to be slow in returning to the circle, you may guide a few more deep breaths and prod them gently but firmly to open eyes and return to the circle

SR 2005

Moving Into Your Own Promise

Theme

This is a ritual to honor the transition from the dark of winter to the light of spring when there is a bursting forth of new life that has been developing deep in the dark of the earth. The egg is a symbol of this process of rebirth and is the focus of our ritual.

Sources of Inspiration

The primary source for this ritual was the Celtic/European symbol of the egg, which was used in pagan religions to symbolize renewal, fertility and the promise of new growth. We drew from pagan May Day and Beltane rituals for the blessing of the flowers.

Altar

- *Cloth for the altar, preferable spring colors*
- *Candles for directions and center*
- *Snuffer*
- *Lighter candle*
- *Matches*
- *Plants or flowers*
- *Petals in bowls around the altar*
- *Basket of boiled eggs, white, if available*

Additional items for sacred space

- *Basket of magic markers*
- *Assorted candles*
- *Small potted seedlings or cut flowers*

Set Up

Set up the altar in the usual manner as described in the introduction. Candles in the windows and around the room help to create a magical atmosphere. We placed the magic markers for writing on the eggs under our chairs or under the altar table as it is less distracting than walking around the room to get them. The seedlings or flowers can be placed on the altar if there is space.

Smudge

Smudging outside the room allows each person a brief clearing and centering before walking into ritual space.

Set up the smudge outside the room. You may appoint a 'smudger', but do not forget to smudge yourself as leaders first. You may use whatever feels appropriate to you. Some suggestions are: sage, paulo santo, or mugwort.

Calling the Directions

Light each candle as you read the direction.

EAST

Leader: I call to the East, the element of Air,
Fill our lungs; help us bring freshness and connection into our lives,
Let us have clear minds so that we may see our paths into new beginnings.

SOUTH

Leader: I call to the South, the element of Fire,
Come into our hearts; warm us with the freshness of spring,
Help us to be caring and strong in connection with each other.

WEST

Leader: I call to the West, the element of Water,
Let the gentle spring rains quench our thirst, and bring us peace, healing and gentle emotions.

NORTH

Leader: I call to the North, the element of Earth,
Make our resolve strong, and keep us grounded as the darkness of winter passes and new life stirs in the earth.

CENTER

Leader: I call to the Center, Above and Below,
Goddess of springtime and new life, bring new beginnings into our lives that we may grow and flower.

Introduction

Leader: Welcome! This is a ritual to honor the transition from the dark of winter to the light of spring. All the elements of life are being brought into new balance, as day and night attain equal length. At the spring equinox, light is gaining, for future days will now be longer than the nights. So a new tide of life begins. We shed what no longer inspires us or is relevant and we keep what still inspires us and moves us along our path. All of nature seeks to bring in what is new, fresh, and revitalized. And so we too make ready for the birthing and rebirthing of our lives.

What we bring forth is often the result of where we have been, what we have done and reflected on previous to this moment. Therefore, the main spring equinox or Oestar symbol is the egg, which symbolizes fertility. It is full of the promise of new growth, yet also shows how plans that were incubating on the inner levels during the winter may now be put into practice in our lives. We may take the first steps towards doing something we have only dreamed about. These eggs show the emergence of life from darkness, of ideas from inner levels. Let us celebrate these transitions, and the rebirthing of the light.

Blessings of the Eggs

Hold up basket of eggs and say:

Leader: Blessed be, the life from within life.
Blessed Be--the egg, symbol of new possibility, fermenting within the shelter of darkness, and a symbol of the transition, the bursting forth of all possibility into new form and new expression. As the possibility inside the egg grows according to its true nature, it is grounded in what has gone before and what is to come. We too grow and bring forth what is in keeping with our true nature and being.

Meditation

The script for the meditation is at the end of the ritual. Remember to leave time at the end of the meditation for people to journal or just sit quietly. This provides a gentle and thoughtful transition into the next part of the ritual. It is also important for their integration of the meditation into current time.

Ritual

Leader: This basket of eggs is like a talking stick. As you hold it you may share what arose for you during the meditation, if you so wish.

After the basket goes around once, pass the basket again, saying:

Leader: We will pass the basket again and you may have an egg to take home with you to plant in your garden to bring fertility and growth to all aspects of your life. For now, place your egg on the altar so it may be a part of the flower ritual.

Flower Ritual

Leader: This is the spring flower spell:

May the blessing of the Spring Queen be upon these flowers,
The fresh blooming of new life.
May there be new understanding on Earth.
May there be new awareness of Mother Earth's needs.
As spring flowers bloom afresh, may this blossom.

May there be a return of joy in life,
The fresh blooming of song, dance and love.
May the beauty of the natural world delight us.
May there be peace on earth.
As spring flowers bloom afresh, may these wishes blossom.

Imagine the return of the freedom and balance of natural life.
Imagine the blossoming of new awareness with the green woods returning.
Imagine people living in harmony with each other and all of life.
Imagine loving kindness spreading across the world.
As spring flowers bloom afresh, may this blossom.

The leader takes some petals and sprinkles some of them on the altar and says:

Leader: May the blessing of the Spring Queen be upon us all.

A pause brings emphasize to the blessing. We then passed the basket of flower petals so that each person might bless the altar.

Leader: I will pass the flower basket so you may each sprinkle some petals on the altar and repeat the blessing:

May the blessing of the Spring Queen be upon us all.

When everyone had blessed the altar, we gave each person a small potted seedling or cut flower.

Talking Stick

We will pass the talking stick and the one who holds it may share any thoughts that have come to you from this ritual or the meditation.

Thanking and Releasing the Directions

Snuff each candle as you read each direction

EAST

Leader: We thank the spirits of the East, the element of Air, and release you

SOUTH

Leader: We thank the spirits of the South, the element of Fire, and release you

WEST

Leader: We thank the spirits of the West, the element of Water, and release you

NORTH

Leader: We thank the spirits of the North, the element of Earth, and release you

CENTER

Leader: Goddess of springtime and new life, thank you for being with us.
The circle is open but unbroken. Blessed be

Meditation

Emerging

And now...begin making yourself comfortable for meditation......you may adjust your position, stretch, or do whatever is necessary to become comfortable........ if at any point you need to dis-engage from the meditation, you may do so by merely opening your eyes........

And so, beginning to bring your awareness to your breathing........inhaling and noticing the feel of the air at your nostrils......and exhaling....again noticing any change in the feel of the air at your nostrils.......allowing yourself to gradually settle into meditation.....each breath bringing you closer to a calm, focused place.......

And taking a deep breath this time......noticing how your belly and chest move and fill......and exhaling slowly.....noticing how your belly and chest release the air and become smaller......
it is possible...with your imagination.....to envision a soft...warm...and soothing mist.....it may have a color or gentle pleasing sound to it.....
And gently.....as your breath moves in and out at its own pace....this soothing yet replenishing mist can flow down over your head....neck....shoulders...... warm and refreshing......and down over your arms....hands...down your torso..... bathing gently as if to mist away a layer of dust and revitalize........and now... down your legs.....your feet....and to the tips of your toes.........

You may notice yourself resting more deeply into your chair.....supported and safe within our circle.......

And now, calling on the fertility of your own imagination...............gradually arriving at a large, warm room or space.......it is comfortable here......protected and very safe....... It is dark..... and quiet....a stillness and darkness that provides shelter and nourishment to your spirit ....a stillness that listens and envelops you gently in the vastness of its possibility....... you may even sense that this space is very much like the inside of your sacred egg..........and you are held within its shell of protection......

Here you can be in touch with your "winter" self............ nurturing the embryo's of your dreams and hopes..........replenishing your energy, your passion and commitment.........

Pause a moment in the stillness.........safe and nurtured within your egg-space........and allow the dreams that have been growing in your inner spheres to rise to the foreground of your awareness..............................and just notice what arises............

Are there new dreams and ideas? Are there any older dreams and ideas that beg for renewed passion and action?

Pause

And now....... still sheltered in your egg-space.............. imagine approaching a time of transition........... suspended in a momentary balance between darkness and light...
Stillness and activity............

You are sensing a stirring that gently becomes louder.......you are beginning to feel the energy of the great spring awakening coursing through your veins............. the anticipation and tension of change.............the desire to burst forth from the shelter of your egg-space and into the growing light and warmth of spring.............. Pause a moment....... suspended in this momentary balance of stillness.. and urge to action...............

Pause

And now................................. imagine the darkness of winter beginning to subside more and more...................................... The warmth of the sun and its light are on the rise....................it is time, and you are free to emerge from the shelter of your egg-space..................................you can push against the edges of your space... ....perhaps feeling them give way.........................freeing you to stretch...................Freeing you from old plans or expectations that no longer serve you................. imagining them falling off like the pieces of shell...................... scattering as you burst forth from your egg-space.......................joyously.........

full of energy.........................you may run, dance and bask in the light and warmth of spring............... ....joining the natural flow of all life in reawakening

Pause

And now let us be open to the gifts offered us from the four directions....that they may help us in our reawakening.........in the cultivating of our hopes and dreams......

From the east--dwelling place of spring and new beginnings. Send us strength and guidance that we might bring forth our hopes and our selves anew...

From the south--home of summer and growth. .... Send us patience and passion to sustain us on our journey

From the west--dwelling place of fall and fruition...send us harmony and joy in the fruits of our labor

And from the north--home of winter, of replenishing and incubating--send us stillness, endless and vast enough to give birth to the future...

Pause

And now it is time to return to current time and place.......so thanking yourself for taking this time........gradually bring your attention to your breath......inhaling with focus...noticing how it feels to inhale....and then exhale....noticing how your body moves as you release your breath....... gradually beginning to notice sensations.....how you are sitting in your chair..... how your feet may touch, the floor.....and breathing again...in and out...each breath bringing you more and more back to here and now.....into the circle.....and now stretching if you like....... opening your eyes as you are ready.....and taking a few moments to look around the space...noticing colors....feeling the air of the room.....and one last big breath in..........filling your belly and chest.....and exhaling...allowing yourself to return completely and wonderfully back to the circle.....

If some people seem to be slow in returning to the circle, you may guide a few more deep breaths and prod them gently but firmly to open eyes and return to the circle

SR2006

Looking Within

Theme

Among the harbingers of spring are the flowers, whose courageous first buds peak through the snow. They bring us hope and reassurance that the seasons are changing and spring is coming. It is the season of new birth and the egg is a symbol of these new beginnings. This ritual uses the egg as a vehicle of divination for what may be budding in each person's life.

Sources of Inspiration

Divination in rituals is world-wide. We combined the practice of divination with the Celtic/European symbol of the egg for this Equinox ritual.

Altar

- *Lace cloth*
- *Direction candles*
- *Four bud vases with the appropriate colored flower at each direction*

  South-red

  West-blue

  North-green

  East-white
- *Matches*
- *Lighting candle*
- *Snuffer*
- *Basket of hardboiled eggs*
- *Markers*
- *Flowers*
- *Bouquet of flowers for the center*

Additional items for Sacred Space

- *Improvised ramp for rolling the eggs.*

Set Up

The altar is set up in the middle of the circle. The vases of flowers may be set up around the outside of the circle. We found this kept the altar simpler and added a fresh dimension to the flower ritual,wrapping us in the call to the Flower Spirits for their help.

Off to one side we set up a small ramp to roll the eggs on. You can improvise with whatever you have handy. We used a towel folded and shaped to form a funnel for the egg and placed it over some blocks to give the ramp height at one end. A gentle slope is advisable, or the eggs will be rolling all over the room.

Smudge

Smudging outside the room allows each person a brief clearing and centering before walking into ritual space.

Set up the smudge outside the room. You may appoint a 'smudger', but do not forget to smudge yourself as leaders first. You may use whatever feels appropriate to you. Some suggestions are: sage, paulo santo, or mugwort

Calling the Directions

Light each candle as you read the direction.

EAST

Leader: I call to the East, the element of Air,
Fill our lungs; help us to breathe deeply the freshness and promise of spring.
Let us have clear minds so that we may see our path into new beginnings.

SOUTH

Leader: I call to the South, the element of Fire,
Come into our hearts; keep the growing light of spring bright within us.
Help us to be caring and strong in connection with each other.

WEST

Leader: I call to the West, the element of Water,
Wash over us; let the gentle spring rains quench our thirst,
Bring us peace, healing and gentle emotions.

NORTH

Leader: I call to the North, the element of Earth,
Feed our bodies; Make strong our resolve, keep us grounded
As the darkness of winter passes and new life stirs within.

CENTER

Leader: I call to the Center, Goddess of springtime and new life
Hold us safely within your cycles; renew us again as spring approaches.
Bring new beginnings into our lives that we may grow and flower.

Flower Ritual

Leader: Among the harbingers of spring are the flowers, whose courageous first buds often peak through the snow and brave the colder spring rains. They bring us hope and reassurance that the seasons are changing and spring is coming. This is the spring flower spell, calling for the flowers of spring to come bravely forward, teaching us as they do of their courage and potential.

The leader moves to the vase of flowers in the east and ceremoniously picks up the vase and holds it forward.

Leader: Let us be one in our hope. May there be new understanding on Earth, new awareness and knowledge of Mother Earth's needs. As spring flowers bloom afresh, may this blossom.

The leader moves to the vase of flowers in the south, raising them ceremoniously

Leader: Let us be one in our search. May there be a return of joy in life, in song, dance, love and the beauty of the natural world. As spring flowers bloom afresh, may this blossom.

The leader moves to the west and raises the vase up for all present.

Leader: Let us be one in our intention. May there be healing and peace on earth. As spring flowers bloom afresh, may this blossom.

The leader moves to the north direction and holds up the vase of flowers.

Leader: Let us be one in our pledge. May there be deeper listening, respect and understanding between all people on Mother Earth. As the spring flowers bloom afresh, may this also blossom.

The leader moves to the center, taking some of the flowers out of the vase and holding them high.

Leader: Let us be one in our blessing. May the blessings of the Spring Queen be upon these flowers and upon us all.

Holding the flowers, walk all around the circle, giving each participant a flower from the center.

When the leader completes the circle, pause and gently place any remaining flowers into the vase.

A short pause here is helpful as a break before moving into the next section of the ritual.

Move to the basket of eggs, picking one of the eggs up and holding it.

Leader: The spring equinox symbol is the egg. It holds within itself the potential for the emergence of life from darkness, of ideas from inner levels. As the life within the egg hatches, we too can crack the shell of our waiting and take the first steps towards doing something we have only dreamt about. As we pass the basket of eggs around you may pick one to hold during the meditation. They are boiled so that you do not have to worry about crushing them.

Pass the bowl of eggs around the circle.

Leader: Now that everyone has an egg to hold, make yourself ready for meditation.

Meditation

The script for the meditation is at the end of the ritual.

Remember to leave time at the end of the meditation for people to sit quietly for a moment. This provides a gentle and thoughtful transition into the next part of the ritual. It is also important for their integration of the meditation into current time.

Be sure that the markers are easily available on the altar. When everyone is sitting with eyes open, start.

Leader: And now in silence, you may write three to four of your ideas or questions onto your egg, one in each quadrant. You may also leave one quadrant empty to make room for possibilities that have not yet been revealed to you.

We have prepared a small ramp for you to roll your egg on. As it settles at the end of the ramp, take note of the idea that is facing you. You may get a message about which of your plans or ideas may be most ripe for hatching.

Have people go up to the ramp one at a time to roll their egg. We had music going in the background for this part. When everyone is done, move to the talking stick. Reassure them they can keep their egg.

Talking Stick

Leader: We will now pass the talking stick. Please share as you are moved. You may want to share something that came up during the ritual, or whatever else is in your heart or on your mind. What is said here stays here in circle. It is all right to pass. Who would like to start?

Thanking and Releasing the Directions

Snuff each candle as the direction is read.

EAST

Leader: I thank the Spirits of the East, the element of Air, and release you.

SOUTH

Leader: I thank the Spirits of the South, the element of Fire, and release you.

WEST

Leader: I thank the Spirits of the West, the element of Water, and release you.

NORTH

Leader: I thank the Spirits of the North, the element of Earth, and release you.

CENTER

Leader: Goddess of Springtime and New Life, thank you for being with us.
The circle is open but unbroken.
Blessed be

Meditation

Looking Within

And now...make yourself comfortable for meditation......you may adjust your position, stretch, or do whatever is necessary to become comfortable........if at any point you need to dis-engage from the meditation, you may do so by merely opening your eyes........

And so, beginning to bring your awareness to your breathing........inhaling and noticing the feel of the air at your nostrils......and exhaling....this time noticing any change in the feel of the air at your nostrils.......allowing yourself to gradually settle into meditation.....each breath bringing you closer to a calm, focused place.......

And taking a deep breath......noticing how your belly and chest move and fill...... and exhaling slowly.....noticing how your belly and chest release the air and become smaller......

And now....beginning to imagine your egg resting in your hand..........feeling the texture of the shell, ...perhaps the temperature.............

Letting the egg in your hand be your egg...............filled with promise.........filled your possibilities..................and the wisdom of the mysteries.........that knowing beyond words......................

And now.....curious....................... you may go inside your egg with your awareness............................perhaps inside is an open and free space ....warm...... illuminated as if it were twilight ....protected and very safe.................... .....you may take a moment.....and notice how the inside of your egg appears................

what does it look like.......are there sounds or fragrances inside your egg.............. noticing any sensations......thoughts or emotions that may arise in your awareness as you rest inside of your egg..........

Your egg is blessed with a comforting sense of stillness and peace............ a life-giving energy that provides shelter and nurtures your spirit.....................that listens and envelops you gently in the immense power of its possibility...........................

You may pause in the stillness and peace of your egg-space..........................bathed and fed by the energy of the sacred..........................and allow any plans........... hopes........or possibilities that have been growing or manifesting to come to the foreground of your awareness.............................

Pause

Are new plans taking form???......................Are there any older plans or dreams that beg for renewed passion and attention???.......................
Are there plans you are in the middle of??.................................You may notice that you are presented with several possibilities...................................a palate of choices that you might make...............or priorities that you might establish......................................

Let these present themselves to you and rest with them for the moment.......... for you may bring them with you for divination when you leave your egg-space............Your egg will soon come to your assistance.................

And now.......gradually notice the currents and flow of energy building in your egg ....it is spring................filled with the energy of birthing and rebirthing........... The warmth of the sun and its light are increasing ....and the balance shifts from inner reflection to outward expression..........................
it is time...........you are free now to burst forth from the shelter of your egg

And so you may pause a moment...................................for you have brought a palate of choices to your awareness..................you may even begin to muse on what this new balance of plans might look like..........

And so.....................holding your egg thoughtfully.....................you may gently blow this request for guidance onto your egg...............................your vehicle for divination........keeper of the wisdom of the mysteries that will soon come to your assistance.....

And as you are finished, gently bring your attention back to your breath...................... Inhaling slowly.........and exhaling gently.........noticing how you are sitting in your chair...any urge to stretch or move........and doing so with relish.........and opening your eyes as you are ready.......taking a moment to look around our room....our circle....and one last breath.......inhaling......and exhaling....returning completely to our circle.

SR2004

Summer Solstice

Summer solstice is June 21st and is the longest day and the shortest night of the year. It marks the first day of summer in the northern hemisphere. At the summer solstice the sun and the earth are considered to be at the peak of their power and fertility. The sun is at its warmest, the earth is moving steadily towards full bloom as it is warmed by the sun, watered by the rains, and tended to by all. We too bloom, we too are warmed by the sun and watered by the rains. We too are finding nourishment, replenishing and enlivening as we go about our days. It is a time of great growth and abundance for all that.

Mother Earth in all of her extravagant finery reminds us that it is a time of playfulness. Here is our opportunity to revel in the light and warmth of the sun, and to feel the magic of the season. We celebrate this in the first ritual in this section. Summer is a time of healing and growth for all living beings including us. It is a time to honor and bless the abundance that we do have in our lives and the many gifts that come to us because we are in a body.

In our second ritual we share a self-blessing that is both light fun, healing and acknowledging of our many gifts.

In our third ritual we acknowledge and celebrate the life-sustaining quality of our caring and loving relationships with each other. This nourishes us and keeps us going in times of difficulty and stress.

As fruits and vegetables blossom and grow, we are reminded of how the "seeds" we have planted in our lives, with hard work and nature's grace, come to bloom.

The Summer Goddess of Playfulness

Note

We did this ritual in the early summer as we both felt that summer is a time of vacations and playfulness. Of course this could be done anytime. We also think that in reading over the ritual, the fun, exploration, insight and lightness that the ritual created for everyone is somewhat lost in the written version. We all had fun and were reconnected to our sense of playfulness. Have fun!!

Theme

As our lives spin ever faster and busier, our work and personal lives may take on a more serious and stressed quality. This ritual reminds us how necessary, how healthy and healing the Goddess of Playfulness is in our lives. Without her we can be dull and dreary. This ritual honors her by all her names.

Sources of Inspiration

Our own sense of summer is that it is a time for play. Our observation of the disconnect from a sense of playfulness in our culture prompted us to write an entire ritual to the Goddess of Playfulness.

Altar

- *Playful and colorful altar cloth*
- *One large candle for the center, playful or whimsical*
- *Tea lights around the center candle, one for each participant*
- *Decorated lighter candle with feathers, beads, or whatever*
- *Bowl of feathers*
- *Bowl of glitter*
- *Basket of yellow flower petals*
- *Bowl of water*
- *Bowl of colored sprinkles*

- *Wand*
- *Snuffer*
- *Matches*

We kept the use of candles to the center of the altar and did not use candles around the edge for the 4 directions because of the possibility of fire due to the scattering on the altar of such things as feathers.

Additional Items for Sacred Space

- *Dress up items, such as feather hair clips, boas, large scraps of fancy cloth to use as scarves, Mardi Gras beads, etc.*
- *Large kid-sized sheets of paper*
- *Crayons and markers*
- *Hard surface such as a book or magazine to draw on placed under the altar*
- *Goodie bags with penny candy and M and M's*

Set Up

We set up the dress up table off to one side of the room, but still clearly in sacred space. Anything goes for dress up items.

We also put candles in the windows and had soft lighting.

Smudge

Smudging outside the room allows each person a brief clearing and centering before walking into ritual space.

Set up the smudge outside the room. You may appoint a 'smudger', but do not forget to smudge yourself as leaders first. You may use whatever feels appropriate to you. Some suggestions are: sage, paulo santo, or mugwort.

Ritual Introduction

Leader: Tonight's ritual is to the Goddesses of Playfulness, and this is the altar to playfulness, mirth and frolicking. We will continue to decorate it this evening and worship earnestly and with vigor the spirits of playfulness that we invite here tonight.

Calling the Directions

SOUTH

Leader: Please stand and turn to the South.
Goddesses of the South, come play with us.
Show us how to delight in the intoxicating perfumes of summer earth and sky, the softness of warm sultry days, and balmy nights.
Show us how to ease gently into mirth and playfulness and warm our insides
with the sounds of laughter.
We welcome you.

Leader or participant playfully sprinkles yellow flower petals over the altar, as she walks around the altar. Pass the basket of flowers so that each person may add some flower petals. Feel free to 'ham it up' and be playful.

WEST

Leader: Please turn to the West.
Goddesses of the West, come play with us.
Splash over us, refresh us with your fluidity, ease and your soft, slippery wetness.
Guide us to celebrate, wildly and outrageously, the joys of fruition, to savor the mellow

joy in wit and cleverness that develops with maturity.
We welcome you.

Leader sprinkles water into the air all over the altar and the participants. Pass bowl of water so that each person may add some to the altar.

NORTH

Leader: Let us turn to the North,
Goddesses of the North, come play with us.
Teach us to find the bottomless wells of humor and mirth within ourselves,
to laugh with the lightness of youth and the depth of age.
Warm yourself with the light of our laughter.
We welcome you.

Leader throws sparkles over the altar. Pass the bowl of glitter so that each person may add some to the altar. The participants may want to put a pinch or two on each other's heads, just for fun and sparkle.

EAST

Leader: Please turn to the East.
Goddesses of the East, come play with us.
Teach us to dance and frolic as the wildflowers do with the gentle touch of your breath.
Teach us to listen as you whisper sweet secrets to the awaiting leaves and grasses.
We welcome you.

Leader throws feathers up into the air, over the altar. Do this playfully and gently. Pass a bowl of feathers so each person may add a feather.

CENTER

Leader: And now, facing the center,
Goddesses of the Center, come play with us.
Dance and romp with us in our circle tonight.
Hold us safely in sacred space so that we might be nourished and healed in the sacredness of play.
We welcome you.

Leader lights one candle. You may want to use a big, playful candle for the middle. We used a candle shaped like a castle. Around the center is a circle of tea lights, one for each participant. Pass the decorated lighter candle for each person to light a tea light.

Pass the Basket

Leader: To help us get into the mood I have here a basket of jokes and humorous readings. Please pick one and after the bowl goes around once, you may read your joke to the group.

Pass the basket of jokes and have everyone draw one and when the basket has gone around the circle, have each one read her joke. If there are enough, the basket can be passed a second time. This was fun and effective in loosening everyone up. Again, use your judgment on jokes, but don't be afraid to be a little bawdy.

Childhood Play

Leader: As a part of our worship of the Goddesses of Playfulness and Frolicking, we will return to childhood, when we knew them intimately and knew how to honor them with abandon and delight. They were our best teachers. To help us get in this playful frame of mind we will have a dress up time. Please feel free to talk and trade dress up items. When you are done, please come back to the circle.

Have a side table set up with all the dress up stuff.

Participants really became involved after the first few minutes of hesitation. It helped that we were dressed up and went back to the table for more. Allow them enough time.

Leader: Now that we are all back at our circle, make yourselves comfortable and take a moment to reflect on what play was like for you as a child. Draw and write what comes to mind. It may be a favorite childhood memory, activity, place where you played, and how it felt. You can spread out around the room, as you are comfortable. We will have a chance to share our musings and spark each other's memories when everyone is done.

Give out paper, markers, paints and crayons and a hard drawing surface if needed. Give them enough time and space to draw or write. We found that they wanted to spread out over the room, almost like kids. We also chose large sheets of paper and lots of kid-like drawing tools.

When everyone is done, gather again in the circle.

Sharing

Leader: We will pass the wand as a talking stick. You may talk about your picture and reflections on play and then place the pictures on the altar to the Goddesses of Playfulness.

Current Play

Leader: Now we will shift gears some. This time sit back, get comfortable, and reflect a moment on what you do for play now. What do you do for fun? How does playfulness feed and nourish you in your current life?

Pass out paper and crayons.

Again give them enough time. We found this part took a little longer and was more thoughtful.

Sharing

Leader: We will pass the wand, inviting you to share your picture and thoughts about current play. When you are finished, place your picture on the altar.

The Honoring

Leader: For the delight and honoring of the Goddesses of Playfulness, for all the gifts you bring into our lives, for joy, laughter, a lightness of being and fresh perspectives, we celebrate your presence in our lives and make this offering.

Leader holds up the bowl of colored sprinkles and scatters some around the altar. Then pass the bowl around the circle for everyone to sprinkle.

Talking Stick

Leader: We will pass the wand again, this time in the usual manner of a talking stick. Please feel free to share whatever you like or pass.

Thanking and Releasing the Spirits

Leader: Please stand.

SOUTH

Leader: Goddesses of the South, thank you for joining us in play.

WEST

Leader: Goddesses of the West, thank you for laughing with us.

NORTH

Leader: Goddesses of the North, thank you for sharing our quiet laughter.

EAST

Leader: Goddesses of the East, thank you for joining us in our dance of joy.

CENTER

Leader: Goddesses of the Center, thank you for sharing our delight in this ritual.

Singing the Circle Closed.

For this ritual we sang the circle closed with the chant, May the Circle Be Open but Unbroken. The music is in the appendix.

Words: May the circle be open, but unbroken

May the love of the Goddess be ever in your heart.

Merry meet and merry part

And merry meet again.

Gift Giving

Pass out the bags of candies. The group loved this as the finishing touch. The candies brought back fond memories.

Celebrating the Dance of Life

Theme

In this ritual we celebrate our own bodies and the joys and pleasures of the dance of life.

Sources of Inspiration

We took a little of this and that from many pagan traditions to craft this ritual. The poetry is from Z. Budapest, a leader in European feminist spirituality. The dance song is adapted from the Yule song, Lord of the Dance, and used to honor the Spring Maiden. The meditation is a self-blessing inspired by Starhawk and other feminist pagans.

Altar

- *Red altar cloth*
- *Matches*
- *Snuffer*
- *Lighting candle*
- *White and red flowers scattered on cloth*
- *Sprinkles or paper confetti in small containers with enough for each participant*

  Paper confetti works best as sparkles are difficult to clean up and itchy, but go for it if you like.

- *Cloth under the chairs in the circle to catch the confetti or sparkles*
- *White candle and the items below at each of the directions*

  Fire or candle at the south

  Water at the west

  Stones at the north

  Feathers at the east

  A Goddess or dancing Shiva at the center

Set up

We set the altar up in the usual pattern with chairs in a circle around the central altar.

On a separate table: A feast of cookies and juice, crackers and wine or whatever foods and beverages seem appropriate to you.

It may be obvious to state, but if wine is served a non-alcoholic choice should also be served. We find that plain water is most popular with the groups we work with.

Smudge

Smudging outside the room allows each person a brief clearing and centering before walking into ritual space.

You may appoint a 'smudger', but do not forget to smudge yourself as leaders first. You may use whatever feels appropriate to you. Some suggestions are: sage, paulo santo, or mugwort.

Calling the Directions

Light each candle before calling the direction

SOUTH

Leader: Please turn to the South.
Energy of Goddess, be hot within us.
Be passion in our hearts.
Be joy and growth and dancing in our being.
Be here with us.

WEST

Leader: Please turn to the west.
Living Waters, blood of Goddess, your heartbeat pulses within us.
Be dreams and feelings flowing forth.
Be sweet and clear and opening within us.
Be here in this hour.

NORTH

Leader: Please turn to the North.
Body of Goddess, be our strength.
Be sacred ground firm under our feet.
Be nectar and nourishment and tenacity within us.
Be here with us.

EAST

Leader: Please turn to the East.
Breath of Goddess, be wind in our sails.

Be divine mind in ours.
Be vision and clarity and lightness of being within us.
Be here in this hour.

CENTER

Leader: Please turn to the center.
From the ground, from the stone, from the windswept sky, from the flaming fire's cone, from the flowing water's sigh, our spirits call, our voices sing, our feet dance to celebrate the solstice.
Join us in the dance.

Reading

Leader: SOLSTICE POEM (with respect to Z. Budapest)
I have slept for ten thousand years.
Now I stretch and waken.
They are calling, calling me, and my heart leaps to greet them.
My forests are my hair, the grasses my heavy eyelashes.
They call me, and I waken.
My body bedecked with a million flowers,
And these many breasts of mine, the mountains joyfully rear their tips.
I long to suckle my young. They are calling.
They will know me!
Earth Mother am I; life springs from me. I carry the seed of creation.
And I awake!

Meditation

Leader: And now lets get ready to celebrate ourselves with a self-blessing.

The script for the meditation is at the end of the ritual. Remember to leave time at the end of the meditation for people to journal or just sit quietly. This provides a gentle and thoughtful transition into the next part of the ritual. It is also important for their integration of the meditation into current time.

This is an active meditation which engages the participants in the meditation. Time needs to be given. For many there is a lightness of being inherent in the self-blessing.

Spiral Dance

Leader teaches the chant by reciting it in its entirety, then reads one line and instructs the group to repeat that line. Repeat until the group is comfortable. It helps to have someone who can sing and knows the melody to lead the group. You may want to appoint this person ahead of time. You may also want to chant more than three times and may want to move in a line around the room or whatever moves you.

Leader: Let us turn to the center, join hands and dance in a simple step dance as we all chant 3 times or more:

Dance, dance, wherever you may be
I am the Queen of the Dance, you see!
I live in you, and you live in Me
And I lead you all in the Dance, said She!

Drop hands.

Music and words are in the appendix. We went outside as it was a beautiful evening and danced the spiral around the churchyard.

We allowed several minutes to walk quietly into the sacred space of our circle and settle in. This seemed to be adequate transition into the talking stick.

Talking Stick

Leader: We will now pass the talking stick. Please share as you are moved. You may want to share what came up during the meditation. Who would like to start?

Thanking and Releasing the Directions

Snuff each candle as you read the direction

SOUTH

Leader: Please stand.

Great Goddess of the South, of Fire, we thank you for your presence.

EAST

Leader: Great Goddess of the East, of Air, we thank you for your presence.

NORTH

Leader: Great Goddess of the North, of Earth, we thank you for your presence.

WEST

Leader: Great Goddess of the West, of Water, we thank you for your presence.

WEST

Leader: May the peace of the Goddess of the Center be in our hearts.

Merry meet,
Merry part,
And merry meet again.
Blessed Be!

You may choose to use the chant "May the circle be open" instead. This ritual should end with a feast that may be served elsewhere in the room or brought to the altar.

Meditation

Self Blessing, Celebrating our Being

And beginning to settle in for meditation.....And so breathe deeply......inhaling and taking in the bounty of the breath....the nourishment of the universe....filling your belly.....your chest......and as you are ready.....exhaling....giving back nourishment to the universe and its beings......

And now....bringing your attention to your feet ....feeling the floor beneath you........ sensing your legs.......up to your knees, your thighs........

And pause.....reflecting for a moment on the multitude of ways your feet and legs have served you on your journey through life.....Of the places and people they have taken you to through the years.....the dances they have danced.....the sensation of new grass, warm sand, ocean waves on your toes....the lessons they have offered........

Sprinkle your feet, calves and shins, knees and thighs, saying:
I celebrate and honor my feet, my calves and shins, my knees and thighs and the joys they have offered me

Pause

And now...bring your awareness to your hips and pelvis...........Pausing a moment at the center of your creative energy........and reflecting on how your pelvis and hips have served you......how they have supported your body..........and reflecting on the multitude of ideas, actions and creations, the life and vibrancy that you have nurtured and brought into the world...........

Sprinkle your hips and pelvis, saying:
I celebrate and honor my hips and pelvis...and all the joys they have brought me.....

Pause

And now...gradually move your awareness to your belly....sense your belly......Reflecting on how this part of your body has served you....digesting the bounty from the earth.... supplying energy and nutrients to your physical body.....energy for all the emotions, the thoughts and activities available to us.........reflecting on the wisdom of our gut feelings that have been freely offered...

Sprinkle your belly, saying:
I celebrate and honor my belly and all the nourishment and joy it has offered me....

Pause

And moving to your chest............your lungs...protected by your ribs....breathing in the universe and breathing out the universe....connecting you to all that is...........
and your heart....ever-beating.....held also in the protection of your ribs and cradled in the love and compassion of the mother......And reflect for a moment on how your chest, has nourished and sustained you...how your heart center has touched, loved, cracked and healed.......both yourself and others.......

Sprinkle your chest, saying:
I celebrate and honor my chest...my lungs and heart..and heart center ....for all the joy and love they have offered me......

Pause

And now....gently moving your awareness to your shoulders....and to your arms....down to the very tips of your fingers...... .....
Pausing and reflecting on the myriad of ways in which your shoulders, arms and hands have served you........the hugs they have given and received.......the bundles they have carried.......your touching......... laboring and creating....loving and healing hands............

Sprinkle your shoulders and hands, saying:
I celebrate and honor my shoulders, arms and hands. And all the joy and wonder they have offered me......

Pause

And now....shifting your attention, with great kindness to your back.....letting your awareness travel the full length of your spine......from the top of your shoulders.....to the tip of your tailbone....... ......

And pausing....reflecting here on the many ways your back has served you....however imperfectly you thought at the time.....how it has supported you in standing and sitting....walking and running....supporting the burdens and joys that you have carried physically and energetically here..

Sprinkle your back, saying:

I celebrate and honor my back and all the joys and strength it has offered me......

Pause

And moving your awareness up to your neck....the back of your neck...and your throat.... reflecting on the many gifts and abilities that your neck and throat have offered you.... supporting your head......turning your head to see, smell and hear.....

And speaking....giving voice to your inner life...your thoughts, feelings, and ideas..... offering you the gift of sharing....connecting....expressing.....

Sprinkle your neck, saying:

I celebrate and honor my neck and my voice...and all the joy, and expression they have offered me

Pause

And now, bringing your awareness to your face.......gently touching your face if you like.......and reflecting on the gift of your senses here.......

your sense of taste...and the many delights that have graced your palate.....

on your sense of smell which guides and remembers.......

on your sense of hearing....listening to music and the sounds of nature...........

and on your sense of sight...seeing the beauty that has enriched and sustained you.....

Sprinkle your head, saying:

I celebrate and honor my head, and face.....and my mind and all the joy and learning they have offered me.....

Pause

Please stand up. And now standing........moving your attention to our circle and this place here......Reflecting on all the joys and experiences you have shared here in circle, whether often or for the first time today......

Sprinkle the altar in our center:

I celebrate and honor all who are held in this circle and this place and all the joy and awe that have occurred and will occur here.

And I dance to celebrate....to honor......to rejoice!

SR, MG 2003

with appreciation
to my co-author
Marcia Giudice

Celebrating the Warmth of Connections

Theme

We gathered for this solstice to celebrate the power of connections with each other and with spirit that were forged through sitting in ritual circle. This is the feminine power of listening with heart, being fully present with another and the shared experience of coming together in sacred space.

Sources of Inspiration

The hand massage aspect of this ritual was drawn from an experiential exercise that was offered at a Holistic Nurses training. The exercise focuses on the mindful practice of presence, which highlights our connections with each other in a powerfully tender manner.

The kinto practice is from the Andean shamanic tradition and is used to offer blessings, make requests, and seek balance and harmony. The calling of the directions was inspired by the Celtic and Peruvian traditions.

Altar

- *Candles for the four directions*
- *Cake with a large candle in the middle of it for the center*
- *Altar cloth*
- *Matches*
- *Lighting candle*
- *Snuffer*
- *Bowls of offering herbs, such as lavender, sage, cedar, mugwart, or others of your choice*
- *Bay leaves for kintos*
- *Sandwich bags for taking herbs home*

Additional items for Sacred Space

- *Hand lotions*
- *Tissues*
- *Plates, silverware, napkins, cups in a basket*
- *Drinks*
- *Pillows and towels for the hand massage*
- *Music of a calm, healing nature*

Set Up

For this particular ritual we chose to have the cake at the center of the altar. We placed a large candle in the center of the cake and lit it for the center direction. The plates, drinks etc. were on a separate table. After we closed the circle, people remained seated and we served the cake and drinks.

Smudge

Smudging outside the room allows each person a brief clearing and centering before walking into ritual space.

You may appoint a 'smudger', but do not forget to smudge yourself as leaders first. You may use whatever feels appropriate to you. Some suggestions are: sage, paulo santo, or mugwort. Have the participants enter the ritual room as they are finished being smudged.

Calling the Directions

Light each candle as the direction is read

SOUTH

Leader: We lift our hands and hearts to the South, home to warmth, passion, and healing.
We call upon Grandmother Serpent.
Be here with us, share your wisdom and ability to change and grow with us.

WEST

Leader: We lift our hands and hearts to the West, guardian of Water, flexible, shape-shifting yet always itself.
We call upon our Mother-Sister Jaguar.
Be here with us, share your gifts and medicine with us.

NORTH

Leader: We lift our hands and hearts to the North, dwelling place of the Mountains, of ancient teachings and ways.
We call upon our Grandmother Hummingbird and Grandfather Dragon.
Be with us and share your joy, sustenance and courage.

EAST

Leader: We lift our hands and hearts to the East, guardian of Air and the rising sun, of invisible sustenance.
We call upon our Brothers Condor and Eagle.
Share your vision and joy with us.

CENTER

Leader: We raise our hands to the sky, to our Star Brothers and Sisters, Sun and Moon, and we anchor our feet upon our Mother the Earth, Pachamama.
Hold us and guide us on our many different paths.
Be here with us tonight.

Ritual

Leader: We offer this ritual and ceremony to honor the spirit and the sacredness of the earth and all who live upon her and within her. It serves as a time and place that unites us in our connection to all of life.

Expressing our gratitude for this privilege of gathering is central in tending to and caring for our relationship with the Spirit that dwells within all things. In offering thanks we give back, we acknowledge, we honor all the many expressions of the sacred: the trees, the waters, the animals and birds, the earth and sky, and our relationship with each other.

We would like to share a process of honoring and giving thanks that we hope you will continue throughout the summer. There are bowls of herbs on the altar which you may use to fill your offering bags. You will make your first offering this evening. Throughout the summer, as you find yourself in a place of beauty, are blessed with good fortune or kindness, or just whenever, you may make an offering. Go out in your yard, stop by the road at a beautiful spot, or on the street, wherever you are, and offer thanks with an herb bundle.

We also have kintos for each of you to make. They are an offering of thanks and honoring to the Spirits of the land, done in the tradition of the Quero Natives in the mountains of Peru. Kintos can also be a request for balance, for right relationship within you, with others, and with all of life. You are invited to use the kinto throughout the summer.

Take three bay leaves that are in good shape, stack them with the front facing you, one on top of the other. As you work the leaves, you are bringing body, mind and spirit, your thinking, feeling and doing into balance and harmony. It is a request to Spirit for help and an honoring of the Spirits for the assistance, beauty and sustenance that they offer us. As you formulate this in your heart, blow the intent of the offering onto the kinto, breathing life into your intentions.

So, as you gather your herbs and kinto now, please do so in silence, and then sit until everyone is done.

We labeled the herbs with their energetic properties. They are located in books, internet searches and in your personal experience. They walked around the altar, choosing and filling their bags and picking up their three bay leaves

Leader: Once you have made your kinto and bag of herbs you are ready to make your first offering of the summer. Go to a spot that calls you and offer your kinto and some of your herbs as an expression of gratitude for the year we have had together and the beauty and abundance that is present in our lives. You may call the directions again if you like, and thank the directions when you are finished.

Return when you are ready.

All the participants went out into the churchyard to make their offerings. This was very meaningful for people and they took their time and care accordingly. One by one they returned to the circle. (It was the end of the year of rituals for us. If that is not applicable to your situation, just leave out those words.)

Honoring our Connections - Mindful Hand Massage

Leader: Now we will have a meditation, an active meditation that is about being with each other with a caring presence. We will be giving each other a hand massage, done with the intention of sharing our caring presence and connection with each other through mindful, compassionate touch.

Please pair up. Let yourself find a comfortable position.

You will each have an opportunity to give a hand massage and receive a hand massage. We will guide you through this exercise to be sure that everyone has plenty of time. We will also let you know when you can switch to the other hand.

You will have a brief time at the end of each massage to share with your partner.

There is lotion and tissues near each of you.

We will also guide you in a brief centering before you start and after you switch roles.

Because this is a very gentle yet powerful exercise, we ask that people not speak. For the giver, this will assist you in bringing your full presence and intention to what you are doing. For the receiver, you will be able to be present with all six of your senses.

Guidance for Hand Massage

This is done as a mindful meditation. You may want calm music in the background to help hold the space. Guide at a relaxed and peaceful pace, as this is the tone that you want to create for the hand massage. We found that timing was helpful to keep us on track as guides. Also, as this can be very meaningful for people, allow enough time for sharing. There may be a variety of responses from intense giggling to tears.

Leader: Arrange yourselves in a comfortable position........decide who will receive first.........

And breathe, filling your belly...your chest......and exhale...deeply and slowly...from your belly...chest ......letting the breath bring you gently inward to just noticing...in this moment...whatever arises in your field of awareness.

For the recipient of the hand massage...this is an opportunity to experience what it is like to receive caring, conscious touch......

I invite you to just notice whatever thoughts, feelings, and sensations may arise....with open compassionate curiosity for yourself........for the next few minutes there is nothing else for you to do.....no place to go........just receiving and noticing......

For the giver of the hand massage................this is an opportunity to offer your full presence to another person.........to be fully present in a caring and compassionate manner................... Bring your awareness to the power of touch and what you can convey through touch...........
I encourage you also to just notice how this is for you.....your thoughts, feelings, any sensations.......
For the next few minutes there is nothing else for you to do.... ...only giving the hand massage and noticing...

This is a time of silence. A gentle gong of a bowl or tingsha is helpful to people to mark the start and end of this massage. A voice or gong at the halfway is a helpful reminder to switch hands. We suggest three to five minutes for each hand and five to ten minutes for the sharing time. We found that sharing is best done in pairs.

Leader: And now switch roles.

For the new recipient.....bring your attention gently to your breath.......a conscious intentional breath...........beginning to switch to the role of receiving.............this is your opportunity to experience what it is like to receive caring, conscious touch..........to receive another's full presence..................

I invite you to just notice whatever thoughts, feelings, might arise.........noticing sensations......... with open, compassionate curiosity for yourself........whatever you notice is wonderful and rich......

And for the new giver of the hand massage ....this is your opportunity to offer your full presence to another person... ...to be fully present in a caring and compassionate manner.................... Bring your awareness to the power of touch and what you can convey through touch........... I encourage you also to just notice how this is for you..... your thoughts, your feelings, any sensations.......

Again, voice or gong halfway through the massage and again at the beginning and end. Allow time for sharing in pairs. When this is complete, stop the music and invite everyone to return to the circle

Leader: I would like to regroup everyone around the altar now, so please draw your conversations to a close and gather. I am turning off the music.

Pause here for a moment of silence to transition.

Talking Stick

Leader: We will now pass the talking stick. Please share as you are moved. You may also pass. Who would like to start?

Thanking and Releasing the Directions

Snuff each candle as you read each direction

SOUTH

Leader: We lift our hands and hearts to the South, to Grandmother Serpent and the Goddess. Thank you for being here.

WEST

Leader: We lift our hands and hearts to the West, to the power of Water and Mother-Sister Jaguar.
Thank you for being here.

NORTH

Leader: We lift our hands and hearts to the North, to the Mountains, and Grandmother Hummingbird and Grandfather Dragon.
We thank you for being here.

EAST

Leader: We lift our hands and hearts to the East, to the Air and our Brother Condor and Brother Eagle.
Thank you for being here.

CENTER

Leader: We raise our hands to the sky, to our Star Brothers and Sisters, Sun and Moon, and lower our hands to our Mother the Earth.
Thank you for being here.

Fall Equinox

The Autumn Equinox is September 21st and is another moment when light and dark are equal. It is at this moment that the turning wheel pauses before it begins its journey toward harvesting the abundance of the spring and summer. Squirrels store their nuts, others eat abundantly in the fall storing fat, the trees shed their leaves providing nourishment for the soil and the plants, we gather and harvest our crops, hunt and store our food. We gather in from the fields and woods and sea of the nourishment that will sustain us through the winter. And we celebrate the harvest, giving thanks for the gifts from our labors and from nature that will sustain us.

There may also be a gentle turning inward, an awareness of a subtle, emerging desire for quiet, for settling in warm and comfortable. Darkness is coming, cold is creeping in, and we naturally begin to turn our thoughts to the introspection and quiet that is food for our hopes and plans for the future.

Our first ritual celebrates the old 'wicker man' of Celtic origins, who is 'plowed under' and harvested so that new life may grow in the spring.

The last two acknowledge the delicate balance of day and night that also occurs on the equinox. A point of equality upon which we can rest to look both backwards and review the spring and summer and look forward to what might be coming.

Honoring the Ancient Wisdoms

Theme

In many Celtic traditions there is a celebration of the Wicker Man, a figure representing the Plant Spirits, in which he is sacrificed so that growth and renewal are possible. He is the image of resurrection following death, and as such is filled with the energy and power of the feminine.

Sources of Inspiration

We drew from the Green Man traditions. Although commonly thought of as Celtic, these traditions are found in all of Europe and Asia.

Altar

- *Gold or any fall colored altar cloth*
- *Fall decorations like leaves, gourds, etc. as the spirit moves you*
- *Plate of honey cake or pound cake cut in small bite sized pieces*
- *Honey in a pot with a honey drizzle stick or small teaspoon*
- *Beeswax candles at the directions*
- *Rattles*
- *Wicker man*

In the past a wicker man was woven from flexible sticks such as willow. You can make a man out of straw, raffia, or dried corn leaves. It is the symbolism and your intent while creating your wicker man that are important.

Additional items for sacred space

- *Fire pit or grill*
- *Small kindling wood*
- *Paper*
- *Matches*

- *Cooking oil to help fire burn quickly*
- *Lavender, sage or other sweet scented herbs*

Set Up

We created the altar using fall colors. Additional items are all representative of the season. Have fun with it. Place the 'wicker man' on the altar for the ritual.

We went outdoors for the fire. It is also helpful to set up the fire in the grill so that it is ready to go. We placed matches, oil and herbs by the grill. If there is inclement weather, an Epsom salts and alcohol fire may be used inside. If this is the case, a paper representation of the wicker man should be used, as the fire is not hot enough to burn the straw or raffia.

Smudge

Smudging outside the room allows each person a brief clearing and centering before walking into ritual space.

Set up the smudge outside the room. You may appoint a 'smudger', but do not forget to smudge yourself as leaders first. You may use whatever feels appropriate to you. Some suggestions are: sage, paulo santo, or mugwort

Calling the Directions

Light the candle for each direction as it is read.

EAST

Leader: We call upon the Spirit of Air who cools us during the heat of summer and chills us in the winter months.
We are in balance on this night of the equinox.
Be with us to clear our minds that we may walk in beauty in all seasons.

SOUTH

Leader: We call upon the Spirit of Fire who heals our hearts in the burning days of summer and gives us hope and light in the dark and cold of winter.
Be with us to nurture our hearts that we may walk in beauty in all seasons.

WEST

Leader: We call upon the Spirit of Water who washes over us in the waves of the ocean during the heat of summer and freezes and sparkles in the cold days of winter.
Be with us to calm and sustain our bodies that we may walk in beauty in all seasons.

NORTH

Leader: We call upon the Spirit of Earth who nurtures us with flowers, fruits and vegetables in the days of summer and sustains and holds us in the cold of winter.
Be with us to delight our eyes and hold us that we may walk in beauty in all seasons.

CENTER

Leader: We call upon the Spirit of the Center, the Above and the Below, who holds the calm of all days in the light of summer and the dark of winter.

Be with us and hold us centered in our being that we may walk in beauty upon the Mother in all seasons.

Ritual

Leader: We gather here to celebrate the fall equinox, the time of the first harvest. Often a feast is prepared and thanks are offered for the abundance that is the result of our labor. The equinox signals the time of gathering and storing this abundance for the times ahead. All of life participates: the squirrels are foraging for nuts, I have been watching them gather the big green ones, the birds are getting ready to fly south, the kids are returning to school. And the bees too have been busy all spring and summer, gathering pollens, making honey and tending the hive. We have been gathering and savoring the abundance of our labor over the spring and summer. Rest and sun have given us new energy, fresh food has fed our bodies. All of nature is dancing the wheel, including us.

Meditation

The script for the meditation is at the end of the ritual.

Remember to leave time at the end of the meditation for people to journal or just sit quietly. This provides a gentle and thoughtful transition into the next part of the ritual. It is also important for their integration of the meditation into current time.

Ritual

Leader: Honey symbolizes the sweetness of the harvest. Honey also symbolizes a process of harvesting that is bigger than any one person alone, for honey is the result of the cooperative efforts of the bees, flowers, rain and sun.

Leader passes the plate of cakes and as each one takes a piece, the leader drizzles a bit of honey on it. If you have two leaders, one can pass the cakes and one can drizzle the honey. All then eat.

Leader: It is also on the equinox that we honor the turning of the wheel of life. We acknowledge the circular nature of these rhythms, now perched for a moment in balance and equality, for the fall equinox signals the tipping or turning of the balance towards the growing night, the growing darkness and the time of composting or turning inward.

But as surely as the Fall Equinox holds the harvest and night deep within its Mystery, it also holds the promise of the spring equinox, sister of the fall equinox. Each holds the promise of the other in a circular, rhythmic movement or dance around the wheel of life.

Nature herself changes outfit at this time. The green man, who arises in the arms of the spring maiden has grown to maturity and makes ready to be harvested and ploughed under for composting new growth. The Green Man is an ancient energy that has taken many forms throughout history, but always he is equated with the wild and passionate nature spirit—the spirit of the woods, fertility and growth. He is known as Enkidu in the Gilgamesh epic, as Robin Hood, the Green Knight of Sir Galahad, as Puck in Shakespeare and as Kokopelli for the Navajo. He is even immortalized on the John Barleycorn album of Traffic. His symbols and representations are everywhere.

It is in the fall that the Green Man changes and with maturity becomes the Wicker Man. In Celtic traditions, the Wicker Man is burned at the fall equinox, symbolizing the death of summer and long days. He is burnt to honor the fruits of the harvest that Nature has given. He is set aflame to ensure and bless our eternal dance around the wheel.

For as surely as his death is honored and he is ploughed under, the crone-mother will bring back the green man as she moves into her spring maiden form. And so the dance of the sacred wheel continues.

But at the equinox, the dance of the Goddess and the Green Man, the dance around light and dark, growth and rest, new and old are held in balance. And we celebrate. We burn the Wicker Man and we dance around the fire with joy and gratitude. We dance and chant to honor the Green Man, the Goddess, and the eternal rhythms of life.

We are going to go outdoors and in ceremony burn the wicker man. I have brought rattles of all kinds for you to use during the fire if you would like. The ashes from the fire will be given to Mother Earth after the ritual.

Let's take a minute and review the chant. It is similar to a responsive reading where I will chant a phrase and you will respond with the refrain. The refrain is

"Hey eh yeah
The beauty way"

For example,.
I say: I dance the turning wheel
And you respond with
"Hey ee yeah
The beauty way"

Words for the chant appear at the end of the ritual.

Leader: Let us go outside in silence and gather around our sacred fire.

We use cooking oil to get the fire going. This can be added ceremoniously. When the fire is going well give the invocation. As the fire begins to die down add lavender or other herbs for the sweet scent and to carry our gratitude and joy to Spirit.

Invocation

Leader: Spirits of the Green Man and the Spring Maiden, be with us. Hear our songs of gratitude, our songs of joy and love for all that is. Witness our dance of honoring the rhythms and the Mysteries that unite all things as one. For we are the dance, we are the light and the dark, the seed and the fruit, the new and the old. And they are we.
HO!

When we started the chant, we began our dance around the fire. We used a simple two step in time with the chant. After burning the Green Man we returned inside in silence.

Talking Stick

Leader: We will now pass the talking stick. Please share as you are moved. You may want to share something that came up during the ritual or whatever else is in your heart or on your mind. What is said here stays here in circle. It is all right to pass. Who would like to start?

Thanking and Releasing the Directions

Snuff each candle as the direction is read.

EAST

Leader: We thank the Spirit of Air who has cleared our minds that we may walk in beauty.

SOUTH

Leader: We thank the Spirit of Fire who has nurtured our hearts that we may walk in beauty.

WEST

Leader: We thank the Spirit of Water who has calmed us that we may walk in beauty.

NORTH

Leader: We thank the Spirit of Earth who has held us that we may walk in beauty.

CENTER

Leader: We thank the Spirit of the Center who has held us centered that we may walk in beauty.

After the ashes have cooled, usually after participants have left, you may offer the ashes to Mother Earth by calling the directions and scattering the ashes in a place that you feel is a place in nature blessed by Spirit. Remember to close the directions.

Chant

adapted from I walk the Sacred Down Trail
by Lisa Theil

Chanter: I dance the turning wheel
Refrain: Hey eh yeah, the beauty way
Hey eh yeah, the beauty way.
Chanter: Dark to Light and Light to Dark
Refrain: Hey eh yeah, the beauty way
Hey eh yeah, the beauty way

Chanter: I dance the turning wheel
Chanter: Hey eh yeah, the beauty way
Hey eh yeah, the beauty way
Chanter: Fall to spring and spring to fall
Chanter: Hey eh yeah, the beauty way
Hey eh yeah the beauty way.

Meditation

The Sweet Wisdom of the Bees

And now, finding a comfortable position for meditation.........please take a moment to settle in.......gradually letting your attention come to your breath........eyes open or closed as is comfortable for you......gently turning inward and inviting your imagination to come forward.......

Pause until people are settled

Begin to imagine for a moment that it is late summer......a sunny warm afternoon......... the sky is a radiant blue, with only soft white puffs of clouds floating by to give it form....................and so settling in......noticing the warmth on your skin as you rest against a sun-warmed rock....................It is easy to let your body soften and rest in this warmth, your eyes may close gently..................

And you can hear the gentle rustle of the breeze in the trees...and smell the sweet fragrances that float on this breeze. And slowly, breathing in.... drinking in this richness... deep into your body.........taking in this warm and soothing peacefulness......... ripe and rich..........and slowly exhaling sending this calm into every nook and cranny of your body/mind..........

As you rest here................you become aware of the buzzing of the bees a safe distance away............so you continue to sit........somewhat curious now ....
and gently opening your eyes you see the bees................as if you were an invisible observer....

One or two bees busy themselves with the flowers in the field.....darting here and there......gently rubbing up against the flowers, gathering their nectar......and off they fly......................on their mission to the hive...............there are several more off to the side........ and this process continues around you....................several more bees arriving to gather and harvest the wild flowers.....

The hive is close by and you can begin to see the activity in and out of the hive............. everyone doing their part.......and the sweetness of the honey begins to tickle your senses..................smelling the sweet fragrance.......the fruit of the sun, rain, flowers, earth and the fruit of the labors of the bees...all this begins to tickle your taste................ how amazing is this process.....this circle of gathering and harvesting....and the sweetness of it all.... ....

And like the bees......you too may have been gathering during the long days of spring and summer......perhaps crops....perhaps moments of warmth and peace in the sun....... perhaps joy filled experiences with friends and play mixed in with the work.......... sustenance for the body and also the spirit, your soul food for the coming times............ you may rest a moment... savoring the sweetness of your spring and summer...... of all of the experiences you have gathered.....even the difficult ones that you have now survived........gather them all for they are all the fruits of your labor filled with wisdoms.... sweetness...learning........and just pause and savor them all..............

Pause

And now.....gently, as you are ready...............begin to bring your awareness to the breath again..........bidding farewell to the scene before you........thanking yourself for the time you have taken to savor your life.................gradually returning your focus to your breath.........each inhale and each exhale bringing you softly back to our circle....... perhaps sensing how you are resting in your seat............moving or wiggling if you like......and now inhaling deeply......and slowly exhaling.........opening your eyes when you are ready.........gazing around and returning completely to current time and place.

SR2005

Honoring the Turning of the Wheel

Theme

Mother Earth pauses at the fall equinox marking the gathering of the harvest and the turning of the seasons. At this harvest celebration we, too, begin to let go into calmer and more pensive times of rest and replenishment.

Sources of Inspiration

The concept of eating symbolic foods in ritual is done in many traditions. For example, the use of the pomegranate seeds is drawn from the Greek myth of Persephone and Demeter. The bag of seeds, which is used as an offering to Mother Earth, is taken from the Peruvian shamanic tradition.

Altar

- *Cloth in fall colors*
- *Colored leaves, acorns, etc. scattered over the altar*
- *Moon cookies*

  We used small chocolate cookies or brownies half covered with white frosting,
- *An apple cut horizontally, dipped in lemon juice*
- *Bowl of apple slices, dipped in lemon juice*
- *Bowl of dried hazelnuts*
- *Bowl of pomegranate seeds*
- *Small sandwich bags of grass seeds, enough for each person, in a basket or bowl*
- *Small sandwich bags, empty*
- *Bowls of dried flowers, grass seeds and dried herbs*
- *Candle snuffer*
- *Small candle for lighting the directions*
- *Matches*
- *Candles for the directions*

Additional items

- *Many candles*
- *Decorate the rest of the room as you please with seasonal colors and items*

Set Up

We had the room dark with just enough light to read by. We had many candles around the periphery. Our goal was to symbolize the growing darkness of autumn. Before the participants arrived, we smudged the room. We find it helpful to prepare the room energetically and spiritually by smudging. It seems to us that it makes a subtle difference in the way that people approach the room and respond to the ritual.

Background music is optional, but may be used to set a quiet, reverential tone.

Smudge

Smudging outside the room allows each person a brief clearing and centering before walking into ritual space.

Set up the smudge outside the room. You may appoint a 'smudger', but do not forget to smudge yourself as leaders first. You may use whatever feels appropriate to you. Some suggestions are: sage, paulo santo, or mugwort.

Grounding

Read this slowly and thoughtfully like a meditation

Leader: Please stand and take a deep breath in…and breathe out…a cleansing breath…relaxation in…anxiety out…Breathe deeply…and bring your attention to your body…down your legs to your feet. Imagine your feet are growing…deep into the ground…like the roots of a tree, down into the earth, deep into the soil. Feel the energy deep within the core of the Mother. Allow it to travel up into your feet, feel it rise up to fill you. Notice how it settles and matures as it spreads up and throughout your being…just as the energy of Mother Earth mellows and settles at this time. Embrace the energy…your energy connected to the earth.

Pause, to allow people to sense and feel the energy.

You may be seated.

Calling the Directions

Light each candle before calling the direction

EAST

Leader: Spirits of the East, of Air, we ask you to be with us.
Air, bring lightness of being to our bodies and minds.
Please join our circle.

SOUTH

Leader: Spirits of the South, of Fire, we ask you to be with us.
Fire, transform us, warm our hearts so that we may grow in compassion.
Please join our circle.

WEST

Leader: Spirits of the West, of Water, we ask you to be with us.
Water, soothe us, wash us with your calming, cleansing touch.
Please join our circle.

NORTH

Leader: Spirits of the North, of Earth, we ask you to be with us.
Sacred mountains, heal us, nourish our bodies, minds and spirits.
Please join our circle.

CENTER

Leader: Gaia, Mother Earth, bring balance and harmony to this circle as we move through the seasons in predictable pattern.
We thank you for the fruits of this harvest season.
Please join our circle.

Meditation

The script for the meditation is at the end of the ritual. Remember to leave time at the end of the meditation for people to journal or just sit quietly. This provides a gentle and thoughtful transition into the next part of the ritual. It is also important for their integration of the meditation into current time.

Ritual

Pick up the hazelnuts from altar and say:

Leader: Within the silence of the coming winter, let wisdom's fruit bring inner knowing. May it strengthen us, as we prepare to descend through the darkness of the winter season. We accept the change that wisdom brings, for such fruit may not be eaten lightly. It is the gift of the Earth. May our harvest be bountiful.

Walking around the circle to pass out the food enhances the feeling of ceremony. We did this for the passing of all foods.

Pick up the pomegranate from altar and say:

Leader: When Persephone, Goddess of Spring, visited the land of the dead, according to the ancient Greek myth, she ate three seeds from the pomegranate and thus had to stay in that land for three months of every year. Her mother's sorrow is our winter, a time of hibernation and deep thoughts. May our harvest prepare us for this time.

Pass out the pomegranate seeds and eat mindfully.

Pick up the apple from altar and say:

Leader: In this time that we think of as the end of summer, the earth is pregnant with the seeds of new life. Within this apple resides a star. Within the star reside the seeds. May these seeds nourish our spirits as the apple nourishes our bodies.

Pass out the apple pieces and eat mindfully.

Pick up chocolate cookie with moon on it and say:

Leader: In this time when light and warmth are held in perfect balance with the dark and cold, we can begin to look towards the richness of the dark time that encourages more introspection and thought. May we honor both the light and the dark as a part of our wholeness and the richness of life.

Pass out chocolate cookies and eat mindfully.

Hold up the basket of sandwich bags filled with grass seeds and say:

Leader: We also honor the harvest, the fruits of our labor and growth that will sustain us through the fall and winter and provide for future growth. The altar holds some of the fruits of the first harvest. In these bags are seeds that will lie dormant during the cold of winter, ready to burst forth in the spring. Following the Incan tradition, you may take a bag and carry it outside to a place that feels right to you. Then you may hold it to your forehead and imagine your gratitude for the many blessings that this place has given you. Then blow your thankfulness and blessing into the seeds, breathing life into your gratitude. Scatter the seeds anywhere on the lawn or where ever you wish. Do this offering ritual in silence to hold the moment as a sacred time.

Everyone goes outside and scatters the seeds.

When all the participants return say:

Leader: Holding the silence, take another bag and fill it with whatever on the altar feels right to you. There are seeds and herbs in the small bowls. At home you may repeat this ceremony of gratitude for your own home or any special place that you hold dear.

Talking Stick

Leader: We will now pass the talking stick. Please share as you are moved. You may want to share what came up during the meditation, what nourishes you through the dark of winter, or the gifts that you may have received during the meditation. Who would like to start?

Thanking and Releasing the Directions

Snuff each candle as you read each direction.

EAST

Leader: Spirits of the East, of Air, we thank you for the breezes that cool us.
Thank you for joining our circle.

SOUTH

Leader: Spirits of the South, of Fire, we thank you for the fire that transforms us.
Thank you for joining our circle.

WEST

Leader: Spirits of the West, of Water, we thank you for the water that soothes us.
Thank you for joining our circle.

NORTH

Leader: Spirits of the North, of Earth, we thank you for the strength of stone that heals us.
Thank you for joining our circle.

CENTER

Leader: Mother Earth, we thank you for the balance and harmony you have brought to this circle.
Thank you for joining our circle.

Meditation

Breathing with all of Life

And now, getting ready for meditation..........gradually bring your attention to your breathing..................just noticing.....curious to follow your breath as you inhale....................and then exhale....................knowing that more and more with each breath....you can leave the activity of the day behind.......moving into a quieter.....more timeless realm......where there is no right or wrong.....better or worse.....where there is just this moment.......this open-hearted, compassionate noticing of your breath........... your inhale....and your exhale.........

And now....as you inhale.... bring your awareness to your body.........becoming aware of any movement in your chest and belly as you breathe in..........and breathe out........... gently sensing or feeling.............observing how your chest and belly are expanding and moving outward as you inhale....... .... and as you exhale....noticing how your chest and belly begin to gradually get smaller ....

And this time, consciously expanding your chest and belly as you inhale..........drinking in the nourishment of the air ......the life force that surrounds you.... ....expanding outward.......................and then exhaling as you are ready.........consciously inviting your body and mind to move inward.......... ....releasing...quieting................fed by the nourishment you have taken in.....

And now............attuning to the richness of this steady rhythm...the rhythm of your breathing...........consciously inhaling....and noticing the pause at the peak of your inhale............clear but subtle............ followed by a slow, purposeful exhale.....noticing now the gentle pause at the end of your exhale......a slight pause to finish your breath.... pregnant with anticipation of your next inhale..........and so the pattern... inhaling.....

expanding outward...............pausing..........and exhaling slowly...contracting and then the pause.....

You may explore this rhythm, its sensations and nuances........inhaling...and pausing....... exhaling....and a pausing....

Our breath.......the rhythm of our breath...... is one with Gaia.........with Mother Earth....... As one of her children, we breathe with her ......as she moves through the seasons of her breathing ...so we breathe in the same rhythm.........And so it is...... just as we pause at the end of the exhale............Mother Earth pauses at the spring equinox.....marking the turning to a new phase....pregnant with her own anticipation of expansion...growth..................
She too inhales with the spring and summer of her seasons..................expanding outward.............drinking in the nourishment that surrounds her..............just as we too inhale...bringing in nourishment for our growth.......

And just as we pause at the peak of our inhaling.......... Mother Earth pauses at the peak of her inhale.......the pause of the fall equinox marking the shift.........the gathering the first harvests...............the preparing and storing.......anticipating the gradual clearing and turning of the seasons...

And so she too moves rhythmically into exhaling ....the long purposeful exhale of her fall and winter as she gathers....stores. ....distributes...... and begins to let go into calmer and more pensive times of rest and replenishment...........we too release...calm and center with our exhale....

And so....let us breathe with her.........we are her children just as we are.........united with her through the breath... ....reminded of our source..........

Pause

And so as you rest..........you can honor and celebrate the teachings of another of her children.......the great tree.................and so you may begin to imagine breathing down out through the soles of your feet...............just as the great tree has breathing roots... your breath can flow down....deep into the welcoming moisture of Mother Earth.......... spreading wide and deep... your roots grow......sustained by her nourishment.....like a living anchor...holding you steady and safe within this source of abundance........and as you breathe your roots grow....spreading.... they may touch the roots of nearby neighbors...........embracing and intermingling just as the roots of the great tree ....becoming a vast, strong ring of connection beneath the surface of the earth.....strengthening your bond with the earth and all of her beings.......and all those here

And your growth too is upward and beautiful, as you breathe in the earth's energy......... breathing in and imagining that your breath can move up to your crown........and you grow up.........

and just as with the great tree.....you too reach for the stars, the sun and moon........ calling in.....breathing in the nourishment and warmth of the universe............letting it feed you and mature you.........your growing energy branching out......full and rich ....nourished by the sun and air that embraces you.......and perhaps your branches gently touch and connect with the branches of your neighbors.....just as the branches of the great tree touch and connect with its neighbors.........

And so it is that we are all children of Gaia...the Great Goddess........and of the Stars, the Sun and the Moon.............Just as with all of life....we too breathe with Mother Earth.... moving through the rhythm and seasons of our breath...reminding us and uniting us with Her............with the stars and sun and moon.......... with the Great Mysteries........

And as we breath with Her, we breathe with all of life.........a part of....and one with all that is of Her.

Pause

And now let us return to our circle.........taking a deep breath in......and out.....this time allowing the breath to bring you back to current time and place..... each breath....... bringing your awareness to sensations in your body......how your feet are resting on the floor.....how your body rests against the surface that supports you.........and moving or wiggling if you want.......and one more deep breath in.........and slowly out........opening your eyes when you are ready......gazing around the room for a moment until you are fully back.........

SR2005

Looking Backward and Forward

Theme

The equinox celebrations are unique in their moments of equality between day and night, only occurring twice a year. This provides us with a unique perspective on the equality between opposites, as reflected in the equal length of day and night. In the fall it is also the time for the harvest and the preparation for the winter's contemplation.

Sources of Inspiration

Much of this ritual stems from European earth-based traditions and a nature orientation to spirituality that is prevalent in the United States. What evolved as we created this ritual is the ease with which these various sources were integrated and found expression for us as a unified whole.

Altar

- *Russet and yellow altar cloths*
- *Directional candles with two in the center*
- *Matches, taper and snuffer*
- *Fall decorations such as acorns, leaves, grains, dried fruit, etc..*
- *Simple feast - homemade bread for the grain harvest*
- *A small fallen tree branch in a vase*
- *Writing materials*
- *Materials for earth painting*

    Containers for dirt that have a flat bottom, like a pie plate, for each person

    Dirt

    Items from nature that may be gathered in the fall, for example fallen acorns and leaves

Set Up

We had the dirt in the pie plates and placed them under the chairs of the participants. The objects from nature were in bowls on the altar.

Smudge

Smudging outside the room allows each person a brief clearing and centering before walking into ritual space. Set up the smudge outside the room. You may appoint a 'smudger', but do not forget to smudge yourself as leaders first. You may use whatever feels appropriate to you. Some suggestions are: sage, paulo santo, or mugwort.

Calling the Directions

Light each candle before calling the direction

EAST

Leader: Spirits and Goddesses of the Winds, blow clean and clear, blow freely through the skies to be with us here.

SOUTH

Leader: Spirits and Goddesses of the Sun and Fire give comfort and brightness.
Be with us here.

WEST

Leader: Spirits and Goddesses of the oceans, lakes and streams, wash clear and bright and fresh.
Be with us here.

NORTH

Leader: Spirits and Goddesses of the mountains, meadows and forests, bring forth life, richness and beauty.
Be with us here.

CENTER

Leader: Star Brothers and Sisters, Sun and Moon shine upon us.
Bless us with joy and wisdom.
Be with us here.
Pachamama, Mother Earth, we call upon you, Queen of the Harvest, Giver of Life.

Bless us with strength, laughter and power.
Be with us here.

Ritual

Leader: The fall equinox celebration is about the harvesting of the effort of our labors during the spring and summer. It is also the moment in the turning of the wheel that daylight and night are equal, poised for a time in perfect balance before the inevitable move from light into increasing darkness, fall into winter, harvesting into reflection and contemplation. It is a time of balance between opposites and perched on this moment we can look back over the spring and summer, with gentle acceptance of all that was there. We can reflect on what brought us joy, what was left unfinished or to be continued, what troubled us and what our response was to these events. Perched here we can also look forward to see how the coming time of reflection will unfold. What seeds from the harvest will be planted, continue to grow and need our tending? This is the intention of our ritual. We will have a meditation and then work with earth paintings to help us explore what comes up for us.

Reading

Adapted from a Mabon Ritual by Scott Cunningham

Leaves fall,
The days grow cold.
The Goddess pulls her mantle of Earth around Her
As the Light of long days moves toward the West
To the lands of eternal enchantment,
Wrapped in the coolness of night.
Fruits ripen,
Seeds drop,
The hours of day and night are balanced.
Chill winds blow in from the North.
In this seeming extinction of nature's warmth and light
I know that life continues.
For spring is impossible without the harvest,
As surely as life is impossible without death.

Blessings upon you, light and summer, as you journey into
The lands of winter and into the loving arms of the Goddess.
Goddess, Pachamama, I have sown and reaped
The fruits of my actions, both sweet and sour.
Grant me the courage to plant seeds of joy and love
In the coming year.
Teach me the secrets of wise existence upon this planet.

Meditation

Leader: During the meditation you will be invited and guided to pick up some things from the altar to represent what you look back upon and what the future might hold. This is a chance to bring your reflections to our Earth Mother as you explore these issues and events: what problems might be present, what stays, what gets developed, and what can be released. The meditation will be followed by a silent period in which you may explore these events in your sand painting.

The script for the meditation is at the end of the ritual. Remember to leave time at the end of the meditation for people to journal or just sit quietly. This provides a gentle and thoughtful transition into the next part of the ritual. It is also important for their integration of the meditation into current time.

Ritual

Leader: Find a comfortable spot. Play, explore, move the objects around on the earth. Find a placement that 'feels right'. Mark an opening in your earth painting for spirit to enter and exit. Explore what thoughts and emotions arise as you move these objects. How does it feel to you? Notice any sensations in your body that come up. I encourage you to draw or journal your objects and their placement in the earth painting and any meaning that might occur. In addition, please journal or ponder any shifts or new insights that may occur over the next few minutes or days while you work with your earth painting.

We gave them 5-10 minutes to explore their earth paintings.

Leader: You are invited to take what you have created home and continue to play and explore. You may want to place your earth painting outside for a while, during the day or overnight, and see if Spirit makes any kind of comment.

At home, when you are finished with your earth paintings, you can return the objects you have chosen to the earth. There may be some things from the past that you will want to release by blowing a 'releasing breath' on them as you place them back in nature.

Another traditional practice of the fall equinox is to walk in wild places and forests, gathering seedpods and dried plants, or whatever strikes you. Some of these may be used to decorate your home, create an altar, or to add to your earth painting as things come up for you. Within 2 or 3 days, your earth painting should be returned to the earth.

Ritual Food

Leader: This bread is a gift of the harvest, to mark the fullness of the season. Life does fulfill its cycle and leads to life anew. The eternal chain of life has stretched and bent but never broken. We give thanks for this, the season of the harvest. That the season of plenty shall return once more, in celebration of life springing ever new from death, I offer you this bread to eat.

Pass the bread

Talking Stick

Leader: We will now pass the talking stick. Please share as you are moved. You may want to share what came up during the meditation or anything else that is happening in your life. Who would like to start?

Calling the Directions

Snuff the candles as you read each direction.

EAST

Leader: Spirits and Goddesses of the winds, we thank you for your presence.

SOUTH

Leader: Spirits and Goddesses of the sun and fire, we thank you for your presence.

WEST

Leader: Spirits and Goddesses of the oceans, lakes and streams, we thank you for your presence.

NORTH

Leader: Spirits and Goddesses of the mountains, meadows and forests, we thank you for your presence.

ABOVE

Leader: Star Brothers and Sisters, we thank you for your presence.

BELOW

Leader: Pachamama, Mother Earth, we thank you for your presence.

Meditation

Looking Past and Future

I invite you to find a comfortable position........either sitting in your chair or on the floor ....and begin to bring your attention to your breathing............perhaps noticing the feel of the air at your nostrils as it moves in.........and then out................just noticing..........................or perhaps noticing the feel of the breath at your belly .....moving in..............and moving out..................gently letting your breath lead you to a space where there is no time.............where there is no place to go......nothing to do................ nothing to become.......... .....there is just this open.......playful...........curious noticing of what comes into your awareness...........moment to moment..............................just noticing.......held in the safety of our circle and embraced by the love of the Goddess....

And gently begin to imagine yourself standing ....poised.....or perched on the balancing point of light and dark, day and night.................. secure and steady in this moment of harmony........suspended ....and as you are ready...breathe deeply...... savoring this moment of balance between opposites...........this holding of both in harmony................................you may repeat to yourself.....I stand in this place as the year balances between the dark times and the light times.........I can look back and remember.............I can look forward and plan.........and I balance the dark and light in my life................

And so.......turning in your mind's eye to the season past.....to summer..........long days of warm sunlight............and remember..........notice what comes up in your awareness as you look back to these times.............perhaps colors, scenes or places arise in your field of vision..............perhaps sounds or smells softly drift into your awareness................ and any sensations as you look back to your summer...............Just noticing what comes up............and noticing what it was that nourished you over this past summer.......... what brought you joy.....and perhaps..maturing

Pause

Perhaps there are events or plans that were left unfinished or abandoned as the summer season unfolded............................notice these also...........gently and curiously...... whatever arises ....

Pause

And perhaps there are plans that are still in progress.............or that began their planning in the warmth of your summer.........................notice what arises here also.......................

Pause

And now...quietly.....I invite you to move to the altar and choose whatever objects you want to represent those things that nourished you............those things that were left undone............and those things that are still in progress............and place them in your cup

This is an opportunity to explore these elements in your life....what may be further developed........how............. what might be released and given thanks for.......this is a chance to explore any problems that might be inherent in these elements or events and ask for help...

Pause

You may pause long enough here for everyone to gather their objects and settle in again in their seat.

And now....gently......return to your breath and again imagine yourself perched or poised in this space of balance between past and future, light and dark........................

And gently turn in your mind's eye to the future................................perhaps noticing any images that might arise as you look forward into fall and the coming winter................ ....any smells,.......sounds...........or sensations that might arise as you hold your fall and winter in your mind's eye..............moving with curiosity to noticing what plans or projects arise for this coming time...................they may be new or a continuation of the summer... .....perhaps ideas from your harvest that need more time to compost ... percolate and quietly develop......

Pause

Perhaps there are new plans or ideas for the coming times that begin to arise in your minds-eye............

What is it that might hold nourishment and joy for you in the coming seasons......

Let it arise as it will to inform you........

Pause

And pause briefly to acknowledge what might remain unseen to you just now.......the possibility that might present to you sometime in the future

Pause-short

And now, quietly move to the altar and choose several objects to represent these hopes seeds, ideas or projects......being careful to choose at least one object to represent what is still unknown to you in this moment..............

Pause

Allow people enough time to gather objects and return

And gently return to your breath.......noticing the breath ....returning completely to your place in circle ......eyes open.......but with an inner stillness and quiet.......... aware of your breath...your sensations....of the objects you have gathered during meditation.........we will move to the earth paintings.

SR2008

Yule

Winter solstice is December 21 and is known as Yule in the European tradition. It is the shortest day of the year, when the sun is at its southern most point. From this time on the light grows, and slowly and steadily with the growing light comes a growing warmth which incubates and sustains the activity that is quietly and surely stirring underneath the blankets of snow and leaves.

The birth of a god-figure reflects the return of the sun and the promise of new growth, of salvation and an end to the hardships of long nights and cold weather. It is the promise that below the snows and cold, buried deep in the earth, are the sleeping seeds waiting for the warmth of spring to stir their souls. Deep within us, the seeds of our growth are incubating and waiting for our new beginnings. New life springs from the fertile darkness of the winter.

In our first ritual we gather together in the darkness of the time and learn what sustains us and what is growing. Celebrating the joys of the season is the theme of our second solstice ritual. And in our third ritual we rededicate ourselves to fostering peace and love in the world, expressed through the use of prayer flags. The last two rituals honor again the turning of the wheel, the darkness and the light in their inextricable union.

A Yule Candle Ritual

Theme

This ritual honors the strengths and qualities that nourish us through the dark and cold of this season. As we are nourished we are able to name the beginnings that may be composting throughout the quiet of our winter. This also allows us to greet our aging with grace and wisdom.

Sources of Inspiration

We drew the chant from the Celtic traditions and from the concept of Yule as the focus for the Winter Solstice. The calling of the directions includes the archetypes from the Andean Shamanic tradition. The reading is from the Lakota traditions.

Altar

- *Black cloth*
- *Small gift bags filled with chocolate*
- *Two candles, red and green, lit for each person*
- *Candelabra decorated to symbolize a yule tree*

We often used a tall candelabra that holds five candles for the winter solstice. We fixed branches of greens to the candelabra so that it symbolizes an evergreen tree. Light the candles in the candelabra as you call the directions. Please adapt as fits you.

- *Two snuffers*
- *Yule tabletop tree*

We used the candalabra as the Yule tree. You may choose to use the tabletop tree and omit the candles from the opening. We were concerned about people reaching over candles to decorate the tree

- *Bowl of star ornaments and/or snowflakes for tree decorations*
- *Talking stick*

We used a tea light or votive in a bowl.

- *A small 'lighter candle' in the bowl with the tea light or votive*
- *Objects at the directions to symbolize the seasons and cycles*

East- seeds = beginnings, newness, birth

South- green plants, flowers = growth, blossoming, young adulthood

West- grains = maturing, harvest, middle age

North- fake snow, mountain symbol = rest, reflection, old age

Center- evergreen = the continuation of life through darkness and light

Set up

We placed the chairs around the center altar, set back so that there is room to walk around the altar with the opening chant. The room was dimly lit except for the candles on the altar and around the room. As leaders for this ritual, we sat opposite each other in the circle so that we could guide the moving chant more effectively. We brought reading lights to read the ritual, as initially it is very dark.

Smudge

Set up the smudge outside the room. you may appoint a "smudger", but do not forget to smudge yourself as leader first. You may use whatever feels appropriate to you. However a winter smudge, such as pine or evergreen is often nice.

Chanting the Turning Wheel

Leader: Once again, the Winter Solstice is upon us. We are going to chant our circle open to honor the turning of the wheel through the seasons of the year and of our lives. The image we may all hold is this: As we chant and walk around the altar imagine that we are helping the wheel turn, moving the wheel through the solstice and into the next season of winter and the promise of spring.

While we walk around the altar clockwise, chanting, each person will snuff a red candle and a green candle, symbolizing the darkness of the season. We will pass the snuffer as we walk the wheel.

And so it is that we create our sacred space here tonight, uniting us with the greater mysteries.

Please stand.

The music for the chant is located at the end of the book. Start the chant and sing through once or twice before walking. Begin walking clockwise around the altar when it seems right. The leaders start by snuffing the red and green candles and passing the snuffer to the person behind them

Chant

Air Her breath
Fire Her spirit
Water Her blood and
Earth Her body

The room is now dark except for the dim lighting of a reading light and the candles placed around the room. If the group is small, you may want to go around the altar twice. The first time around, snuff the red candle, and the second time around snuff the green candle.

Change the spoken directions accordingly

Calling the Directions

Light each directional candle as the direction is read

NORTH

Leader: Goddesses of the North and Hummingbird and Dragon- we stand now in the North, at the Winter Solstice.
Help us learn from nature to honor the darkness of Life's Mysteries without losing faith.
Show us how to recognize the seeds of growth and nurture them in our own inner warmth until the Light returns.
Lead us to honor and face our own old age with serenity, faith and power.
Once again help us to see that even in the darkest moments, peace and healing energy are available when we focus on them with positive intent.

EAST

Leader: Goddesses of the East and Condor and Eagle- bring to us the morning dew and the sweet, clear breath of the dawn, new and full of promise.
Breathe into our circle the energy of new beginnings, the joy of birthing and bringing forth, as all of life rejoices in Spring.

SOUTH

Leader: Goddesses of the South and Sachamama- bring to our circle the warmth and growth of summer, of maturing and moving towards our full potential, just as all of life moves steadily towards developing, blooming and growing into fullness.

WEST

Leader: Goddesses of the West and Jaguar- bring to us the waters and fruits of the harvest, so that we might celebrate the bounty of the harvest and savor the fruits of our labor with all of life.

CENTER

Leader: Goddesses and Gods of the Oneness, Sun and Moon, we ask that you watch over us and hold us here in our circle.
We give thanks for our Brother Evergreen who shows us that life continues through darkness and light, solid in its being throughout the seasons, offering us hope and wholeness as we too move through the phases of our lives.

Please be seated.

Meditation

The script for the meditation is at the end of the ritual. Remember to leave time at the end of the meditation for people to journal or just sit quietly. This provides a gentle and thoughtful transition into the next part of the ritual. It is also important for their integration of the meditation into current time

Ritual

Leader: The gift of the Gods and Goddesses may help you endure and appreciate the darkness that leads you replenished into the light. Therefore, we are passing a candle for the talking stick. Each person may light a green candle on the altar for what you feel you need for support to continue through the darkness. The light is coming, even as we rest in the darkness.

The candle in the bowl, with a lighting candle worked very well. Wax did not drip on people or clothes, and lighting the green candle on the altar helped everyone pause before they spoke. A tea light or votive candle may be placed in any attractive bowl and lit. A short 'lighting candle' is placed in the bowl, unlit, so that each person may light it from the bowl and light their green candle

Reading/Prayer

Adapted from a meditation from Lakota Native Americans

Leader: And so we honor the season of winter, of endings and agings, composting and new beginnings.

Short pause

Great Spirits of the Winter and of the North, hear us as we come asking for the wisdom and the courage to age gracefully in our lives and in our endeavors.

Honor us with your presence as we stand in the sacred dark of the Season and of our Earthwalk.

Permit the crystal clarity of winter snow to bring clarity to our lives and thoughts, and healing to our bodies and to our world.

Help us to turn the lessons we have learned and the knowledge we have gained into wisdom and abundance.

Allow us to understand the dignity of being.

Help us to learn the truth and beauty of not doing.

Teach us to fly with quiet grace and seeing eyes through the dark times of our lives.

Give us the patience to share our selves and our knowledge with those who can use them. Give us the faith and the courage to continue our journeys gracefully to the end, so that our energy may once again arrive in the Dawn of the East.

Show us how to find joy in darkness and in endings, as well as in light and in beginnings

Pause here for a few moments to let people reflect on the reading and to rest in the feeling of prayerfulness and honoring.

As you transition, the leader picks up the bowl of decorations and holds them up

Ritual

Leader: We will pass this bowl of stars and snowflakes to decorate our tree. They represent the light of beginnings. As you place them on the tree, you may speak of new beginnings that you seek. Then you may light a red candle for the coming light and new beginnings.

Gift Giving

Leader: It is hard for some of us to appreciate the sweetness of the winter season, the gifts and teachings of the dark. Our gift for you is to remind you all that this may be so. Enjoy and learn to find peace and sweetness within you. Happy Yule. Happy Solstice.

Pass out gift bags.

Thanking and Releasing the Directions

Snuff each candle as you read each direction

Leader: And now we will thank and release the directions.

NORTH

Leader: We thank the Goddess of the North and Hummingbird and Dragon for being with us.

EAST

Leader: We thank the Goddess of the East and Condor and Eagle for being with us.

SOUTH

Leader: We thank the Goddess of the South and Sachamama for being with us.

WEST

Leader: We thank the Goddess of the West and Jaguar for being with us.

CENTER

Leader: We thank the Goddesses and Gods of the Oneness and Mother Earth and Sister Moon, Father Sky and Brother Sun, for being with us.

Chant

Leader: Please stand and join hands

Leaders start the final chant that is in the back of the book. We suggest you sing it through 3 times or more, as feels right to you.

May the circle be open
But unbroken
May the love of the Goddess
Be ever in your heart
Merry meet
And merry part
And merry meet again.

Leader: And now we feast!

Yule Feast

Serve cookies and drink and send participants out into the winter cold in the warm glow of the ritual

Meditation

Journey to the Inner Goddess

Please take a moment to get comfortable for meditation............ gently noticing your breath moving in........and moving out.........finding a comfortable position in your seat......... you may let yourself sink into the chair or surface supporting you........... noticing the support that is offered you...........breathing in........and out..... following your breath as it gently and steadily finds the soft and quiet spaces
within ....held gently within our sacred space... Surrounded by the love and peace of our circle here...safe within the Great Wheel and Her understanding.

And on this evening as we move into the dark phase of the wheel .....let us sit together in the dark, quietly, and listen to the stillness within.

Pause

And so...following your breath.........letting it lead you to an image of a path..........
you may imagine walking down this path............ a well trod path shimmering in the moonlight........perhaps in a forest, or along the ocean's edge........
It is winter..... the snow beneath your feet creaks and crunches, breaking the exquisite silence of a winter's evening.............All around you is a dusty white softness to your eye.............. and the feel of the night air cool on your skin..........

You walk here in safety and with the blessings of the Goddess as she leads you gently to the beginning of a large circular path.............

You may pause a moment as you remember your quest........your journey to the home of the Goddess who resides deep within the earth.........you are coming with a simple gift of appreciation in return for Her wisdom and sustenance................
as you enter the path you are reminded of the Sacred Wheel................your deep connection to the Mysteries..........to the rhythms and cycles of all life........

and so it is that you enter in the east...walking along the path of beginnings...of spring...birth and rebirthing...longer days and growing warmth........you may notice the intoxicating smell of spring earth and life beginning to reawaken........you might even notice an energized, and expectant air about things.

Pause

As you move steadily around the path...you become aware of a growing warmth and light............summer is surrounding you.....plants are becoming a rich and vibrant green.......flowers bloom.........fields are growing high and full.......and the waters are cool and refreshing to touch... you may sense that all of life seems to be thick in the work of growth and the tending of growth.

Pause

And so you continue further around the path.........perhaps sensing a slightly cooler breeze on your skin.........gradually realizing that autumn is at hand...the fields are bearing all sorts of grains and fruits.......and abundant seeds .... all of life is mature and full.......you may notice a desire to gather in the richness of the earth's growing............to celebrate the harvest.......to gather with others...and to pause and take stock.........all this to make ready for the growing darkness....

Pause

And so it is that you move back into winter...the sounds of the snow beneath your feet...........the cold air upon your cheeks..........all this beginning to draw you inward... drawn to the warmth and strength that lie within you...as within all things..... For all of life seems asleep........quiet.......waiting.........while deep within life continues...... forming....reforming.......changing..............perhaps tending unseen seeds of possibility.

Pause

And so...as you pause here on the darkest day of the year............a sensing or knowing from deep within you begins to whisper and stir..........and you know that you are a

part of something much greater than yourself .... the path you travel is sacred..... connecting you to sacred and universal rhythms.......... for all of life travels this path...........over and over.........through days......years..........and lifetimes.
So it is here that lies our connection with all that is.

A light beckons you from within the Great Circle........... you continue...travelling safely and easily towards the center...........down the path gradually towards a beautiful cave in the center of the wheel.....with gems and stones sparkling in the moonlight..... illuminating the way in......... perhaps lending an air of magic and mystery.

You may enter the cave as you are ready......... walking down the long entryway of the cave......... noticing the dampness........ the cool warmth..... perhaps hearing the gurgle of a stream gently spilling into a pool further down the corridor.
And you come upon an inner chamber, softly lit by a crackling warm fire......there are blankets and furs arranged near the fire............and a shimmering pool ....The fruits of the harvest are present here for you also.

You may be drawn to rest near the fire...or perhaps by the pool... nestling into the blankets and furs.........perhaps enjoying the bounty of the harvest laid out before you.

And so you may rest... held by the Great Mother Goddess....for this is Her cave and you are cradled gently and lovingly in Her embrace.
She has blessed you with the gift of darkness... of quiet... watching over you as you rest,

Pause

As you pause here...she invites you to reflect and to ask...........she will answer in her own time.......perhaps now......perhaps as you move through your coming days.....
You may reflect on any or all of these as you rest...........

How might I make space within for the wholeness of life...How might I hold both the light and the dark...the bitter and the sweet... the beginnings and the endings with compassion, understanding and great wisdom?

Where do I find deep peace and renewal?

What wisdoms may be seeking to reveal themselves to me at this time?

How might I tend to my inner growth, and re-emergence as I move into the coming light?

Perhaps you have a question that is uniquely yours.......you may ask it now......

Pause

She has listened carefully ...perhaps offered guidance.....held you gently as you searched and watched over you as you rested............ You may give Her your gift in return.... thanking Her for Her help and presence...................And She in return has a gift for you... to sustain and nurture you on your journey through the dark nights into the growing light.

And now it is time to return........... you rise easily.....moving out past the gurgling stream..............out into the winter's night..........cool and white.........steadily walking down the path still shimmering in the moonlight............around the wheel to the very edge of the Great Wheel............
You pause here ....surveying for a moment the Great Wheel from your vantage point in the North.......................and then turning as you are ready............returning back to current place...current time............

You may bring your attention to your breathing.........noticing your breath moving in..... and your breath moving out..........and as you notice your breath....noticing that each breath is bringing your awareness more and more to sensations........noticing how the air feels as you breathe.......how you are sitting in your chair.........perhaps noticing that you would like to move or wiggle...and doing so with delight......

And once more.....a deep breath in.......filling your belly and chest.........and exhaling ......letting your belly and chest become smaller........returning completely to our circle...to here and now.....opening your eyes.......gently looking about the room.........

Pause here and wait for everyone to open their eyes and return. If need be, suggest another deep breath and opening the eyes to return, relaxed and refreshed

SR2004

Celebrating the Gifts of the Season

Theme

The theme is one of celebrating the aspects of the winter that you find nurturing and joyful. Your thoughts might include memories of seasons past, your favorite family traditions or finding time for introspection.

Sources of Inspiration

The winter solstice has been observed around the world in a beautiful tapestry of ritual and celebration. In some areas it has taken on many religious traditions such as Christmas, Kwanza, and Hanukah. The evergreen is a German symbol for the continuation of life through the hard winters.

Altar

- *Undecorated evergreen in the middle.*

  We used a candelabra with five candles around the center pole at different heights for our direction candles. We tied evergreen boughs to the center pole and around the candleholders to make the 'tree'.

- *Many votive candles, tied with red bows circling the table*
- *Small ornaments for decorating the evergreen*
- *Matches*
- *Cauldron, with alcohol and Epsom Salts*
- *Symbolic items at directions and labels for each direction*

  West - shells, water, sea glass

  North - rocks, earth,

  East - feathers, bird statues

  South – candle, symbol for sun

Additional items for Sacred Space

- *Marzipan or other candy, wrapped as gifts or in small gift bags, placed under the altar*
- *Words to the carol, 'Deck the Halls with Boughs of Holly'*

Set up

Decorate the room as festive as you wish and have a separate table set up with cookies and mulled cider for the Yule feasting that ends this ritual.

Smudge

Smudging outside the room allows each person a brief clearing and centering before walking into ritual space. Set up the smudge outside the room. You may appoint a 'smudger', but do not forget to smudge yourself as leaders first. You may use whatever feels appropriate to you. Some suggestions are: sage, paulo santo, or mugwort

Calling the Directions

Leader: In the spirit of the season of sharing joy, we invite you to join in the calling in of sacred space. You may choose the direction that speaks to you and place a votive candle at that direction and light it calling in whatever god, goddess, archetype or other sacred image you may want to call in. Please let your heart-mind speak to you as you choose the direction and what you wish to say. You may speak from your inner being openly and truthfully.

We have labeled the directions, and I will tell briefly the element, the season and images associated with each direction.

Leader goes around the altar and speaks about each direction

Leader: North is winter, mountains, stones, reflection and introspection, hibernation, darkness and long nights. The Quechua archetypes are Condor and Eagle.

East is spring, air, beginnings, birthing and planting. The Quechua archetypes are Hummingbird and Dragon.

South is summer, fire, passion, healing, warmth and growth. The Quechua archetype is Serpent.

West is fall, water, maturity, harvest and fruition. The Quechua archetype is Jaguar.

Center is above and below, God and Goddess, Sun and Earth, and our own center. We will call the center. Let your imagination and creativity be free as you take a turn calling the direction of your choice. Who would like to begin by calling in the North?

We found that we needed to encourage those who wanted to speak. The suggestion would be to have one of the leaders start.

Leader: Who now would like to call in the East

Continue around the four directions in this manner.

Leader: And we call in the center, the Oneness and union of Above and Below. Be here with us Mother Earth and Father Sky, Sun and Moon and our Brothers and Sisters the Stars. Bless our gathering.

Introduction

Leader: Our ritual this Yule is one of celebration and joy. As in the past and as we do today, we celebrate the returning of the light. It is reassuring as we watch the days become longer and warmer, certain of the promise of spring.

However tonight we are also going to honor and celebrate the gifts and delights of winter, the time of darkness, rest and a slowing down for reflection, composting and gathering in the warmth of a fire with a friend. So, I ask you all to get comfortable and pause a moment for this quiet meditation.

Meditation

Please see the end of the ritual for the meditation. This is a meditation to bring people to a deeply peaceful place. It need be nothing more but a caring and gentle holding of this space for them to feel peaceful.

Give them enough time at the end of the meditation to return and sit for a moment before moving onto the next part

Ritual

Leader: As much as winter brings us the gift of solitude and inner reflection, it also brings us the joys of the Solstice season, a time of parties, warm evenings by a fire with family and friends or time to read a good book. Tonight we invite you to tap into the joys of the season that nourish you, body-mind and spirit, that bring you joy, peace and perhaps moments of transcendence. Perhaps it is how the cold helps us to cocoon and be at peace in the warmth of our homes, and to gather nourishment from moments stolen for reflection and quiet. Perhaps it is how the season encourages us to gather with friends. Think of the smells from the kitchen, your favorite and traditional meals and gatherings. These may be from your childhood, youth or current situations. Perhaps it is the beauty of new snowfall, the patterns of frost on your windows, or the primal safety of a fire on a wintry day. What are the gifts of winter and this season in your life? What nourishes you during this season?

As you reflect, look at the altar and all the decorations on it. Think of what each ornament might symbolize for you. Please select one ornament from the altar that you would like to place onto the tree, sharing your thoughts and memories as you do so. We will go around as many times as you wish, because we find that as we share and listen, new memories awaken within each of us.

Decorate the tree one at a time so that the speaker is honored with attentive listening. At the end we had some ornaments left over, so we all stood and decorated the tree and chatted. It was a very pleasant time together.

Celebrate

Leader: Let us sing in the light with this old pagan Carol, 'Deck the Halls with Boughs of Holly"

Light the cauldron. We used an alcohol and Epsom salts fire, which is fun and fairly dramatic. The song is in the appendix

Gift Giving

Leader: Look under the altar and you will find a small gift bag that is our gift to you to celebrate the season.

Take a few minutes for them to find and open their gifts. It can be anything you wish, but we usually use candies or sweets of some sort

Talking Stick

Leader: We will pass the talking stick. Please share, as you feel comfortable, what has come up for you during the ritual or anything else that feels right.

Thanking and Releasing the Directions

Leader: Please stand. We will pass the snuffer around and whoever is at the direction may snuff the candle as that direction is called. We can join together saying, Thank you for celebrating with us.

NORTH

Leader: To the North.

Group: Thank you for celebrating with us.

EAST

Leader: To the East.

Group: Thank you for celebrating with us.

SOUTH

Leader: To the south.

Group: Thank you for celebrating with us.

WEST

Leader: To the east.

Group: Thank you for celebrating with us.

CENTER

Leader: And to the center, above and below.

Group: Thank you for celebrating with us.

Sing

Leader: Please join hands and sing our final closing.

May the circle be open
But unbroken
May the love of the Goddess
Be ever in your heart
Merry meet
And merry part
And merry meet again.

Leader: These cookies and this mulled cider are to warm your body, mind and spirit before venturing out into the cold and dark.

You can leave any other candles burning, and bring the cookies and cider to the altar to share

Meditation

Held in the light

Invite people to find a comfortable position, sitting, lying down, with blankets or whatever. Center yourself with an abdominal breath and intention to share this imagery in a 'heartfelt" manner.

And now, gently begin to bring your attention to your breath...............noticing the feel of the breath as you inhale...............and the feel of the breath as you exhale............. Just noticing sensations, how your body moves as you inhale..................and as you exhale..............noticing with a detached and curious manner.........the breath moving in, filling your belly..... your chest.............and the breath moving out as you exhale....feeling the gentle falling of your chest....and belly

Gradually connecting with the soothing and calming rhythm of the breath......so that thoughts, emotions, concerns begin to fade into the background of your awareness........ and your breath becomes your anchor...........so that for a moment.....the mind and emotional self can pause............there is quiet and open space....and you are blessed with a stillness and silence ......soft and deep like a shimmering smooth lake at sunset.............

Pause

And now.....imagining a place where you feel safe and peaceful..........either from your memory or make believe.........allowing the place to gradually become more real to you... at its own pace.......gradually noticing images, colors, scenery

Pause

And noticing the sounds of your safe, peaceful place.........just pausing to notice whatever sounds might arise in your awareness.........................And fragrances........ smelling the rich fragrance of your nurturing, peaceful place........

Pause

And as you become more and more comfortable, safe and protected in your special place.... notice any sensations........perhaps the surface you are resting on...........is it warm or cool,..............soft or firm.....

Pause

And so resting, comfortable here................you gradually become aware of a beautiful, shimmering light that permeates your peaceful place..............you sense its gentleness.........its caring and compassion................. .... and from the light there is an invitation to just pause.....to just be ....for the light is here to soothe.....to nourish you in body, mind and spirit.....

pause

And so, gently....as you are ready..... the light gathers at your crown.............moving gently down your scalp soothing and softening..................and down your forehead........ bathing your eyes...... soothing beneath and behind your eyes.........down to your nose... your cheeks and over to your ears......................soothing and peaceful the light bathes your jaw...right down to the tip of your chin...........

And once more this gentle nurturing light gathers at your crown and this time begins to bathe your mind....soothing and calming your mind...................letting your mind just pause a moment.....inviting a deepening sense of peace and calm.......

And gently the light moves down your neck.....to your shoulders.........moving softly through layers of muscle, soothing....comforting...........warm or cool as needed............. filling muscles and bones with a deep peace.......................down your arms....your upper arms.......elbows.......... lower arms............your wrists and hands.....to the tip of each finger and thumb......... bathing muscles and bones in this soft, nurturing light.......filling cells with a deep peace.

This gentle, soothing light moves from your hands over to your belly.............soothing and softening muscles and gently filling your belly with light........with a deep sense of peace and harmony...........................

And up to your chest......bathing skin...muscles and bones with light......moving gently to your lungs and to your heart.....gently cradling your heart in light....filling your heart with light and love and peace.

And the light continues to gently flow up over your shoulders and down your back.....................rippling out from your spine.....soothing and calming muscles......... ....at your shoulders..........down to your midback.......to your waist area.........
So that your back begins to soften... and sink into the chair or floor that is supporting you........................and so the light moves steadily and purposefully down your lower back.....bathing bones and muscles .....down to the tip of your tailbone....you may even sense a softening here also.......

And from your back gently over to your hips.......bathing both hips.......down each thigh.......moving quietly through the layers of muscles in your thighs....soothing and filling your muscles and bones with light and peace.......down to your knees.....your calf and shins......ankles........and down to your feet....to the top of your feet........soothing and calming your feet down through to the soul of each foot.........to the tip of each toe.

And so your entire body is filled with this soft.....peaceful light.........radiating out and wrapping you gently in its embrace like a soft.... ....shimmering blanket of breathing light.....
And so you can just rest here.......safe... and held in the light of your special place.........

You may want to pause and count or check the time, but a full minute here is lovely and may seem like an eternity when you are offering the meditation to others.

And now it is time to return to current time and place............gently beginning to bring your attention to your breath........noticing the breath as you inhale.........filling your belly

......your chest.......and noticing your breath as you exhale.... slow and easily.............each breath returning you more and more to current time and place....Noticing how your body feels......if anything would like to stretch or wiggle.....and enjoying this movement..

Again............breathing in.........deeply and breathing out.......each breath returning you to this place and this time.............And opening your eyes when you are ready......gazing about the room for a moment.............

And one last deep breath........................in......and out......and returning completely.. ...refreshed and calm.....

It is helpful to guide them back slowly. I found that I sometimes needed to repeat the taking of a deep breath in and out to cajole the more deeply relaxed and reluctant participants back to the circle. Enjoy!

SR2007

The Promise of Peace

Theme

The theme of the altar, and the ritual, is to reaffirm and rededicate our selves to bringing forth peace and love in our own lives and the lives of others. As UU's we respect all faith's search for peace. This ritual brings together several spiritual traditions in prayers for peace.

Sources of Inspiration

The Buddhist practice of prayer flags inspired this ritual. Flags are filled with prayers for peace, prosperity, health or whatever, and hung outside so that the wind may take the prayers to be answered. The calling of the directions is a blending of Goddess traditions and the Andean traditions of the Quechua.

Altar

- *A large table, oval if possible*
- *Direction candles*
- *Work space at the altar for participants to create their individual prayer flag.*

  This is sacred work therefore it is appropriate to create the flags at the altar dedicated to peace, compassion and wisdom. Working in meditation with focused intention imbues our actions and the flags with the sincerity of our prayers we are sending to Spirit.

- *Fabric pens*
- *Fabric squares--red, yellow, green, blue and white, about 8"x8"*
- *Rope or cord-to hang the flags on*
- *Stapler-to staple the flags onto the rope for hanging*
- *Matches*
- *Candle snuffer*
- *Buddhist prayer flags, available in many spiritually oriented stores.*

If you cannot get the Buddhist prayer flags, you may get a picture. This is helpful for participants to have a mental picture of what they look like

- *Symbols of peace and the season from all faiths, Set up*

For example a menorah, Quan Yin (Chinese Goddess of Compassion), Mohamed, Om symbol, Jesus as infant, the Virgin Mary, Tara figurines and Tara Thonka's (the Mother of All the Buddhas and the Tibetan Goddess of Compassion), the evergreen, dove, peace pipe... Be creative, inclusive and have fun.

Set up

Place hooks or nails in strategic places outside to hang the string of flags from. Appoint helpers for hanging the flags. You may also want to place many candles around the room, so that the room is lit by candlelight. This enhances the feeling of prayerfulness.

The tone is enhanced if you have some chant music playing inside the room. If you have the Om Mane Padme Hum chant, you can play that. It is a prayer for compassion and peace, and available at most music stores or online.

Smudge

Smudge outside the ritual room, as a preparation for entering sacred space. An official 'smudger' may be appointed. You may ask participants to wait outside the room until it is time to start the ritual.

Calling the Directions

One leader may read as the other lights the directional candles. Our preference is to light the candle first and then read.

NORTH

Leader: Goddesses of the North, mothers of wisdom and deep inner knowing, Hummingbird and Dragon, bring to us your strength and perseverance.
Bless us with the wisdom of the Goddess.
Replenish our hearts and minds and bodies.

EAST

Leader: Goddesses of the East, mothers of vision and beginnings, Condor and Eagle, share with us your insights and vision.
Bless us with the lightness and clarity of the Goddess.
Clear our hearts, minds and bodies of cloudy confusions.

SOUTH

Leader: Goddesses of the South, mothers of our passion and flowering, Sachamama, Great Grandmother Serpent, show us how to grow and cultivate our compassion.
Infuse us with the warmth and vitality of the Goddess.

WEST

Leader: Goddesses of the West, mothers of healing and dexterity, Mother-sister Jaguar, walk with us on our journey, leading us to greater depths of knowing and wisdom.
Bless us this evening and wash us with your healing and refreshing nectars.

CENTER

Leader: Great Goddesses of the Center, above and below, Mothers of all who nurture our being, Pachamama, Mother Earth, Inti Tutu and Mama Gela, Sun and Moon.

Bless us with your presence here tonight.
Carry us closer and closer to our true inner nature.

Ritual

Leader: Tonight we are gathered to celebrate Yule- the winter solstice and the turning of the wheel towards increasing light and warmth. It is also Christmas, celebrating the birth of Jesus and his teachings of Love and Peace. Hanukah is at this time of year, which celebrates the miracle of light. In the Hindu nations, Dawali, a celebration of lights, is celebrated in late fall. Most indigenous peoples had or still have celebrations of the solstice that fit their culture and spirituality. This ritual respectfully and intentionally brings together several spiritual traditions in prayers for peace. As UU's we respect all faiths desire for peace, and search for ways that we can honor all people's expressions as well as our own desire for peace.

All of these celebrations are concrete events that hold the promise that Peace, Love and Compassion are available to each and every one of us. So Yule and the Solstice is a wonderful opportunity to rekindle our inspiration, to rededicate ourselves to cultivating love, compassion, and peace within our own lives. As we work to bring these qualities forward in ourselves, our actions and attitudes with others begin to shift and reflect this growth. It is a new way of being in relationship. As we interact with others in this subtle new way, our communities begin to shift. As our communities begin to shift, cultures begin to shift and a ripple is nurtured and encouraged to spread and grow throughout the world.

Tonight we will focus on the rekindling and reaffirming of our desire to move toward the light, to cultivate peace and love and to seek help for our journey through our prayer flags, which are here on our altar.

We'd like to spend a minute on the altar. Our altar has many symbols of the promise that peace and love are available to all of us regardless of where we live, our faith or race. These qualities dwell within us, and around us. We need only to turn our attention and intention in their direction.

Please take a few minutes to point out the different symbols of celebrations from around the world that are represented on your altar. You may pay specific attention to the commonality of symbolism of peace, love, and compassion that seem to weave through these celebrations

Cultivating these values within ourselves may often seem a daunting process and we can use all the help we can get, which brings me to the prayer flags on the altar. These particular prayer flags are from Northern India, from McLeod Ganj, which is the home of the Dalai Lama.

Prayer flags are everywhere in areas where Buddhism is practiced. They are at the peaks of the mountains, on stonewalls of homes, on trees and between trees, on poles at entrances to villages. They seem omnipresent. The most common prayer flag is the Prayer for Compassion, which is Om Mane Padme Hum. It is the one we have here and is the chant that you listened to as you entered.

Compassion is a deep understanding and commitment to the wellbeing of all sentient beings, including yourself. And it is a source of profound wisdom, giving our compassion an earthy and pragmatic vibrancy in the real world. The prayer flags are a constant reminder that compassion is alive and well, it is being asked for, sought after, and cultivated.

There are also prayer flags for Good Fortune, called the Wind Horse. Then there are some for Harmony and Balance in the area in which a person lives, and so on. They are almost always the five colors: green, blue, yellow, white and red that relate to requests from the five elements or directions.

When the flags are raised and open to the breeze, the wind carries our hopes, requests and prayers to Spirit and all that is Sacred. We will hang these flags that come from McLeod Ganj. We will also make our own prayer flags here tonight, focusing on rekindling and rededicating ourselves to move towards peace and love. We seek help for our journey through our prayer flags. We will hang them side-by-side, on a continuous piece of twine, sending our prayers for peace and love out for all peoples.

We will pass the Tibetan prayer flags around first. You may blow your intentions onto the Tibetan flags so they will be filled with our prayer. Infusing the flags in this way, with the breath, is an Andean shamanic practice. It is also referred to in the Bible, when God breathes life into Adam and Eve, and so around the world, in many cultures. We breathe life into our beliefs and hopes and make them real, and so we breathe our prayers into the flags and make them real.

One of the leaders picks up the Tibetan flags, holds them up for all to see, and speaks the following. Then the leader blows upon the flags their intention

Leader: We rekindle and reaffirm our desire to shift toward the light. We ask for help on our journey, for strength, hope, and perseverance, that we might continue, each in our own way, to the best of our ability, to move toward greater peace, love and wisdom.

Pass the flags around so that each person may rededicate and reaffirm their desire for peace, love and wisdom by blowing this intention onto the flags.

Meditation

Leader: This meditation ends with an invitation to make your own prayer flag. The art supplies and materials are on the altar. We ask that the silence of the meditation continue during the making of the flags in order to keep our focus on our prayers.

The script for the meditation is at the end of the ritual. Remember to leave time at the end of the meditation for people to journal or just sit quietly. This provides a gentle and thoughtful transition into the next part of the ritual. It is also important for their integration of the meditation into current time.

Ritual - Making Prayer Flags

Prayer flags are created at the altar dedicated to this purpose, and silently-as part of the meditation. When people are done, go around the circle, inviting people to say what they have put on their flag if they want to. The leaders will attach it to the rope with the stapler. When this is complete, a leader holds up the flags that have been made and says:

Leader: We rekindle and reaffirm our desire to move towards the light. We ask for help on our journey, that we might continue, each in our own way, to the best of our ability, to move towards greater love, compassion, and peace.

The leader blows her intention onto the flags. Pass the flags around the circle so all participants can blow their intentions onto the flags.

Leader: We will now go outside and hang the prayer flags. As we hang them, we will chant the Om Mane Padme Hum chant.

The words for the chant are Om Mane Padme Hum sung four times each verse. The chant is in the appendix. Sing the chant several times before going outside so that people are fairly comfortable. We hung the flags between our Church and Parish House. You can find any suitable place at the ritual site to hang them. Proceed outside, chanting, the leaders with the flags and helpers first, to hang the flags. When this is complete, return inside and sit.

Talking Stick

Leader: We will now pass the talking stick. Please share whatever feels right to you. Who would like to start?

Thanking and Releasing the Directions

Snuff each candle as you read each direction

NORTH

Leader: Goddesses of the North, mothers of wisdom and deep inner knowing, Hummingbird and Dragon, thank you for being here with us and sharing your gifts.

EAST

Leader: Goddesses of the East, mothers of sunrises and beginnings, Condor and Eagle, thank you for being here with us and sharing your insights and vision.

SOUTH

Leader: Goddesses of the South, mothers of our passions and flowering, Sachamama, Grandmother Serpent, thank you for showing us how to grow and cultivate our compassion.

WEST

Leader: Goddesses of the West, mothers of healing and dexterity, Mother-sister Jaguar, thank you for being here with us tonight, for sharing with us your healing nectars.

CENTER

Leader: Great Goddesses, Mothers of all who nurture our being, Pachamama, Mother Earth, Inti Tutu and Mama Gela, thank you for being here with us tonight.

Leader: Please stand and we will sing the closing

May the Circle Be Open
But Unbroken
May the Love of the Goddess
Be ever in your heart.
Merry meet and merry part,
And merry meet again.

The closing chant is in the appendix.

Meditation

Your Prayer Flag

Leader:

The meditation is a time to reflect and contemplate from the quiet of your own inner sanctuary. Consider what you would like to put on your prayer flag. What do you and all of us need to sustain us and nourish our hope and commitment to peace and love? We will pass around the fabric and fabric pens after the meditation, and we invite you to work at the altar, for this is sacred work. We ask you to work in silence, treating this as a part of the meditation.

And now, make yourself comfortable......bringing your attention to your breathing........ Just focusing on your breath.......noticing the feel of the air at your nostrils...each breath calming and guiding you gently to this pause............and one more breath..................... signaling to your entire being.....your body....mind and spirit that it is a time to pause...........to step out of the business of the season..........to pause and enjoy the gift of quiet and reflection, safe here in our circle.......

Short pause

And for just now gradually allow yourself to become more deeply aware of this day, this evening that is the Solstice... This evening when the Wheel turns and the days will be gradually and steadily longer.........this is the evening that reaffirms our knowing of the truth of change......................and the cycles that nourish us into periods of growth and then periods of rest.................. This is the evening that reconfirms the power of our knowing...that deep within each of us lies a bottomless pool of abundant love compassion and wisdom...........perhaps incubating .....waiting to be tapped and grow with the growing light......

So take a moment.....breathing deeply...as if into the very center of your being......... Following your breath deep within........moving lightly and gently.............. inward with the breath toward your core..........guided by a shimmering light that seems to radiate from deep within you............ ...and you move easily now on the current of your breath toward this light......and into your inner sanctuary........

As you enter your inner chambers.......you are struck by your own beauty and simplicity. There is much light here....... much love and compassion and you are gently enveloped by its warmth and understanding........You are quite safe here.....and you begin to relax and soften ....filling with this warmth and understanding.......and the awareness of a deep inner wisdom that dwells here within you ....the sacred within.......

Pause here.........as images and scents or sensations may arise......notice them...... Savor them.......And let yourself find a comfortable place to settle down and reflect...
Tonight you are here to re-energize and rededicate yourself to cultivating a deeper knowing of the love, compassion and wisdom that dwells within you........that this is the source of your own inner peace and happiness............Pause for a minute and let yourself fill with the light and love that is here.........

Pause

As you rest here................you may ask for guidance......for insight................for tonight you have a task.......you will soon be making a prayer flag.................and you may have a question....

Pause

And so, you may notice that an enlightened one.....a goddess figure...or a deep inner knowing arises to help you...............for this is the home of the sacred within........
And you are free to ask and ponder.......What do I need to sustain me on this journey? What will help myself and others in our quest towards greater peace and happiness........

Reflect and ask, as it is right for you to do so..............Accept the suggestions and teachings in whatever form they come.........

Pause

And now it is time to begin your journey back to our room and our altar, so that you might act on your learning.............

So thank your Enlightened ones.......your knowing....and gently turn your awareness to your breathing..........this time following your breath out.......gradually becoming more and more aware of how you are sitting in your chair.............taking a deep breath in........and then slowly exhaling............each breath bringing you more and more into our circle here this evening.................and another deep breath in and a slow exhale out......returning more and more to here and now.....to the winter solstice.......
And now stretch if you would like to............open your eyes slowly and gaze about for a moment.......... you may start on your prayer flag whenever you feel ready.

SR 2009

The Turning of the Wheel

Theme

The theme of the ritual is celebrating the turning of the wheel through the seasons. The winter solstice, on Dec. 21, marks the turning of the wheel from growing darkness and long nights, to increasing light and longer days. We are gently and persistently drawn inward in the winter season, giving us opportunity for our inner realms to expand. The richness of our imagination and dream states are where the seeds of what is to come are conceived and nourished. And so, the darkness holds the promise of new growth in its embrace. We honor the darkness and the gifts of reflection and inner growth that come with winter.

Sources of Inspiration

The Aum breath has roots in a Hindu and Buddhist practice that we incorporated into this ritual. The use of candles is a universal spiritual practice. We wove the evergreens into the ritual, which are a European symbol of the continuance of life through the dark and cold of winter.

Altar

- *Black cloth for the altar*
- *Sparkles or sprinkles for the altar that will shine and reflect the candlelight*
- *Many dark candles*
- *Direction Candles*
- *Tibetan singing bowls, or any meditation sounding 'gong' such as Ting Tsaws, a chime or bells*
- *White ribbons, pinned in shape of a necklace with evergreen-a symbol of life continuing through the winter season, enough necklaces for each participant*
- *Journaling paper, crayons, pens, pencils or whatever*

Additional items for Sacred Space

- *Small gift boxes filled with chocolates and a candle*

Set up

We followed our traditional pattern of a center circular table used as the Altar and the chairs arranged in a circle around the Altar. The table/Altar is lower than a usual table so participants can easily see each other around the circle. We hid the small gift bags under the Altar table.

Smudge

Set up the smudge outside the room. You may appoint a 'smudger', but do not forget to smudge yourself as leaders first. You may use whatever feels appropriate to you.

Grounding

The AUM breath is a lot easier than it sounds with the written explanation. It is a powerful grounding and centering and helps the group become more fully present to the ritual.

Leader: We will now ground with the AUM breath. This is a three part breathing meditation.

We will break it down into its three parts initially. So, breathe deep into your belly, expanding your belly and make the sound of "Ahhh" as you exhale from your belly, letting your belly become small.

On the second inhale, expand and fill your belly. When you exhale, make the "Uuuuhhhh" sound as your chest becomes smaller.

On the third breath, expand and fill your belly. As you exhale, say the "Mmmmm" sound as the breath reaches your throat and head, and notice how it resonates in the throat and head area.

Demonstrate the breath, and then coach them through an entire sequence.

Now we will combine this all in one breath. Inhale a deep belly breath. Exhale, and make the sound of the "Ahhhh" and focus on your belly, moving up to your chest and making the "Uuuhhh" sound. As your exhaling moves upward to your throat and head area make the sound of "Mmmmm" and let it resonate through your throat and face.

Invite any questions. When everyone is ready, sound the singing bowl to signal the beginning of the centering meditation. The vibration of the bowl also helps to move the group into a centered state.

Then proceed to guide the group through three consecutive Aum breaths, voicing the AUM on the exhale. Sound the singing bowl at the end of the three breaths. This lends a definitive structure to the grounding, helps return them grounded to the circle and sounds great.

Calling the Directions

Light each candle as the direction is read

EAST

Leader: Guardians of the East, Air Spirits, breathe warmth and wisdom into the darkness of winter and nourish the growth of our spirit

SOUTH

Leader: Guardians of the South, Fire Spirits, burn bright with the growing light so that the seeds that have grown in the fertile ground of winter may flower in a new day

WEST

Leader: Guardians of the West, Water Spirits, flow deep into our being and nourish us that what flowers within us will be beautiful and strong.

NORTH

Leader: Guardians of the North, Earth Spirits, keep us strong and grounded so that our new growth will have deep roots and be strong

CENTER

Leader: Guardian of the Above and the Below, Goddess, be with us as we look at what grows within us and as we look outward towards what we will manifest

Meditation

The script for the meditation is at the end of the ritual.

Remember to leave time at the end of the meditation for people to journal or just sit quietly. This provides a gentle and thoughtful transition into the next part of the ritual. It is also important for their integration of the meditation into current time.

Ritual

Leader: Please stand and we will celebrate our passage through the season of winter into the growing light. We will go around the circle with each person lighting the next person's candle and saying: "Let us celebrate the light that is growing in the world." Your candle is on the altar in front of you. When we have gone full circle, please place your candle on the altar. I will start.

We started with a candle lit from the altar. Then turn to the person next to you, light her candle and say, 'Let us celebrate the light that is growing in the world.' This person turns to her neighbor and lights her candle, repeating the phrase. After the candles have been placed on the altar, the leader picks up the white ribbons and holds for all to see.

Leader: Let us celebrate the light that is growing within each of us. We gift you with a white ribbon symbolizing the light, and holding a piece of evergreen to symbolize the promise that life continues throughout the winter.

We liked the sense of ceremony that is added as the leader or leaders walk around the circle placing a ribbon around each person's neck, saying....may you celebrate the light within you.

Leader: Let us be seated

Talking Stick

Leader: We will now pass the talking stick. Please share as you are moved. You may want to share what came up during the meditation, what nourishes your life and growth through the dark of winter, or any gifts that you may have received during the meditation. Who would like to start?

When everyone who would like to speak has had a chance, read the poem.

Leader:

For as the world is dreamt awake,

From year to year and age to age,

And the Sun shall come up early,
May silver vision be granted to me,
In this darkness.
I dance for birth, for the returning Sun
And for the earth in dawn beauty.
Now the womb of night gives birth to life and light
And all shall be renewed. It begins here, now.
Womb of the night brings forth new life and light.
I share in the renewal of all life.
With all creatures, I am cherished
By the Mother Goddess
May I grow in love and wisdom
Pagan child of the Sun and Moon.
I am reborn in freedom,
I am nourished in sweetness.

Source unknown

Gift Giving

We gift you with these gifts of the Yule season that symbolize the sweetness of the dark time and the rebirth of the light.

Thanking and Releasing the Directions

Snuff each candle as you read each direction

EAST

Leader: Guardians of the East, Air Spirits, thank you for being with us and helping us on our spirit journey

SOUTH

Leader: Guardians of the South, Fire Spirits, thank you for being with us and helping us on our spirit journey

WEST

Leader: Guardians of the West, Water Spirits, thank you for being with us and helping us on our spirit journey

NORTH

Leader: Guardians of the North, Earth Spirits, thank you for being with us and helping us on our spirit journey

CENTER

Leader: Guardian of the Above and the Below, Goddess, thank you for being with us and helping us on our spirit journey

Meditation

So now....begin to make yourself comfortable for meditation.......Finding a comfortable position.......gradually bringing your awareness to your breathing...........Noticing your inhale..........your exhale........taking a moment to observe with curiosity.........the feel of the air at your nostrils as you inhale..........and the feel of the air at your nostrils as you exhale..........each breath drawing you gently inward........calming and leaving you room to just notice your breathing at your nostrils.........

And now.......traveling in your imagination...........imagine walking down a path.... a well trod path lit by the moonlight.... perhaps in a forest, or along the oceans edge...... There is a familiarity to the path...... a sense of security and assurance as your feet move effortlessly along.......As you walk, your awareness turns to the feel of the earth beneath your feet..... the coolness of night air.... soft and slightly damp on your skin........and to the smells of the darkness....crisp, clear.......and now the sounds of the night..... perhaps a stray owl or bird..... the wind in the trees..... the crack of a twig or branch as the creatures of the night go about their routines......throughout you are aware of your sense of peacefulness and comfort at moving along this path.........and you realize deep within you that your travel down this path is guided by your inner knowing, your Goddess within........you walk here in safety and with Her blessings.

And with all your senses awakened and relaxed.... you travel, safely and easily down the path towards the entrance of a cave...... A beautiful, sacred cave... with gems and stones sprinkled generously around the entrance.......illuminating the way in and lending an air of magic and mystery.

You may enter the cave as you are ready.......walking down the corridor of the cave.. ....noticing the dampness......the cool warmth...... hearing the trickling of a stream spilling into a pool further down the corridor.

And you come upon an inner chamber.... softly lit by a crackling, warm fire...... There are blankets and furs arranged near the fire for you to rest on........the fruits of the harvest are present here for you also.........And you gradually move towards the fire.... nestling into the blankets and furs......finding your place of comfort.......perhaps enjoying the bounty of the harvest laid out before you.

And you may rest here.....within this cave in the Earth........for this is Her cave and you are cradled gently and lovingly in Her embrace.........she has blessed you with the gift of darkness......of quiet....as she watches over you...

From the detached safety of Her embrace.........you can reflect upon what has been happening in your life over the last year..........Just observing thoughts......events.... feelings.....with open curiosity.......unattached and uninvolved in the moment........

As you reflect on what has happened over the last year.......your attention begins to turn to where this may lead you........ What is it that enlivens your spirit? What is it that nourishes your whole being, your body, your mind, emotions and your spirit? And so, what is growing and seeking expression from deep within you?......

You may pause, and listen to what has been growing and bubbling up into your awareness.

Pause

And wondering now, what small steps might you take?.... What small seeds might you plant to nourish your spirit and growth into the coming light?.........For the wheel turns... and on this day we begin the gentle... steady return to the light....the warmth.........to renewal and the reemergence of new growth for ourselves.

Yule is also a time of celebrating this turning of the wheel..........it is customarily a time of sharing gifts...........The Great Mother Goddess has a gift for you to nourish and sustain you on your journey....... .You are free to receive this gift........ it may be an image, a song, a mystery that will become more clear and known in the coming days.........And you in return may gift her........ with a song, a kiss or embrace....... a dance or a blessing...... some symbol of your gratitude.

And now it is time to return......so thank yourself and our inner light for being present....and begin to return along the path you came on........down along the ocean or through the forest........again noticing the cool night air....the call of the owl......and the exquisite peace and still of the evening.......

As you reach the beginning of this journey....gently return your awareness to your breathing........inhaling and noticing the feel of the air at your nostrils...and exhaling... again noticing the feel of the air at your nostrils.....
And taking a deep breath in...filling your belly...chest...and throat.......and exhaling a long and deep exhale........noticing if your body would like to stretch or move.......and another deep breath.......opening your eyes when you are ready....noticing the play of the light and shadows.........

And as you are ready please find journaling materials at your seats. Please write, draw or muse on your experience as it seems right for you.

Please do this in silence.

SR 2006

Honoring the Darkness

Theme

The theme of this solstice ritual is honoring the darkness as an opportunity to rest, reflect and replenish ourselves. When acknowledged as a process that is necessary, this reflection and rest allows us to thoroughly get ready for the coming light and burst of growth that is so invigorating in the spring. It is an opportunity to look back over the year, reviewing the positive legacy that you have accrued over the months. In this way, we release attachments to the past, open to the present and prepare for the future.

Sources of Inspiration

The spiral is a feminine symbol of the never-ending cycle of change and growth that so characterizes women's lives. It is found throughout history in many cultures worldwide. Walking the spiral was inspired by two things. One was the spiral dance used in old pagan rituals, and the other was walking a labyrinth, that has returned to us as a healing and spiritual vehicle

Working with the Stone People is taken from the Andean Shamanic traditions.

We were also inspired by the various meanings of Namaste. The meaning we used speaks to the uniting and honoring of Spirit within each of us.

Altar

- *Gifts*
- *Stones, scattered on center altar*
- *Tea lights scattered around the center altar*
- *Four tables each with a direction candle and 6 or 7 tea lights*
- *Lighting candles with drip plates on each table*
- *Snuffers*
- *Bowl and large candle for the center altar*

Additional Items

- *Gift bags with a candle decorated as you wish. We wrapped each candle with a holiday bow and holly..*

Set up

The concept of walking the spiral into the center lies at the heart of this calling of the directions. Moving inward along the never-ending spiral path to the center of our sacred space reflects both our path through the seasons of our lives and our path into the heart and soul of who we are.

The altar table is set in the middle, with the candle for the Center. Chairs are placed around the altar to form a circle for participants.

There are four tables holding the direction candles, one placed in each direction around the outside of the chairs. Leave enough room between the directional tables and the back of the chairs for people to walk.

We lit all the tea lights on the direction tables before the ritual started. The effect of putting out the tea lights during the processional gives participants a symbolic sense of walking into darkness.

Please see the diagram at the end of the ritual for our version of this spiral.

Adapt and enjoy your creativity.

Smudging

Any appropriate smudge may be used. Some suggestions might be Paulo santo, sage, cedar, or pine. The Smudge Mistress smudges outside of the ritual room. People gather here, so that they will all enter together for the casting of the circle and the processional into the center of the spiral.

Calling the Directions

We found that having quiet music playing helped to set the mood. People enter and stand at the north of the spiral. We enter in the north to celebrate the gifts of the winter season and the solstice. When all the participants are standing at the north, it is time to call the directions. At this time we stopped the music.

One leader reads and the other (or a volunteer) walks the outer edge of the spiral lighting the large candle on each directional table. We suggest lighting first and then reading

NORTH

Leader: We call upon the Spirits of the North, of Earth and Mountain, who dwell in the dark and cold of midwinter.
In the quiet darkness, help us to send our roots down into Mother Earth, past rocks and water into the molten fires deep at Her core.
Help us to gather strength and sustenance here, that we may look quietly within and nourish our own inner strengths.

EAST

Leader: We call upon the Spirits of the East, of Air, who dwell in the wind and warmth of spring.
Blow on the cold earth and the icy snows of winter to soften and reawaken all creation.

SOUTH

Leader: We call upon the Spirits of the South, of Fire and Sun, who dwell in the heat and passion of summer.
Warm the earth, that the seeds born of winter's dormancy may grow and the passion in our hearts may awaken.

WEST

Leader: We call upon the Spirits of the West who dwell in the rains and still waters of fall.
Heal, cleanse, and nourish all of creation.
Receive our tears that they become one with your healing waters, and so heal us all.

Walking to the Center

Leader: To complete the calling in of our sacred space we will walk the spiral inward to the center of our circle, the altar of the Goddess deep within. We walk into the time of darkness, the time of turning inward to reflect on our lives, and all that has happened in the past year.

As we proceed through the spiral we will chant:

Air her breath

And fire her spirit

Water her blood

And earth her body

Please see the Appendix for music.

The leader starts the processional in the north,

1. *The processional walks around the backs of the chairs, inside the direction tables, to the East, South, and then West.*
2. *When the leader is back to the opening, (near the north), She/he walks inside the inner circle walking around the altar, and stopping to stand in front of a chair. See diagram.*

One leader headed the processional and the other leader, or volunteer, walked at the end.

As we walked the spiral each of the leaders snuffed several of the small candles on the direction tables. The leader who was last, finished snuffing the small candles or tea lights.

It becomes a real 'walking into the dark of winter' as participants walk to their seats.

CENTER

Leader: We call upon the Spirits of Above and Below, who dwell at once at the core of our being and the fulcrum of the world.

Keep our planet and us in harmony that we may hear the music of the spheres.

After a timely pause, pick up the bowl with the tea light from the altar and hold it up in front of you with the candle lit. The candle may be lit ahead of time or you may choose to ceremoniously light the candle before you pick it up

Leader: Flame of the Sacred Within. May you provide light on our journey of turning inward to the center of our knowing. May you offer guidance and renewal for the work of long nights and short days.

We invite each of you to light a candle on the altar to acknowledge your own Sacred Inner Light.

Inside the bowl place a short 'lighting candle'. Each person may light this 'lighting candle' from the bowl and then light their candle on the altar. One of the leaders may want to start, or invite the person next to you to start and offer a brief instruction beforehand.

When everyone has had a turn and the leader has the bowl back, place it on the altar and pause briefly.

Leader: And now, we will join in an honoring of each other. Please bring your hands to your heart center, palms together. This is an almost universal prayer mudra. And so holding your space of Inner Light, prayerfully at your heart, let us honor the Light within ourselves and within each other. Repeat after me

When I am in this place within me,

all repeat

and you are in this place within you

all repeat

we are one

all repeat

NAMASTE

all repeat

As you finish this, bow respectfully to the Light that resides within all who are present.

Short pause to let this settle. When we did this in ritual it was quite moving and the pause allows time for the experience to complete

Leader: Please be seated

There are a number of stone people scattered on the altar. They have been gathered in ceremony. They have volunteered to be present here at our ritual and to be passed on to one of you. A word about stones and stone people; some of you may be drawn to stones, others to Trees, Animals, or other totems and symbols of The Sacred. Tonight we explore the Stone Nation, patient, slow moving, observant, grounded and solid. This is suitable for our ritual of the North, where the Spirits of Mountains dwell. The North is also a time for seeking inner vision and the truths that guide our lives, best done quietly, when we are grounded and centered.

It is our belief that Spirit is in all that is. We are gifted by Nature each moment we take the time to be open to those gifts and simply observe, work with and respect the truth of non-human teachers. Tonight we are working with these stone people that come from the meeting place of Earth and Sea.

How do we work with stones? Be open. Ask. Listen. Be Patient. Just holding the Stone Person you've been drawn to, in an open and respectful way, will begin to release its gifts to you. We walk along a beach and out of thousands of Stones, we find one or two that we just feel compelled to pick up and hold. And most often we do, finding the feel of the stone person comforting in some way. Touch is a way of energy transfer and Stones respond to touch just as humans do. When we hold our Stone Person there is a sharing of energy, a connecting and transfer that often transcends words.

So our stones talk to us by sight, touch or sound. We invite you to walk around the table, one by one, and find the stone that draws your attention. You may hold your hand a few inches over the stones and feel the energy from your stone. (Demonstrate) It may be a visual connection. Or you may hear a stone calling you, choose me! choose me! Perhaps you already know which stone is yours and can pick it up right now. Which stone is your heart stone? Who will begin?

As you speak this part, you may demonstrate how they might walk around the altar and feel the energy of each stone with their hand. Allow plenty of time for each person to pick their own stone person

Meditation

Leader: And now we will get ready for meditation. So make yourself comfortable in your chairs, holding your new stone friend with an open heart and mind. Listen carefully to the inner knowing voice of your stone.

Pause a few minutes as they begin to get comfortable.

Pause after the meditation ends until you sense that everyone is completely back or present in the circle.

You may also time this, giving the group at least a minute to recollect after you stop speaking.

See Meditation at end of ritual.

Ritual

Leader: Spirit and life have gifted us with many talents and skills to make us who we are. You may light a candle for each gift, each talent or strength that is yours. It may be a gift of learning, a gift of something you do well, your strengths as seen through the past year or year to come. Name it that we all may acknowledge your strengths and power. Do not be afraid to name these gifts, for you are unique in the world, and Your Spirit guides you to live in balance and harmony with the gifts that you possess. In naming, and claiming, you affirm self-awareness and the knowledge that you are also to share these gifts with others, so that all may benefit from your earth walk.

Allow each person to go around, lighting a candle and naming their gift or gifts. Some people may need the encouragement of a leader modeling before they are comfortable enough to freely speak their gifts.

Talking Stick

Leader: And now we will have the talking stick. You may share whatever feels right to you, and you are free to remain silent in your reflection.

Presentation of Gifts

This Yule we celebrate the North, the time of darkness and nurturing inner selves, just as the seeds rest and incubate within Mother Earth. Although it is the shortest day and longest night of the year, we look forward to the growing of the light. In that spirit we gift you with this small symbol of that miracle. Together with your stone, you can create a magic place in your home.

Pass out the gift. We gave a candle, wrapped with a bow and the stone person they chose from the table.

Thanking and Releasing the Directions

Leader: Please stand. We will thank and release the directions, chanting as we leave the center altar and proceed out the spiral and into ordinary space and time.

Snuff the center candle.

Leader: We thank and bless the Spirits of the Center.

The last person into the circle starts the procession out. For us this was one of the co-facilitators. We started out and around the outside of the chairs, back to the entrance. The rest of the circle will walk around some of the altar and then out and around the outside of the chairs.

Air her breath

And fire her spirit

Water her blood

And earth her body

One leader lights every other candle on the directional tables as the procession winds slowly out of the spiral. The other leader, going last, lights the rest. If there is one leader, appoint a helper to be at the end of the procession to light the remaining candles. When all arrive outside the circle of chairs, pause at the north direction and signal to others to stay where they are.

The leader/volunteer bringing up the rear snuffs the direction candle as each direction is released.

NORTH

Leader: We thank and bless the Spirits of the North.

EAST

Leader: We thank and bless the Spirits of the East.

SOUTH

Leader: We thank and bless the Spirits of the South.

WEST

Leader: We thank and bless the Spirits of the West.

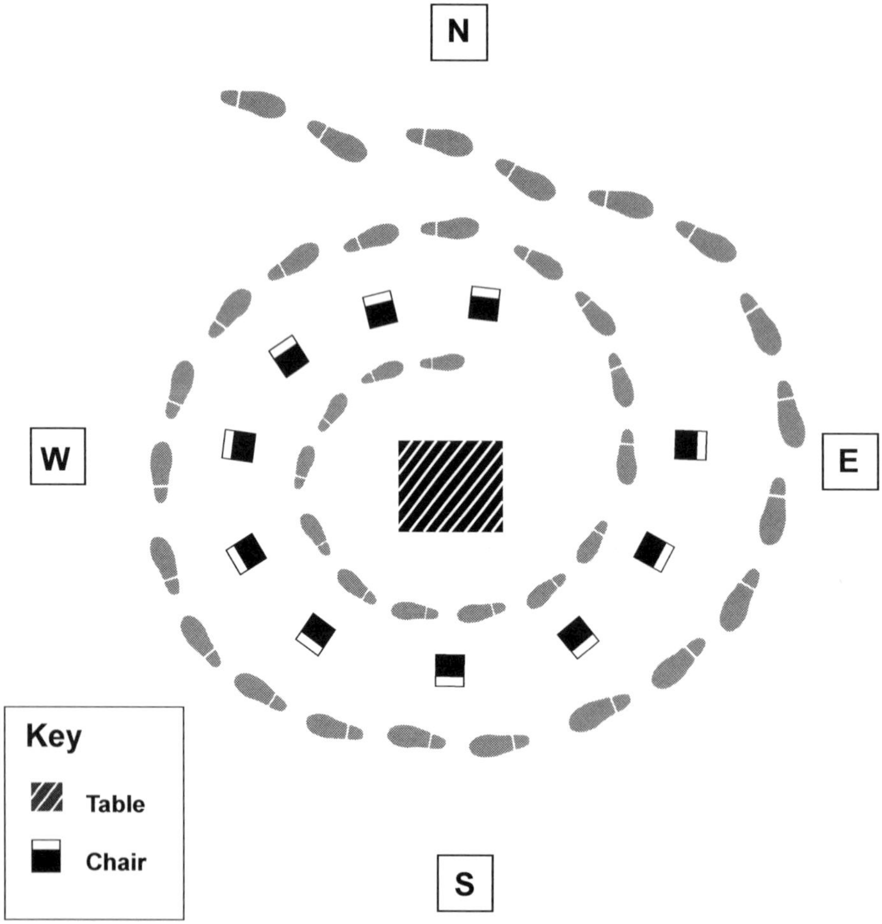

Meditation

Exploring our Positive Legacy

I invite you to make yourself comfortable......settling in for a short meditation.................. perhaps adjusting your position or stretching some as you get comfortable.

And now, bringing your attention gradually to your breath........Noticing your breath..... the inhale....followed by the exhale..........

Just noticing your breath moving in..........perhaps the feel of the air at your nostrils....... and then the breath moving out........again noticing the feel of the air at your nostrils......

This is a gentle turning in ....moving gradually into a space where there is no right or wrong...better or worse............ for this moment there is only your breath in...... and your breath out...........there is no place to go....nothing to do....... nothing to become for the next few moments........................

There is only your breath.... each breath carrying you gently inward......... beginning to imagine yourself outside.........on a beautiful, clear night.........the skies are decorated with a thousand twinkling stars.......and all that is around you glimmers in the moon-light......................

The night air is slightly warm............. balmy and moist on your skin..............
You gaze about you......taking in the landscape...............gradually becoming aware of a beautiful, majestic mountain nearby.... ....with a multitude of smaller rocks strewn upon the ground near your feet...as if a mischievous spirit had scattered them before you as a reminder......................and you remember the sacred stone that you hold...........sensing it in your hand...........feeling the texture .....smooth or rough........... its temperature......its energy connecting you with the stones and mountain in your meditation....... You begin to sense a deep peace and connection with all

that is around you......an ageless wisdom, solid and grounded as it makes its presence known to you.........

As you look about.....you notice a cave entrance off to one side of the mountain... beckoning you to enter.........and so you walk down the path towards the cave entrance......... you notice how beautiful it is............with gems and stones sparkling in the moonlight.....lending an air of magic and mystery.......................And you are reminded of the stone person you hold in your hand and its connection to the greater whole...........

You pause here at the entrance for a moment......noticing a well-trod path before you, spiraling inward................marked by radiant standing stones of all shapes and colors.....................you enter the spiral........the light from the standing stones guides your way...........and so moving ever inward............feeling the cool warmth of the air on your skin........... perhaps hearing the gurgle of a stream gently spilling into a small pool in the distance....................................

And you come upon an inner chamber.... softly lit by a crackling warm fire.
In this special place there is just what you need................. a colorful nest of blankets and pillows near the warm fire ....another by the beautiful stone pool....gurgling and singing.....................you may settle into any of these spaces that feel right to you..........................

And so making yourself comfortable............ holding your sacred stone being..........
you settle in....making ready for the work of the season.........you call upon the spirit of your stone being for assistance as you review your year.........
And so Calling....... "Spirit of the stone people, wise one, share with me your wisdom and guidance as I reflect upon my year......lend me insight...... show me deep knowing........help me to see the positive legacy that I have left this year.....that I might grow and see my wholeness."

So it is that you begin to reflect back on your earthwalk through the seasons and events of this past year......................paying particular attention to the positive legacy that you have left...............as you look back on the seasons.....the spring and summer......... the fall and winter................you begin to notice what you have done well.........what it is that you feel good about........and how this taps your gifts and strengths........

Pause for some time to allow them to look back

And now inquire of your stone person........ "Wise one, guide me with your insights.....what gift or strength shall I nourish throughout the long nights, in preparation for spring?"

Pause

And taking a few more moments as you need............you begin to make ready to leave your inner sanctuary of the Goddess........calling to the stone spirit that you cradle in your hand........thanking this spirit for the insight, the knowing and patience with which it has assisted you.................................blowing your gratitude onto the stone..........

And thus starting your journey back to current time and place.......walking out around the spiral marked by the softly glowing standing stones......
Slowly spiraling around and out...........moving steadily towards the entrance of the cave......................and then out the entrance into the beautiful, clear night......
.................and breathing, as if you could fill your belly......your chest, and even your throat with the clean clear air of the night............and then exhaling slowly............ feeling your stone person held safely in your hands.........and breathing in again...... deeply.......and slowly exhaling.........noticing if you would like to stretch or move in any way.........savoring this............and opening your eyes when you are ready......take a moment to look around our circle....noticing colors, light and dark......and take one more deep breath......returning fully to our circle within the sacred spiral.

SR 2003

Graditude

Giving thanks is a life long practice and one that will connect us on very deep levels to Spirit, both within and without. A robust and alive relationship invites us to do this as a way of acknowledging the give and take of being in relationship with Spirit that exists around us. And it is good for our Inner Spirit that yearns for connection with Spirit in Nature.

We can express gratitude in many ways, through ritual, through the use of kinto's or flowers, or any object that we choose to symbolize our gratitude. Each of us will find our own way with this. I have friends who will stop and offer flower petals, or small bundles of herbs, to places where they have felt a special connection. Or sprinkle clean potable water to say thank you for a beautiful sunset, or the peace and grandeur of mountains. Any expression or symbol of gratitude may be offered. Sandy and I often leave kinto's out in nature at a beautiful site or at special places that we each sit to commune.

And there are times, often times, that we come to commune and ask for help or guidance…and we can offer a "pay forward" and say thank you ahead of time. It is like going to a dear friend and bringing a gift. It might be cookies, or flowers or whatever. We are taken in, fed and nourished, and perhaps our questions will be answered there and then or perhaps later.

And so it is that as we ask for help or guidance from Spirit either inner and/or outer, we give back a thank you…we see a beautiful sunset and we give back a thank you for that beautiful sunset. By giving thanks we cultivate a healthy and robust relationship with Spirit, both within and without.

In this grouping of rituals, we give thanks for the physical forms of our bodies that allow us to experience the gifts around and within us. In the second ritual we offer thanks through the form of a ritual meal, and in the third we honor the gifts that are handed down to us from our elder women about connecting to the earth.

Enjoy!

Celebrating the Physical Form as Sacred

Note

This ritual fits nicely into a spring or early summer ritual, which is filled with new growth, anticipation and joy.

Theme

The theme flows from the concept that everything, including us, is an expression of the Goddess or the Sacred made manifest. She lives within us and within all things, providing a common thread that unites us. This ritual celebrates and gives thanks for the physical world around us and for our bodies, which afford us the ability to experience this life, to learn, to feel, to act and interact. As goddess-within, we bless these gifts that have been given us.

Sources of Inspiration

We were inspired by such leaders of the Neo-Pagan movement as Starhawk and Z Budapest, who have explored self-blessings as a form of women's earth-based ritual.

Altar

- *Fabric of spring or summer colors*
- *Direction candles*
- *Matches*
- *Snuffer*
- *Lighting candle*
- *Flowers of all colors*
- *Basket of paper packets of confetti to take outside*
- *Bowl of flower petals or flowers for hair*
- *Bowl of water with flower essence or Rescue Remedy in it.*

Rescue Remedy is a homeopathic liquid often found in health food stores.

- *Paper confetti in small bowls for each participant for the meditation*

  Paper confetti works best as sprinkles are difficult to clean up and are itchy

- *A large piece of plastic or cloth under the chairs in the circle to catch the confetti*
- *Objects for the directions*

  Fire or candle at the south, sun medallion

  Water at the west

  Stones at the north

  Feathers at the east

  A Goddess or dancing Shiva at the center

Additional items for Sacred Space

- *Food for a feast after the ritual.*

Set up

We decorated the room further to enhance the feeling of spiritual space, calm and quiet. Flower petals were scattered on the altar. A bowl of confetti was placed in front of each place, along with a flower. The bowl with flower essence water was on the altar to be passed around. On a separate table we arranged a feast of cookies and juice, crackers and wine or whatever foods and beverages seem appropriate to you.

Smudge

Smudging outside the room allows each person a brief clearing and centering before walking into ritual space.

Set up the smudge outside the room. You may appoint a 'smudger', but do not forget to smudge yourself as leaders first. You may use whatever feels appropriate to you. Some suggestions are: sage, paulo santo, or mugwort

Calling the Directions

Light each candle as the direction is read.

SOUTH

Leader: Please stand and turn to the South.

Energy of Goddess, flow through us and warm our hearts and the hearts of all your children.

Be joy and growth and dancing in our being. Be here in this hour.

WEST

Leader: Please turn to the West.

Blood of Goddess, move nourishment and healing throughout our bodies and the bodies of all things.

Be the movement of feelings flowing forth, sweet and clear and opening within us.

Be here in this hour.

NORTH

Leader: Please turn to the North.

Body of Goddess, bring the solidness and substance of your mountains to us and to all beings.

Be our strength and form, sacred ground firm within us.

Fill us with insight and vision.

Be here in this hour.

EAST

Leader: Please turn to the East.
Breath of Goddess, wind in our sails.
Be divine mind in ours.
Be vision and clarity and lightness of being within us.
Be here in this hour.

CENTER

Leader: Please turn to the center.
From the ground, from the stone, from the windswept sky, from the flaming fire's cone, from the flowing water's sigh, our spirits call, our voices sing, our feet dance.
Hear our celebration of gratitude.

Ritual of Celebration and Gratitude

Leader: Please take a small bag of confetti from the basket we are passing. We will take our offerings of confetti outside to give to Spirit in gratitude for the gift of a world that we can touch, see, smell, taste, hear and interact with. In order to hold space, we will walk outside in silence and gather in a circle.

It was helpful for one of the leaders to go first and establish the place for the circle.

Leader: I want to share this poem by Z. Budapest that speaks to the form that the goddess and sacred feminine may take. Listen to the words of the Goddess.

I have slept for ten thousand years.
Now I stretch and waken.
They are calling, calling me, and my heart leaps to greet them.
My forests are my hair, the grasses my heavy eyelashes.
They call me, and I waken.
My body bedecked with a million flowers,
And these many breasts of mine, the mountains joyfully rear their tips.
I long to suckle my young. They are calling.
They will know me!
Earth Mother am I; life springs from me. I carry the seed of creation.
And I awake!

Leader: Take your packets of confetti, find a place that calls you and sit or stand with this place for a while. You may pick a tree, flower, grass or whatever has physical form and notice it. Use your intuition and all of your senses to interact with the place and form you have chosen. Smell it, touch it, feel it. What does it feel like? What does it look like? Look carefully. Does it have a smell? Can you taste it? Does it speak to you? Listen. What do you sense about its inner nature?

Read this slowly so people can take in the directions. Pause briefly.

When you are ready, offer your packet of confetti to your chosen place. You may sprinkle your confetti with a few words of thanks to Spirit for the joy of her physical form. When you are ready return to the altar inside.

Meditation

The script for the meditation is at the end of the ritual. Remember to leave time at the end of the meditation for people to journal or just sit quietly. This provides a gentle and thoughtful transition into the next part of the ritual. It is also important for their integration of the meditation into current time

Talking Stick

Leader: We will now pass the talking stick. Please share as you are moved. You may want to share something that came up during the ritual or whatever else is in your heart or on your mind. What is said here stays here in circle. It is all right to pass. Who would like to start?

Thanking and Releasing the Directions

Snuff each candle as the direction is read

SOUTH

Leader: Great Goddess of the South, of Fire, we thank you for the energy of Goddess expressed within us and around us.

WEST

Leader: Great Goddess of the West, of Water, we thank you for the flow of healing and nourishment that sustains all physical forms of life.

NORTH

Leader: Great Goddess of the North, of Earth, we thank you for the gift of groundedness that comes with our physical form.

EAST

Leader: Great Goddess of the East, of Air, we thank you for the breath that flows through all physical form bringing life.

CENTER

Leader: May the peace of the Goddess of the Center be in our hearts, as we
Merry meet,
Merry part, and
Merry meet again.
Blessed Be!

You may choose to use the chant, May the circle be open, instead. We closed the ritual with a feast to further celebrate the joy of the multitude of physical forms that we can enjoy, such as good food. It may be served elsewhere in the room or brought to the altar.

Self Blessing Meditation

Make yourself comfortable in your seats.....wiggle and adjust as you need.....and gently allow your eyes to close for a moment........gradually bringing your attention to your breath.......noticing your body as you breathe in.....and breathe out.........

And now......inhaling and taking in the bounty of the breath....the nourishment of the universe....filling your belly.....your chest......and as you are ready.....exhaling....giving back nourishment to the universe and its beings......Each breath bringing you gently to your inner sensing........noticing how your body moves or doesn't move as you inhale.......and exhale..........reassured that as you enter this domain you are held in the sacred inner core of who you are..........that unites you with all life and the heart of the goddess..........so just noticing....knowing deeply that there is no judgment here......only acceptance.........and compassion........

And knowing this, you can now bring your attention to the privileges and gifts that your body provides...........bringing your attention first to your feet....... feeling the floor beneath you.......... sensing your connection to the earth.......and to your legs ....
........sensing your calves, knees and thighs..........

And pause.....reflecting for a moment on the multitude of ways your feet and legs have served you on your journey through life.....Of the places and people they have taken you to through the years.....the dances they have danced.....the sensation of new grass, warm sand, ocean waves on your toes....the lessons they have offered........

Pause

Placing your hands gently on your thighs..........feeling the touch..........saying silently with me........

I accept my legs and feet just as they are.........

I celebrate the joys of movement

I give thanks for the places and opportunities they have brought me to.

With the bowl of sprinkles in front of you, sprinkle your feet, calves and shins, knees and thighs in celebration.

And now...bringing your awareness to your hips and pelvis...........Pausing a moment at the center of your creative energy......and reflecting on how your pelvis and hips have served you......how they have supported your body..........perhaps brought children into the world.......and on the multitude of life, ideas, actions, creations, that you have nurtured and brought into the world...... ......

And placing your hands gently on your lower belly and hips...........sensing the warmth of your touch.........saying silently
I celebrate my feminine body.......
I give thanks for my creativity and passion
I bless all that is feminine in me.....

Sprinkle your hips, pelvis in celebration

And now...gradually move your awareness to your abdomen.......your belly....sense your belly......Reflecting on how this part of your body has served you....digesting the bounty from the earth....supplying energy and nutrients to your physical body.....energy for the emotions ,thoughts and activities available to us.......and for offering us the wisdom of our "gut feelings"

And gently bringing your hands to your belly, saying silently with me
I bless my belly
I give thanks for the gift of transforming food into sustenance......energy...
I give thanks for the wisdom of my 'gut feelings'

Sprinkle your belly in celebration.

And now....moving your awareness to your chest............your lungs...protected by your ribs....breathing in the universe and breathing out the universe....connecting you to all that is.......feeding your body and mind with breath........and your heart....ever-beating.....held also in the protection of your ribs and cradled in the love and compassion of the mother......And reflect for a moment on how your lungs have nourished and sustained you...how your heart center has touched, loved, cracked and healed.......yourself and others.......and how your heart has faithfully continued to beat and feed your body.

Sprinkle your chest, saying:
I celebrate and honor my chest,..my lungs and heart..and heart center ....for all the joy and love they have offered me......

And now....gently moving your awareness to your shoulders....and to your arms....down to the very tips of your fingers...... .....and
Pausing and reflecting on the myriad of ways in which your shoulders, arms and hands have served you....the hugs they have given and received.......the bundles they have carried.......your touching......... laboring and creating....loving and healing...........

Sprinkle your shoulders and hands, saying:
I celebrate and honor my shoulders, arms and hands, and all the joy and wonder they have offered me......

And now....shifting your attention, with great kindness to your back.....letting your awareness travel the full length of your spine......from the top of your shoulders.....to the tip of your tailbone....... ......
And pausing....reflecting on the many ways your back has served you....however imperfectly you thought at the time.....how it has supported you in standing, sitting....walking and running....supporting the burdens and joys that you have carried physically and energetically here..

Sprinkle your back, saying:
I celebrate and honor my back and all the joys and strength it has offered me......

And moving your awareness up to your neck....the back of your neck...and your throat.... reflecting on the many gifts and abilities that your neck and throat have offered you....Supporting your head......turning to see, smell and hear.....And speaking....giving voice to your inner life...your thoughts, feelings, and ideas.....sharing....connecting....expressing.....

Sprinkle your neck, saying:
I celebrate and honor my neck and my voice...and all the joy, and expression they have offered me

And bringing your awareness to your face....gently touching your face....reflecting on your sense of taste...and the many delights that have graced your palate.....your sense of smell which guides and remembers....... your listening and hearing.....the joy of music and nature...........and the sense of seeing... the beauty that has enriched and sustained you.....and the central home of mind....visioning and envisioning.... thinking.... wondering....learning and resting.

Sprinkle your head, saying:
I celebrate and honor my head, and face.....and my mind and all the joy and learning they have offered me.....

And one last sprinkle of your wholeness.......I celebrate all that I am....my body, mind and spirit....I celebrate my wholeness in this moment......

Please stand up. And now...standing.....moving your attention to our circle and this place......Reflecting on all the joys and experiences you have shared here in circle, whether often or for the first time today......and for the place......the trees and flowers......the buildings......and all that has been held in this place.....

Sprinkle the altar in our center

I celebrate and honor all who are held in this circle and this place and all the joy and awe and caring that has occurred and will occur here.

And I dance to celebrate....to honor......to rejoice!

SR 2004

MG & SR 2001

with appreciation
to my co-author
Marcia Giudici

Giving Thanks for the Gifts of Mother Earth

Theme

This Giving Thanks Ritual is a partaking of the gifts of Gaia, the Earth Goddess. Through symbolic ritual feasting we share the many gifts of our Mother, the Earth, and celebrate our oneness with all of life.

Sources of Inspiration

We were inspired by the idea of the Jewish Seder, a ritual dinner, where certain sacred foods are a symbolic part of the prayers. We were also inspired by the Buddhist Loving Kindness Meditation that we felt blended nicely with the abundance of nature's harvest.

Altar

- *Plates*
- *Napkins*
- *Wineglasses- filled with water or sparkling cider*
- *Pitchers of water and sparkling cider*
- *Bowls of rose petals*
- *Goddess statue*
- *Five white candles*
- *Runner or tablecloth*
- *Bowl of soft rolls*
- *Plate of saltines*
- *Plate of sour pickles (slices)*
- *Plate of fruit marzipan*
- *Platter of small cups of firewater*
- *Blue bowl of water*
- *A Rose at leader's place, by blue bowl.*

Set Up

Set up the altar as a dinner table, each place with wineglass of water or sparkling cider, a bowl of rose petals, plate and napkins.

In the center, we placed a decorative runner, a Goddess statue with rose petals scattered around Her, and a row of five white candles as if set for a dinner party. We placed the rose and the blue bowl at leader's seat. We placed the food around the altar table in a visually pleasing manner.

Smudge

Smudging outside the room allows each person a brief clearing and centering before walking into ritual space.

Set up the smudge outside the room. You may appoint a 'smudger', but do not forget to smudge yourself as leaders first. You may use whatever feels appropriate to you. Some suggestions are: sage, paulo santo, or mugwort.

Calling the Directions

Light each candle as you read the direction

SOUTH

Leader: Let us stand and toast the Directions
Please raise your glasses.
We drink to the South, to fire, warmth and long days of light.
We drink to the passions and actions that fuel our growth and nourish our hearts.
Hear our prayers of thanks, Goddesses of the South, great grandmother Sachamama, for we are grateful for your presence in our lives and the bounty of your gifts.
Let us all drink.
Salud!

WEST

Leader: We drink to the West, to soft mists and fog, to rain and snow, for they are the waters that bring life to all beings.
We drink to the lakes, streams and oceans that bathe our bodies and heal our spirits.
Hear our prayers of gratitude, Goddesses of the West, Mother-sister Jaguar, we are most grateful for your presence in our lives and the bounty of your gifts.
Let us all drink.
Salud!

NORTH

Leader: We drink to the North, to the mountains and rocks, to the trees and the plants, the riches beneath the earth's surface, for they provide us food and fuel, and a place to live in abundance and beauty.

Receive our offerings of gratitude, Goddesses of the North, Grandmother Hummingbird and Grandfather Dragon, for we are grateful for the bounty of your gifts and your presence in our lives.
Let us all drink.
Salud!

EAST

Leader: We drink to the East, to the warm and gentle breezes of summer, and the winds of all the seasons, for they bring messages of change and the turning of the wheel of seasons.
We drink to the clouds that flow on the breeze and leave their rains.
Receive our offerings of gratitude, Goddesses of the East, Brother Condor and Brother Eagle, for we are truly grateful for the bounty of your gifts and your presence in our lives. Let us all drink.
Salud!

CENTER

Leader: We drink to the Center, to Pachamama, Earth Mother who is the great Goddess, for She has held us in Her embrace through good times and bad times.
We drink to the Center, to our Star Brothers and Star Sisters, to the Sun and Moon, to the Heavens and Father Sky, for they have watched over us and shed their light and wisdom down upon us.
We receive and give in oneness with the sacred.
Let us all drink.
Salud!

Ritual

Leader: Bread is called the staff of life. It is a gift from a seed, planted deep in the earth; a gift from the sky, the sun and rain...and a gift from the labors of our brothers and sisters. Let us break bread together within our circle as a symbol of our interconnectedness with all of life.
After we pass the bread to everyone we will guide you in the ceremony.

Pass bread

Leader: With the first taste, we strive to practice loving kindness.

Eat

Leader: With the second taste, we strive to relieve the suffering of others.

Eat

Leader: With the third, we strive to see others' joy as our own.

Eat

Leader: With the fourth, we strive to learn the way of nonattachment and equanimity.

Eat

Leader: In the Jewish Passover Seder, traditional foods are eaten to symbolize the pain and tears of the Jew's existence in Egypt. A bowl of salt water with a sliced hardboiled egg in it symbolizes the hardness of the life and the tears that are shed by all peoples in all cultures. Our meal is symbolic of the trials and joys in our own lives.

Pass dish of salty food:

Leader: Let us partake of this salty cracker to remind us that our tears cleanse us of anger.

Pass sour food:

Leader: Let us partake of this sour pickle to remind us that out of the sourness of loss and grief come new beginnings

Pass bitter food:

Leader: Let us partake of this bitter herb to remind us of the bitter times we have lived and survived, stronger and wiser than before

Pass sweet food:

Leader: Let us partake of this sweet dessert to remind us to acknowledge and give thanks for all that is sweet in our lives

Leave time after everyone has eaten the sweet to let the experience of the foods settle.

Leader: As we have acknowledged both the difficulties and the sweetness's of life through the foods we have shared, let us now turn our attention to the Loving Kindness meditation, in which we give ourselves and others our prayers for compassion and kindness.

Instructions

Leader: There are four phrases that are repeated silently during the meditation. I will guide you through the phrases, so you will not have to remember them.

*May I find safe haven. This refers to freedom from the torments of the external world, such as violence, greed, hunger.

*May I have peaceful mind. This refers to freedom from the mental/emotional issues that plague most of us in our daily lives.

*May I have harmony with my body. This is a prayer for physical well-being and peace with our physical state, whatever that may be.

*May I be filled with loving kindness. This is an intention for balance and harmony in our day-to-day life. We will first offer loving kindness to ourselves, then out to other people.

Loving Kindness Meditation

Pacing is important, and participants will respond more deeply if not rushed. It gives them time to be present with the phrase and images.

And so making yourself ready for meditation........ finding a comfortable position................. either closing your eyes or leaving them open as is comfortable for you.

And notice your breath, the inhaling and the exhaling......

If you would like, and are able, you may place your hand over your heart......

Let a smile come to your lips as you remember a happy, joyful experience...... a birth... a beautiful day... an especially meaningful moment with a loved one.... any experience where you felt a great deal of joy and love........ Now give this love to yourself..... Imagine that this love is flowing out to you from your heart, filling your entire body....... gently and slowly...... and breathe....... Be with the following intentions/prayers for yourself...... I invite you to repeat each phrase silently to yourself as we move through the meditation.

Leader: Sending this loving kindness to yourself, repeating to yourself

May I find safe haven

May I have peaceful mind

May I have harmony with my body

May I be filled with Loving Kindness

Now bring to mind someone in your life, past or present who has supported you in times of need, or that you love and care for. Share your intentions for joy and love with them, repeating to yourself

May this person find safe haven

May this person have peaceful mind

May this person have harmony with their body

May this person be filled with Loving Kindness

Now bring to mind someone you are upset or angry with—or that you feel has wounded you or given you critical messages. Gently begin to turn this love and joy in their direction and repeat silently

May this person find safe haven

May this person have peaceful mind

May this person have harmony with their body

May this person be filled with Loving Kindness

And sending this loving kindness to everyone here....

May all of us find safe haven

May all of us have peaceful mind

May all of us have harmony with their body

May Loving Kindness manifest throughout all of our lives

And lastly, sending this prayer or intention out to all of life, people, animals, plants, earth, sky, to all things

May all of life find safe haven

May all of life have peaceful mind

May all of life have harmony with their physical body

May all of life be filled with Loving Kindness.

And now breathe, gently and deeply filling your belly, your chest---and exhale.......

Breathe again........ Opening your eyes when you are ready...

Talking Stick

Leader: As we pass this bowl of gratitude, You may take some of the rose petals at your place and add them to this bowl. As you do, you may talk about what you are grateful for, or how or when gratitude has been in your life. What is said here stays here in circle. It is all right to pass. Who would like to start?

Pass bowl. When everyone has shared, the leader holds the bowl and says

Leader: The bowl is now filled with the gifts and joys of our gratitude. As our bowl is passed for a second time, please bless the person next to you by sprinkling them with the waters we are imbued with our thanks. This is done so that they might always remember to take time to be grateful for the abundance in their lives. Bless and say, "I bless you with the waters of gratitude. May you know joy and abundance."

When all have spoken, say:

As you leave, we invite you to express gratitude to Spirit with an offering of the rose petals from this bowl, placing them anywhere outside with a prayer sent out on a gentle breath. We will pass the bowl one more time so that you may take some petals for your blessing.

Pass the bowl again.

Thanking and Releasing the Directions

Snuff each candle as you read the direction

SOUTH

Leader: Raise your glasses.
Hear our prayers of thanks, Goddesses of the South, great grandmother Sachamama, for we are grateful for your presence in our lives and the bounty of your gifts of warmth and passion.
We thank you and release you.
Let us all drink.
Salud!

WEST

Leader: Hear our prayers of gratitude, Goddesses of the West, Mother-sister Jaguar, we are most grateful for your presence in our lives and the bounty of your gifts of nourishing waters.
We thank you and release you.
Let us all drink.
Salud!

NORTH

Leader: Receive our offerings of gratitude, Goddesses of the North, Grandmother Hummingbird and Grandfather Dragon, for we are grateful for the bounty of your gifts of food and fuel and your presence in our lives.

We thank you and release you.
Let us all drink.
Salud!

EAST

Leader: Receive our offerings of gratitude, Goddesses of the East, Brother Condor and Brother Eagle, for we are truly grateful for the bounty of your gifts gentle change and clarity and your presence in our lives.
We thank you and release you.
Let us all drink.
Salud!

CENTER

Leader: Receive our offerings of gratitude, Pachamama, Earth Mother who is the Great Goddess, for you have held us in your embrace through good times and bad times.
We thank you and release you.
Let us all drink.
Salud!

Blessed be!

Women's Wisdom

Theme

This ritual honors feminine wisdom and the passing down of guidance by the wise grandmother to the spring maiden. It is often that this sharing is done in the kitchen at the kitchen table. It seemed appropriate to honor this place of feminine wisdom by making it the altar for this ritual. This can be a powerful feminine altar in our daily lives.

Note

When Sandy and I held this ritual, one of our participants was so moved that she went home, made an altar on her kitchen table, and relayed the story of the ritual to her two daughters.

Sources of Inspiration

This ritual developed after we had been introduced to Naomi Rachael Remen's book, Kitchen Table Wisdom. The title was a source of musing and inspiration about how much of our wisdom as women is passed down at the kitchen table.

Altar

- *Red checked tablecloth*
- *Mugs*
- *Lemonade, or some beverage*
- *Oatmeal cookies*
- *Tall candle for the center*
- *Flowers*
- *Wooden spoon*
- *Snuffer*
- *Matches*
- *Lighting candle*
- *Four tea lights for direction candles*

Many small objects arranged around direction candles for participants to choose

- *East –feathers*
- *South –sand in small decorated boxes*
- *West –shells*
- *North –rocks*

Additional items for Sacred Space

- *Blankets*
- *Pillows*
- *Materials for journaling or drawing*

Set Up

Set up the altar as a kitchen table with cookies, beverage, mugs and the four direction candles with their objects set up around the edge. Have some throws draped on some of the chairs and add homey touches, as you like.

Calling the Directions

Light each candle as you read the direction

EAST

Leader: Please stand and face the east.

I call upon the East, the warm winds of springtime that encourage us to plan new beginnings and unfold in harmony with all of life.

SOUTH

Leader: Please face the south.

I call upon the South, the hot sun of summer that helps us to relax and slow down to walk lightly and joyfully upon the earth.

WEST

Leader: Please face the west.

I call upon the West, the nourishing rains of fall that help us appreciate the bounty of Mother Earth and the wisdom of her teachings.

NORTH

Leader: Please face the north.

I call upon the North, the solid rocks of earth that teach us the slow ways of inner strength and the knowledge of the ancients.

CENTER

Leader: Please face the center.

I call upon the center, the Great Mother Goddess.

Be with us here tonight, smile upon us and share with us your love and wisdom, connecting us with the Wise Woman archetype that resides within us all.

I call upon the Oneness that is in all things.

Embrace us and hold us in your love and compassion as we journey through our evening.

Please be seated.

Ritual

Leader: This evening we gather to honor the Wise Grandmother, the keeper and teacher of feminine wisdom. We gather to honor the manner of sharing feminine wisdom at the kitchen table. And we gather to honor the maiden who re-emerges within us each spring. The Wise Grandmother is the support, the ground and the anchor for the maiden as she starts out on her journey of growth and unfolding. The Wise Grandmother offers support and guidance that is feminine in nature, rich, vibrant and deep in the knowing of the mysteries of the earth and her creatures. All of us have a wise grandmother within who nourishes our re-emerging each spring and launches us on our journey through a year of unfolding.

This evening the Wise Grandmother meets us at her kitchen table, the place of so much sharing and growing for women. This is the place where we are nurtured and nurture others, where we tell our stories and our insights to each other. It is the domain of feminine wisdom, the altar to the ways in which it is passed from generation to generation.

And, as in childhood, when we sat around the kitchen table and ate and drank and felt loved, so now I will read you the story of a small girl who lived with her wise grandmother. There are blankets and pillows for you to gather and make yourself comfortable with. Feel free to lie on the floor, put your feet up, cover up, or whatever moves you to a place of comfortable quiet listening. Let your child find her place.

Give people time to spread out, cover up or do whatever they need to become comfortable. When we did the ritual there was some laughter and lightness as people were given permission to become young and listen to a story. They all enjoyed it.

Leader: The Story of the Spring Maiden

Adapted from a story by Ginny Guenette

Once upon a time, there lived a young girl who was known as the Spring Maiden. She lived with her grandmother who was a wise woman, a crone. She lived in a town where she noticed that the people were of all kinds, short and tall, light and dark, fast and slow. She noticed that they all seemed to be busy with very important things and they rushed and frowned and had no time to laugh

The Spring Maiden asked, why does everyone rush so? Her wise grandmother brought out some cookies and lemonade and they sat at the kitchen table to talk. Spring Maiden cherished these moments with her grandmother, the ritual of the food, the kitchen table and the sharing of stories and wisdom. Her grandmother explained that the people had lost their connection to Spirit. The Spring Maiden wanted to help her people. Wise Grandmother told her in order to gain earth wisdom she would need to go on a long journey alone to learn the gifts of Mother Earth, the air, sun, water and earth. She knew she must go.

In the morning, she kissed her grandmother goodbye. Walking alone for the first time in her life, she felt overwhelmed. She sang as she walked towards the east, "Wind blow the clouds away. Wind, help me see clearly."

After several days she came to a deep green forest. She found a clearing where the winds blew gently and there she made her new home. She watched the birds soar and in her mind she flew with them. She found a feather on the ground and kept it as a symbol of the clarity of vision that was growing within her.

All during the springtime, the wind sang her to sleep in the evening and walked with her in the daytime. But she woke one morning, and the wind whispered gently, and she knew that it was time to journey onwards towards the south.

On and on she walked until she found herself in the desert. When an oasis appeared before her she made her camp and rested. She learned the different language of this new land and she learned to see that this land that, at first, seemed to be so barren, was filled with the bounty of the desert. She learned how to partake of the fruits offered her in the heat of sun and the shade of the palms. She listened to the murmur of the sands and the creatures of the desert as they came and went. And she danced under the sun as it journeyed daily across the sky.

Soon the sands whispered to her, she knew it was time to move on. She gathered a small decorated box filled with the sands of the desert. These were her reminders to listen, to see the everchanging beauty and bounty where ever she might be, and to walk lightly and joyfully upon the earth. Then she walked West.

When she found herself besides the sea, she made her camp. The sound of the waves lulled her to sleep and in the morning the waves washed over her as she swam in the healing waters. Now she learned to live in harmony with the creatures of the sea and shore. The waves taught her that she was part of the ebb and flow of life. She collected a shell to symbolize the wisdom to flow with the cycles and rhythms within her and around her.

As the autumn nights became colder she knew her time by the waters was over. She walked on going north to the mountains. Finally, she found a mountain cave to shelter in. The living rock spoke to her, sharing its ancient wisdom, and the depth of her understanding increased. She felt grounded and in touch with Mother Earth. She found a stone to remind her of the ways of inner strength and the teachings of the elders.

In the dark of the cave, in the dark of the night, the mountain spoke to her. "Listen to all that you have learned. Remember the lessons of the wind, the water, the sun and the mountains. Remember your strength comes from Mother Earth."

And so the Spring Maiden walked. She walked down the mountain, by the waters, through the desert, and felt at one with the winds of the earth. She thought about all that she had learned and experienced. And when she was home she ran into her grandmother's house. They embraced and danced and sang their delight at being together again.

Grandmother brought glasses of lemonade and cookies to the kitchen table. Spring Maiden told her Wise Grandmother how she had learned to appreciate the unending wheel of cycles and the ebb and flow of life, the beauty that always surrounded her, the clarity of vision that the east taught her and the wisdom of the elders that was deep within the earth and stones. She laid her treasures out on her Grandmother's kitchen table: flowers, feathers, shells and stones. She arranged them carefully so that they might share their wisdom and beauty with all who came to visit.

Her grandmother saw that the Spring Maiden was full of love and a deep connection with the Spirit in all things. They would celebrate this with all the people, the tall and the short, the young and the old, the fast and the slow.

Pause here for a few moments for them to rest in the story and allow a transition time into the next phase of the ritual

Meditation

Leader: Now we are going on a journey to the Wise Grandmother. Before the meditation you may pick up an object from the altar that symbolizes a question, situation or issue that you would like to take to the Wise Grandmother during our meditation. In the East there are feathers, which represent clarity of vision, a lightness of being and envisioning. In the south small boxes of sand, which represent seeing and listening to ones urgings for growth, and beauty. In the west are shells that represent the healing waters, and ability to flow with the ebb and flow of change. In the north are stones that represent stability, power, and ancient wisdoms.

You may take a few minutes to consider what you would like to take to Her. If nothing comes up easily, choose what you are drawn to and notice that. Let Her comfort and care for you. It does not have to be a big, earth shattering question or situation. Anything you take will be heard and tended to. Also, if you like, you may return to your blanket or wherever you made yourself comfortable for the story.

When the meditation is done, you may take a few minutes to journal, draw or reflect on your time spent with the Wise Grandmother at her kitchen table.

Give them time to reflect for a few minutes, choose their object to hold and generally make themselves comfortable for meditation. The floor is fine.

The script for the meditation is at the end of the ritual.

Remember to leave time at the end of the meditation for people to journal or just sit quietly. This provides a gentle and thoughtful transition into the next part of the ritual. It is also important for their integration of the meditation into current time.

Talking Stick

Leader: As you finish with your journaling, gather around our kitchen table altar and make yourself comfortable as we serve lemonade and cookies. Tonight we have a wooden spoon for our talking stick. You may share about your objects from the table or what came up in the mediation or anything you would like.

Expression of Gratitude

Leader: Please take the object that you are holding home to your own kitchen table as an expression of your gratitude for the power of the feminine wisdom offered at your own kitchen table.

Thanking and Releasing the Directions

Snuff each candle as you read the direction

EAST

Leader: Please stand and face the east.

East, the warm winds of springtime, we thank you for being with us on our journey and bless you

SOUTH

Leader: Please face the south.

South, the soothing sun of summer, we thank you for being with us on our journey and bless you

WEST

Leader: Please face the west.

West, the nourishing rains of fall, we thank you for being with us on our journey and bless you

NORTH

Leader: Please face the north.

North, the solid rocks of earth, we thank you for being with us on our journey and bless you

CENTER

Leader: Please face the center.

Great Mother Goddess, we thank you for being with us on our journey and bless you

Meditation

Women's Wisdom

So now, moving and adjusting as you need to, find a position of comfort as we get ready for meditation. Gradually inviting your awareness to come to your breath........ breathing in and noticing ....where you feel your breath....perhaps at the nostrils..... or your chest...or belly............and then letting the breath go......again noticing any sensations as you exhale gently and slowly. And again,......breathing in.........breathing out and just noticing.........as we gradually move inward we begin to open to a space without judgment......a place within that is the home of our open-heart......a place of deep listening to ourselves....filled with respect and curiosity for our own process.

Your breath is like a portal, or doorway into these realms...and so you quiet and balance and move easily to inviting an image to come forward of the wise grandmother's kitchen.

The feminine wisdom as wise grandmother is a deep knowing........she is warm and nurturing,......gentle in her invincibility and power. Take a moment and gaze around Her kitchen....letting the images unfold before you....comforting you as they unfold.... wrapping you in a sense of peace and love...

And being held in the grandmother's kitchen engages all of your senses ....and so it is, that you may also hear sounds.....perhaps the sounds of your wise grandmother busy in the kitchen....perhaps she is chatting....or there are the sounds of water running in the sink.....spoons and bowls meeting as the batter for cookies is stirred....And there may be smells....delicious smells in your wise grandmother's kitchen....bread...soups....oatmeal cookies...nourishing and comforting smells that sooth the muscles in your body and complete the sense of being part of a warm, loving and embracing place............the window is open and the curtains flutter in the breeze as it floats in to cool and caress you. As you begin to settle into your wise grandmother's kitchen table....she serves you cookies and lemonade....and pulls up her seat to be next to you as you talk......

She may even touch your hand in a gesture of readiness to listen....and she listens completely and attentively....

And you feel free to share with her whatever you have brought with you....

For she knows as well as you that you have a story to share....perhaps one of joy and gratitude that you want to tell her......or perhaps a question or issue that is troubling you and you have come to gain insights about.....

And so you are free to commune....in your own way and time.....

Pause

She listens carefully......nodding sometimes......and she shares with you.....your joy and gratitude....your confusion or sorrow.....

She may offer you insights.....with symbols....tasks....or ideas......given in a way that will unfold for you tonight or over time.....Regardless of how it is given or when.....her sharing will assist you in your unfolding through the coming seasons.....

Longer pause

And now, she signals that it is time to start your journey back to current time and place....to resume your journey in everyday reality....and so you thank her for listening and helping you....

And you can gradually bring your attention to your breath....noticing your breath moving in as you inhale........and moving out as you exhale.........the breath is your portal for returning also. As you notice your breath....you may also check in with your body.... how you are sitting in your chair.........and perhaps there is a part of your body that would like to stretch or move......you are free to do so...and savor the experience.......

And again...this time taking a deep breath in.......and then out.....becoming aware of the feel of the air around you.....the sounds in the room........and opening your eyes as you are ready........gazing for a moment around the room.......

And one last breath to bring you fully back to our circle, to this evening...

SR 2006

Healing Rituals

Most of the rituals in our book have a healing quality within them. The ones listed in this area we put together specifically for the healing of various aspects of the natural world and of ourselves. We are all one, so healing on any level will create healing for all of us.

For example, the Peace Mandala is a prayer for peace created within the Mandala. It is a prayer for world peace and for our own inner peace. We will not have one without the other. Our own inner peace radiates out to others and is reflected back to us from those we touch and those they touch. Our lives are inextricably interconnected with all other lives; there can also be no world peace on earth without a growing inner peace within all of Her inhabitants.

There is another ritual that asks for personal healing, and then healing of a friend or loved one. This is similar to a prayer circle in our way of seeing it, only it is much more experiential and it is openly shared with all the participants. We have found this ritual very moving for everyone.

We are all in need of healing at one time or another. We heal in relationship with each other and with the Sacred. The power of healing rituals is tangible and wondrous to participate in.

A Practice in the Loving Kindness Meditation

Theme

We all need help in approaching all of life, including ourselves, with a compassionate and non-judgmental perspective. The Buddhist Loving Kindness Meditation is a gentle and powerful way in which we can guide ourselves to do this.

Sources of Inspiration

The loving kindness meditation has many different versions used world wide in basic Buddhist practices.

Altar

- *Green cloth*
- *Direction candles*
- *Bowl of rose quartz pieces*
- *Snuffer*
- *Matches*
- *Lighting candle*

Additional items for Sacred Space

Additional items may be used to enhance the feeling of a quiet, reverential space in which to do the ritual. Many candles around the room work well. Quiet background music may be used.

Set Up

We set up the altar simply and in a straightforward manner. You may use a Buddha or other Eastern Diety statue in keeping with the eastern-Buddhist meditation.

Calling the Directions

Light each direction candle as it is read.

Leader: Please stand and face the direction we are calling.

EAST

Leader: We call upon the Spirits of the East and bless them and ask that they blow away the fog of self-doubt that we may see clearly.

SOUTH

Leader: We call upon the Spirits of the South and bless them and ask that they help us create a lightness of being that is truly healing.

WEST

Leader: We call upon the Spirits of the West and bless them and ask that they encourage a shift in our way of being that invites us into flow, to come to both ourselves and the world with compassion and forgiveness.

NORTH

Leader: We call upon the Spirits of the North and bless them and ask that they ground us in the concrete, material world while living with awareness of the spiritual realms.

CENTER

Leader: We call upon the Spirits of the Center and bless them and ask that they help us to experience the self as essence and to live in balance, integration, and love.

Ritual

Leader: Our ritual this evening will center on the Loving Kindness Meditation. The meditation is from the Buddhist tradition, and has been beautifully written about in a book by Sharon Salzberg called Loving Kindness. The phrases we are using today are adapted from her book.

In our times of difficulty, it can seem that loving kindness, these acts of caring and thoughtfulness, are especially needed and cherished. The Loving Kindness meditation invites us to connect with, to nourish and cultivate our own reservoirs of Loving Kindness, and to bring this into expression in our daily lives.

There are four phrases that are repeated silently during the meditation. I will guide you through the phrases, so you will not have to remember them.

May I find safe haven. This refers to freedom from the torments of the external world, such as violence, greed, hunger.

May I have peaceful mind. This refers to freedom from the mental/emotional issues that plague most of us in our daily lives.

May I have harmony with my body. This is a prayer for physical well-being and peace with our physical state, whatever that may be.

May I be filled with Loving Kindness. This is an intention for balance and harmony in our day-to-day life.

We will first offer the loving kindness to ourselves, then out to other people.

Meditation

Pacing is important, and participants will respond more deeply if not rushed. It gives them time to be present with the phrase and images.

Leader: And so making yourself ready for meditation........ finding a comfortable position,................. either closing your eyes or leaving them open as is comfortable for you.

And notice your breath, the inhaling and the exhaling......

If you would like and are able, you may place your hand over your heart......

Let a smile come to your lips as you remember a happy, joyful experience...... a birth... a beautiful day... an especially meaningful moment with a loved one.... any experience where you felt a great deal of joy and love........ Now give this love to yourself..... Imagine that this love is flowing out to you from your heart, filling your entire body....... gently and slowly...... and breathe....... Be with the following intentions/prayers for yourself...... I invite you to repeat each phrase silently to yourself as we move through the meditation.

Leader: May I find safe haven.

May I have peaceful mind

May I have harmony with my body.

May I be filled with loving kindness.

Now think of someone in your life, past or present... who has supported you in times of need or that you love and appreciate....... Allow an image of this person to form in your mind's eye...... Send them this prayer of loving kindesss from your heart. In your mind substitute the name of the person for the phrase 'this person' as you hear it.

Pause.

May this person find safe haven

May this person have peaceful mind.

May this person have harmony with their body.

May this person be filled with loving kindness.

Now think of someone that you are upset or angry with.....someone that you feel has wounded you or given you critical messages that are still running your life. ... If comfortable... allow an image of this person to arise in your mind's eye. Using just their name is also effective. Gently begin to turn this love and joy in their direction and repeat the four phrases to yourself.

Pause.

May this person find safe haven

May this person have peaceful mind

May this person have harmony with their body

May this person be filled with loving kindness.

And now... send this loving energy out to everyone in our circle... imagining that the energy can flow easily from person to person as your hear the phrases.

Pause.

May everyone here find safe haven.

May everyone here have peaceful mind.

May everyone here have harmony with their body.

May everyone here be filled with loving kindness.

And lastly, send this loving kindness out to all living beings

Pause

May all beings find safe haven

May all beings have peaceful mind and heart

May all beings have harmony with their body

May all beings be filled with loving kindness.

Pause for a moment and allow the participants to notice and absorb the gentle power of this meditation. You may easily notice the shift in the ambiance or energy present in the circle.

Gifting

Leader: Rose quartz is one of the minerals associated with the heart chakra for its purity and its symbolism of unconditional love. As you receive this bowl, hold it to your heart and send into the quartz the love that you have for yourself and for all living things.

Pass bowl. When it goes around the full circle hold it up and say:

Leader: This bowl is filled with the love within our hearts and with the love from Spirit. We will pass it around again and I invite you to share in the power of love by taking a crystal. Keep it with you as you depart as a symbol of what we have shared today and the abundance of love around you always.

Pass the bowl again. Return it to the altar.

Talking Stick

Leader: We will now pass the talking stick. Please share as you are moved. You may want to share something that came up during the ritual or whatever else is in your heart or on your mind. What is said here stays here in circle. It is all right to pass. Who would like to start?

Thanking and Releasing the Directions

Snuff each direction as it is being read.

Leader: Please stand and face the direction we are releasing.

EAST

Leader: We thank the Spirits of the East for the clarity that you brought us.

SOUTH

Leader: We thank the Spirits of the South for the passion that brings lightness of being.

WEST

Leader: We thank the Spirits of the West for washing us with the waters of forgiveness.

NORTH

Leader: We thank the Spirits of the North for grounding us in the material world that we may be strong.

CENTER

Leader: We thank the Spirits of the Center for helping us to live in balance, integration, and love.

Blessed Be!

The circle is open but unbroken

The song, May the Circle be Open is a good ending to this ritual. See index.

Full Moon Fire Ritual

Note

This can be a very powerful ritual of releasing. We have done this ceremony many times and each time is slightly different, slightly adapted to the situation. But it is consistent at its core in the intention to release the energetic of that which keeps us stuck and call in help or sustenance for one's journey. We found that it is most effective if done outside in nature, near the time of the full moon.

Preparation of the leader(s) and the space is important. Prepare and clear the space for the fire before the ritual, in whatever manner you are accustomed to. We often smudge and/or use specific drumming or rattling patterns to call in Spirit and supportive energies.

First there is an energetic clearing of a person's field of old patterns that may be keeping them stuck in unhealthy ways of being. In addition there is a setting of intention to release attachment to a situation or belief. On the inner planes this releasing of attachment can enable a person to turn their intentions and their actions in the world toward a more balanced and healthy way of being. The calling in of supportive energies helps to fuel and sustain the journey forward.

Theme

The core theme of the ritual is a releasing to Mother Earth of the energetic patterns that no longer serve a person's growth and healing. This is followed by a calling in of qualities or energies that will assist the person in their growth and effort to live a balanced and harmonious life.

Sources of Inspiration

This full moon ritual is an adaptation of the Andean/Quechua fire ceremony.

Altars

Contemplation altar

- *Altar cloth*
- *Longish pieces of string*
- *Pieces of paper, small*

- *Pens or pencils*
- *Herbs for the fire*

    Mugwort

    Sweetgrass

- *Herbs for bundles- the herbs can be used to call in any positive quality or energetic that the participant is asking for. They are first and foremost a gift to Spirit.*

    Lavender

    Sage

    Cedar

    Tobacco

    And whatever herbs you desire that will draw positive energies to you

- *Paper for rolling herbs in*
- *Rattles*

Fire altar

- *A fire pit or grill may be used*
- *Sticks of wood*
- *Matches*
- *Oil*
- *Paper to help start the fire, optional*
- *Sacred items, such as medicine bundles, or statues to place around the fire*
- *Cover for the grill or fire pit*

Set Up

We found that setting up with the concept of two altars was helpful. The first one is for contemplation and quiet reflection. This is often indoors. It may be in a circular arrangement or it may just be an altar with the rattles, string, paper and pens, herbs and paper for making herb bundles set up on it. Participants may find chairs or sit wherever they like in the room to do their personal work with their death arrow.

The second altar is outside. It is best if the fire is ready to go, and the leader can build the fire in a quiet and reflective space before the ritual starts. Clearing both spaces in whatever manner you are used to, such as smudging, rattling or other methods helps to remove heavy energies and create balance and harmony in the area.

Smudge

Smudging outside the room allows each person a brief clearing and centering before walking into ritual space.

Set up the smudge outside the room. You may appoint a 'smudger', but do not forget to smudge yourself as leaders first. You may use whatever feels appropriate to you. Some suggestions are: sage, paulo santo, or mugwort.

Calling the Directions

We did not light candles for this ritual.

SOUTH

Leader: We call the Spirits of the South, Great Grandmother Serpent.
Help us shed what we no longer need that we might move forward on our earthwalk unencumbered, so that we might grow and continue to blossom into our new skins.
Fill us with your healing wisdoms and perseverance to know when and what to shed.

WEST

Leader: We call the Spirits of the West, Mother-Sister Jaguar.
Let us release our old patterns so that we might approach all of our relations with an open heart and mind, seeing their gifts and strengths that we might learn and grow from them. Fill us with your patience, your keen observing and ability to act when the time is right so that we may stalk our medicine.

NORTH

Leader: We call the Spirits of the North, our Brothers Condor and Eagle, help us to release our old patterns that we may drink in the wisdom of the ages, and come to see the sweetness and beauty that sustains us on our earthwalk.
Fill us with optimism and share your wisdom that we may know where to find nourishment for soul and body.

EAST

Leader: We call upon the Spirits of the East, Grandmother Hummingbird and Grandfather Dragon, Ancient Ones.

Fly down from your sky journey and wrap us in the soft down of your wings.
As we release and become lighter, teach us to soar so that we too, might have your vision and ability to see beyond ourselves.
Fill us with your gifts of vision and envisioning our lives and our world.

CENTER

Leader: We call the Spirits of the Center, Pachamama, Mother Earth, hold us gently as we work, bring us your stability and groundedness.
Fill us with the abundance of your fruits, that we may be nourished body, mind and spirit on our earthwalk.
And we call to our Star Brothers and Sisters, to the Sun and Moon.
Shine down upon us as we work, filling us with the light of Spirit and the knowing of our true natures.

Ritual

Preparing the death arrows

Leader: Tonight's ritual is a full moon ritual, adapted from the Andean tradition of the mountains in Peru. Fire is a cleansing. The full moon in many cultures is a time of heightened energy for doing such ceremony. Tonight you will each prepare your own death arrow, which represents those energetic patterns, beliefs or events that are keeping you stuck, that are keeping you from moving forward and connecting with your true inner nature. We all have these patterns or situations in life that seem to take over and side track our best efforts. We will offer our death arrows to the sacred fire, to be transmuted. The ashes will be offered to Mother Earth, who will further transform the energies.

So this is a powerful ceremony of releasing on an energetic level, and also on a mental/emotional level, as we declare our intention to let go of our attachment to these patterns and beliefs that keep us stuck. Serpent is able to shed her skin when it gets too tight and restricting, preventing her growth. We can do the same here tonight.

Once we have shed our attachments and energies, we will call to Spirit, to Mother Earth, for assistance. With a bundle of sacred herbs to offer Spirit, we ask for help, for whatever qualities or energies that might support us on our journey.

So, first, everyone can go outside and find a stick, not too big, to use as your death arrow. When you find one, come back here and take a piece of string and as you reflect on your state or situation, tie knots in the string around your death arrow. The knots in the string represent the energy that is 'tied in knots' around the specific pattern or situation you are working with. Tie as many as you need as you reflect. If you like, you may also take pieces of paper, write what you are releasing to the fire, and tie these to your death arrow. These will all unravel in the fire as the energy is cleared.

Once your arrow is ready, return to the altar and make your herb bundles as you contemplate what qualities or strengths might assist you on your journey. As you are ready, choose a rattle, bring your death arrow and herb bundle, and come out to the fire.

Because this ritual is reflective and contemplative we will continue in silence.

If the weather is really inhospitable, you can have a selection of sticks on the altar for people to choose. We have gone outside in the snow and cold, and had very meaningful fire ceremonies. We have also brought extra gloves and scarves on occasion.

It is best if the person leading goes out to the fire while the participants are working with their death arrows. While out at the fire, the leader can further clear and prepare the space by smudging or rattling. As participants join the leader at the fire, silence should be maintained, or a chant may be started

Calling the Archetypes, Second Altar

The fire ceremony

When everyone has gathered, the leader can again briefly call the archetypes to be present. This enhances the feeling of sacred space

SOUTH

Leader: Great Grandmother, Sachamama, be here with us as we work to release that which we no longer need.
Guide us well in your ways.

WEST

Leader: Mother Sister Jaguar, be here as we work.
Teach us to stalk our medicine patiently and with dedicated intent.

NORTH

Leader: Brother Condor and Brother Eagle, be here with us this evening.
Share your vision with us that we might see clearly.

EAST

Leader: Grandmother Hummingbird and Grandfather Dragon, be here at our fire.

Teach us to drink up the sustenance of life and walk with courage on our earthwalk.

CENTER

Leader: Pachamama, Mother Earth, be here with us.
Bear witness to our work tonight and hold us gently in your embrace.

Star Brothers and Star Sisters, Sun and Moon, be here with us.
Shine the light of your love and wisdom upon us as we work tonight.

Participants are gathered in a circle around the fire, with their death arrows and herb bundles. Pour some oil over the fire, (canola oil is fine) and light it. As you light it, start the chant. The sweetgrass may be placed on the fire at this time so that the energies may be released to Spirit sweetly.

The melody is in the appendix, along with other suggestions.

Once the fire is going well, participants may place their death arrow into the fire. It is often helpful if the leader goes first to model the behavior.

When all have offered their death arrows to the fire, pause.

Nitche Tie Tie

En U I

Oreneka, Oreneka

Hey Hey, Hey Hey

Oo oo I

Leader: Now is the time to offer our herb bundles to Spirit, one by one. Your request for help, for qualities that might assist you, will be heard as the sweet smoke of your bundle rises to Spirit.

At this point we like to change the chant to one of praise for Spirit. We have used 'Oh Great Spirit' that is in the appendix.

When everyone is done, and the flames have died down, the leader can offer some lavender or sage to the fire.

Leader: I am offering some lavender and sage to the fire so that everyone can smudge with the sweet smoke and intention of our fire.

Releasing the Directions and the Archetypes

SOUTH

Leader: Spirits of the South, Great Grandmother Sachamama, thank you for being here with us tonight and teaching us your wise ways.

WEST

Leader: Spirits of the West, Mother Sister Jaguar, thank you for being here with us tonight and helping us to stalk our medicine.

NORTH

Leader: Spirits of the North, Brother Condor and Brother Eagle, thank you for being here with us tonight and sharing with us the clarity of your vision.

EAST

Leader: Spirits of the East, Grandmother Hummingbird and Grandfather Dragon, thank you for being here with us tonight and helping us in our search for the sweetness of life.

CENTER

Leader: Pachamama, Mother Earth, thank you for being here with us tonight and for holding us safely in your embrace.

Star Brothers and Star Sisters, Sun and Moon, thank you for being here with us tonight and shining your love upon us.

If it feels incomplete to you to end the ritual outside, you may go inside for refreshments.

Candle Magic Ritual

Theme

By using candle magic we can call forth help and support in breathing life into our hopes and goals for each other and for ourselves. We did this ritual in the spring because this is a time when people plant the seeds for new beginnings.

Sources of Inspiration

We were inspired by the celebration of Imbolg, also known as St. Brigid's Day. This is a ritual that traditionally lights many candles and uses divination and ceremony to celebrate the beginning of spring.

Altar

- *Light colored cloth*
- *Many candles*
- *Candles for the directions, with two special candles for the center*
- *One lit candle*
- *Bowl of paper hearts*
- *Envelopes with one blank paper heart in each*
- *Pens*
- *Spring flowers.*

Additional Items

- *Sheets of honeycomb bee's wax*
- *Candle wicks*
- *Scissors*

Set Up

We set the altar in the center of the room with chairs around it. There were lots of flowers on the altar and scattered about the room. A table off to the side of the altar had the sheets of honeycomb wax, wicks, and scissors. You may also scatter flowers on this table.

Smudging

Smudging allows each person a brief clearing and centering before walking into ritual space.

You may appoint a 'smudger', but do not forget to smudge yourself as leaders first. You may use whatever feels appropriate to you. Some suggestions are: sage, paulo santo, or mugwort.

For this ritual we smudged participants as they entered the room. When everyone was seated we smudged the altar and the room in preparation for ritual

Leader: We welcome the Triple Goddess, Maiden, Mother, Crone. We celebrate and we acknowledge her as Maid. For this is the First Stirring of the Light, the dawn of spring. The Goddess is again young. She leaves behind all that is outworn. In Her name, we clean and smudge and we prepare a sacred place.

The leader slowly moves around the altar and the room smudging the circle. Music or chants could be used for this to heighten the sense of the occasion.

Calling the Directions

Light each directional candle as the words are read

EAST

Leader: We call upon the Goddesses of the East to breathe new life into the breeze and prepare the way for the warmth of spring.
Be with us on our journeys into new ways of thinking and seeing.

SOUTH

Leader: We call upon the Goddesses of the South to warm the earth and prepare the seeds in the dark earth to grow and flower.
Warm us too so that our seeds of new beginnings may grow and flower.

WEST

Leader: We call upon the Goddesses of the West to melt the ice and snow and prepare the waters of the earth for the rushing joys of spring.

Melt the frozen and immoveable within us, so that we may flow with the joys of new growth and creation.

NORTH

Leader: We call upon the Goddesses of the North to awaken the frozen earth and prepare the ground for abundance and growth.

Awaken us from the long sleep of winter and guide us in preparing for the coming of our blossoming.

CENTER

Leader: In the Center, we first call upon the Triple Goddess of the Circle of Rebirth, She who brings all life into being.

She is the one who shines in the night sky with beauty and enriches all the Earth with mystery.

She is the one who is the wisdom of the stars, the pulse of blood and the slow growth of the trees.

May Her presence guide us and may her blessing be upon us, for we are of Her creation.

Ritual

Leader: This is a ritual of silence, meditation and creation. After the meditation we will be creating our candles that will be filled with the candle magic of our intentions and love. We will pass the bowl now so that you may take a paper heart, envelope and a pen.

Pass the bowl.

Meditation

Now we will have a meditation, after which we will work with the hearts and candles. Please maintain silence until we finish with the candles.

The script for the meditation is at the end of the ritual.

Remember to leave time at the end of the meditation for people to sit quietly for a moment. This provides a gentle and thoughtful transition into the next part of the ritual. It is also important for their integration of the meditation into current time.

Leader: We invite you to take a moment and think of what you would like to grow in the life of your sisters and brothers in this circle. Then write a word or two on the heart and put it in the envelope. You will notice a blank heart is already placed in the envelope, but leave it there for now. We will explain why after we again pass the bowl to collect your envelopes. You may keep the pen for now.

Pause and allow everyone time to reflect and write.

Leader: Now we will pass the bowl again and you may take an envelope and see what message is there for you. On the blank heart write what you wish to grow for yourself.

Pause and allow people time to reflect and write.

Leader: On the table there are sheets of beeswax and wicks. You may make a candle by placing the wick on the end of the sheet. Then scatter your two hearts on the beeswax, so that as you roll the sheet of beeswax up, the wick and hearts are inside the candle. We will do this as part of our meditation, in silence, and when you are done, you may return to your seat at the altar.

We invite you to use your candle magic when you get home. In our experience, it is best when you invite the Goddess, or whatever names you use for Spirit, to be present, thus establishing a sacred space. Then light your candle and hold your hopes in your awareness. As your candle burns, your intentions are released to the Goddess.

Talking Stick

Leader: In this sacred space you may share what is in your heart and mind and we will hold it within the circle to support you and your dreams. The Talking Stick is always used in a spirit of trust and confidentiality.

Thanking and Releasing the Directions

Snuff each candle as the direction is read.

EAST

Leader: Goddesses of the East we thank you and release you.

SOUTH

Leader: Goddesses of the South we thank you and release you.

WEST:

Leader: Goddesses of the West we thank you and release you.

NORTH

Leader: Goddesses of the North we thank you and release you.

CENTER

Leader: Brigid, the Triple Goddess, here as the Maiden, we thank you and release you.

Leader: Let us sing May the Circle be Open, three times.

The chant is in the appendix. We used to hold hands to form the circle and sing the chant.

Merry meet and merry part and merry meet again

Blessed be

Meditation:

Held in the Growing Light

I invite you to find a comfortable position to get ready for meditation.......if you would like, you may rest on the floor or sit in your chair.......just taking a moment to discover where your place of comfort is.........you may shift and adjust as you need......

And then gently bring your attention to your breath.........breathing in deeply..... expanding your belly....your chest.......and then exhaling deeply and slowly....... and again, breathing in..............and exhaling slowly as you let this be a letting go of the day's business........................and now allowing the breath to flow as it will......and just noticing...........you are still breathing in.....and breathing out............and a sense of safety and sureness gradually takes hold...................gradually sensing this sense of safety permeate your muscles, bones, and inner being........

And so in your mind's eye, a place that is safe, protected and sheltered begins to form........a sense of place............. perhaps outside.. .....known or unknown to you...........a very special place where you can feel close to the natural world....close to all that is sacred..................a place that holds the Great Mysteries ....and is a place where you can be at one with the sacred feminine.....the Goddess..........protected by Her......held by Her......

And gently She begins to offer you Her soothing light........first at your crown...... down your face...... and down the back of your head this light begins to spread and soften.........gently flowing down your neck........your shoulders........bathing your shoulders with a soft massage of light and warmth.................and down your arms........... your upper arms.........bathing your elbows......lower arms........your wrists.....down to your hands.........and out to the tip of each finger and your thumbs...........

And again, She baths your back with this soothing..........your upper back may soften slightly........spreading gently down your mid-back.......your waist.......down to the very tip of your spine.......as she gently guides your awareness and Her Light to soothe and comfort......

and gently spreading around to fill your chest......bathing your heart and lungs.....ribs ...... and flowing down to your belly.........filling your belly with light and soothing.......... softening and nourishing...............and flowing down to your pelvis....and now your hips...both hips.....the joints here.......and down each leg.........your thighs....the front and back of your thighs.........your knees........your calves and shins..........down through your ankles to your feet........the top of each foot..........the soul of each foot..........and down to the tip of each and every toe......

And so, safe and protected in your sacred place........... you can pause, ...just rest a moment.... safely held and bathed in this light,................to just be with yourself and your exquisite, inevitable unfolding.....................each step a little different.............a little more opening...........at one with this ageless process of renewal..........growth......... release........ and then renewal...........

Just being with your own evolution..........witnessing.......... observing with great curiosity and compassion your unfolding..............again into fresh, new, growth.........................

Pause

And embracing this experience..........savoring this gift of resting....of accepting and opening.........this gift of a pause in the fray...........and thank yourself for taking this moment...........and offering thanks to the light and to Her for offering this moment to you........

Pause

And, when you are ready come back to this sanctuary and to our group sitting together here .... joined in a community of the feminine.........allowing yourself to return gently........your breath bringing your awareness to how you are sitting.......any desire to move or stretch........and then gently opening your eyes.........

SR 2002

Healing Stones

Theme

This is a healing ceremony that calls upon the Stone People to assist us in an energetic mind/body/spirit healing.

Sources of Inspiration

This ritual is adapted in part from the shamanic/spiritual practices of the Quero People of the mountains of Peru. The Loving Kindness Meditation is a core Buddhist practice.

Altar

- *Smudge set up*
- *Stones of all sorts scattered on altar*
- *Healing stones in basket*
- *Candles for the four directions and the center*
- *Snuffer*
- *Matches*

Set Up

Healing stones for the altar may be gathered at any site that you feel is especially beautiful or healing. When we gathered them, we called the directions to open sacred space at the site. We then made offerings and called for stone people to come forward to be healing stones for our sisters and brothers. There will be a response and your eye may fall to a particular stone that is volunteering its service. Gather it up. When all the stones are gathered an offering of thanks must be left for the Spirits of the stone people. The offering may be herbs or any other object of beauty.

Calling the Directions

Light each candle as you read the direction

EAST

Leader: Spirits of the East, of Air, cool us with gentle breezes that our grief may dissipate in the air.

SOUTH

Leader: Spirits of the South, of Fire, warm us that the anger that chills our bones may be burned away.

WEST

Leader: Spirits of the West, of Water, wash over us that we do not cling to past hurts.

NORTH

Leader: Spirits of the North, of the Mountains, support us that we may be grounded and solid in all that we do.

CENTER

Leader: Spirits of the Center, Earth and Stars, keep our feet on the path of healthy living.

Smudge

In a ceremonial way smudge the altar. Then go around the circle smudging each person with the leaders saying for each person:

Leader: I smudge you to cleanse you of that which keeps harmony and wholeness from being in your life.

Ritual

Leader: Please be seated. We have healing stones on the altar and in this basket. In the tradition of the Quero of the high mountains in Peru, it is understood that all things have energy or spirit and are an expression of the sacred. In this tradition, stones, and the spirit of the stone, can be used in healing, as they thrive on heavy, dense un-harmonious energy.

These healing stones have volunteered to be gathered and to be here. I will share how they got here. One day this fall, after careful deliberation and meditation, we traveled to a very sweet and powerful rocky beach. On behalf of all of us, we made offerings to the spirit of the land, the stones and the Oneness that is all things, called the directions and opened up sacred ceremonial space. We declared our intention for being there and made a request, asking for healing stones to come forward for our sisters, who are in need of their service in these times of change and disruption. And so calling to the Spirits of the Stone People, we walked from spot to spot between the larger rocks and boulders on the beach, calling each time, "Who will come forward to be healing stones for our sisters?" And each time stones would begin to light up, almost chatter and jump up to volunteer. And again at the next spot between the boulders, "Who will come forward to be healing stones for our sisters?' And again, several would glisten with the ocean waters and offer themselves to be of service. It was as if the stones of the earth, washed in the healing waters of our Mother, the ocean, had colluded to gift us with these stone spirits.
When we had gathered all the stones you see here, we thanked the spirits of the land, the water, the directions and the Oneness and left. And so we have here this basket of healing stones.

We will pass the basket around the circle. Each of you may share a story, quality or strength that has helped you or supported you through a difficult time, helping you to hang on and persevere, to heal, and to move toward resolution and wholeness. This is our gift to the stones. They will be the keepers of our collective experience and energy.

pause

Leader: We would like everyone to just reflect for a moment. Start by focusing on your breathing, noticing.... Now think back to time in your life when you needed healing.. and reflect on what it was that helped you get through it...... What qualities nourished and enabled you to continue?...... What events or actions of others sustained you?...... This can be anything that helped you to keep going and dealing.

Pause

Leader: I invite you to share your story or quality, holding the basket of Stone People close to your heart, knowing that your gift will be received by all the stones.

Pass the basket.

Leader: I will pass the basket a second time and I invite you to take the Stone Person that you are drawn to.

Pass the basket.

Leader: Here are some suggestions on how you might want to use your healing stone. At home you will want to open sacred space by calling the directions. We are already in sacred space so we don't need to do that now. Hold your stone, which will start to absorb any heavy, disharmonious energy. You may move the stone to touch any part of you that is hurting or move it to a space in your energetic field that feels heavy or disrupted. Take a moment to try this.

Loving Kindness Pratice

Pause at the end of each sentence as the participants use their stones.

Leader: Please be seated. Now let us use the stone to practice a Loving Kindness Meditation.

Holding your stone to your heart, thinking of yourself, repeat these words silently after me
May I find safe haven.
May I have peaceful mind.
May I have harmony with my body.
May I be filled with loving kindness that flows into every aspect of my life.

Thinking of the women in this circle, repeat these words silently
Just as I seek safe haven
May everyone here find safe haven.
Just as I seek peaceful mind
May everyone here have peaceful mind.
Just as I seek harmony with my body
May everyone here have harmony with their body.
Just as I seek to be filled with loving kindness,
May everyone here be filled with loving kindness.

Thinking of the people in the wider world, repeat these words silently
Just as we seek safe haven
May all people find safe haven.
Just as we seek peaceful mind
May all people have peaceful mind.
Just as we seek harmony with our bodies
May all people have harmony with their bodies.
Just as we seek to be filled with loving kindness,
May all people be filled with loving kindness.

Talking Stick

Leader: And now come back to the present time and place and think of your experiences here tonight and share with us whatsoever you will. Who would like to start?

Pass the stick

Thanking and Releasing the Directions

Snuff each candle as you read the direction

EAST

Leader: Spirits of the East, we thank you for your cool and gentle breezes that help to heal us.

SOUTH

Leader: Spirits of the South, we thank you for your warmth that helps to heal us.

WEST

Leader: Spirits of the West, we thank you for your waters that help to heal us.

NORTH

Leader: Spirits of the North, we thank you for your Stone People that help to heal us.

CENTER

Leader: Spirits of the Center, Above and Below, we thank you for helping to keep our feet on the path of healthy living

Healing with Heart

Theme

This is a ritual that gives participants a chance to call to Spirit for their own healing and the healing of others. This was an especially meaningful ritual for everyone.

Sources of Inspiration

We were inspired by two different practices. One was the Native American practice of the Healing Vortex, which is a way of sending out healing prayers to Spirit. The second practice is the calling of the four chambers of the heart, developed by Brugh Joy, author of Joy's Way. This is a way of opening our hearts and invoking healing qualities into the circle.

Altar

- Light colored cloth
- Red cloth in center swirled to represent 4 chambers of the heart
- Tea light candles for each chamber of the heart
- A label with the name of each chamber
- Tea light candles for directions
- Goddess candleholder in center
- Candles to take home, perhaps with a ribbon tied on them or placed in a basket
- Paper hearts, two to three for each participant
- Pens
- Snuffer
- Matches
- Lighting candle

Additional items for Sacred Space

Additional items may be used as you see fit and should enhance the feeling of a quiet, reverential space. Any heart shaped decorations may be placed on the altar or placed in an appropriate manner around the room. Music of a quiet and healing nature is often helpful, as are candles.

Set Up

We used a red cloth to represent the four chambers of the heart, Compassion, Innate Harmony, Healing Presence and Unconditional Love. The cloth was swirled into a four leaf clover pattern. The whole cloverleaf was elevated on the altar by perhaps two to three inches. We used a pizza pan and rested it on a couple of wooden blocks. A tea light and a label for each chamber of the heart were placed in the middle of each clover leaf.

We placed the directional tea lights around the edge of the altar with the center candle in the middle of the four leaf clover pattern. The paper hearts and pens were arranged around the edge of the altar to be within easy reach of each participant. Dimming the lights and playing soft music in the background enhanced the feeling of quiet reflection.

Smudge

Smudging outside the room allows each person a brief clearing and centering before walking into ritual space.

Set up the smudge outside the room.You may appoint a 'smudger', but do not forget to smudge yourself as leader first. You may use whatever feels appropriate to you. Some suggestions are: sage, paulo santo, or mugwort.

Calling the Directions

Light the candle for each direction as it is being read.

SOUTH

Leader: Welcome to the Spirits and Archetypes of the South, bringing us the healing warmth of the sun.

WEST

Leader: Welcome to the Spirits and Archetypes of the West, bringing us the healing waters of rain and ocean and tears.

NORTH

Leader: Welcome to the Spirits and Archetypes of the North, bringing us the healing strength of rock and stone.

EAST

Leader: Welcome to the Spirits and Archetypes of the East, bringing us the healing coolness of wind and fresh air.

CENTER

Leader: Welcome to the Spirits and Archetypes of the Center, bringing us the song of the stars, the tides of the moon, the help of Mother Earth.

Ritual

Teaching the Healing Vortex

Leader: As a part of our ritual you will be placing yourself and one other person into a gentle yet powerful vortex of healing energy that lies between your hands. This is a Native American practice for sending healing energy.

Please stand and we will go over how to do the vortex.
Raise your hands and place them in front of you so the palms are together in front of your heart. Now bring them gradually apart, so that the back of your hands touch the back of the person's hands next to you. Imagine an X extending from the fingers of both hands to the heels of the opposite hand, crossing in the middle. Where the lines intersect is a vortex of energy called the Field of Plenty. As we intention for ourselves, or for another, to be placed into the vortex, we are reassured that Spirit will provide whatever is needed for this person's wholeness and healing.

The distance between your hands should be close to shoulder width apart. If there are not enough people in the circle to maintain this distance, then do not have people touching the back of the hands next to them.. The group synergy of this ritual is still vibrant even though the participants are not touching each other's hands.

Leader: Now slowly bring the palms of your hands together in prayer position in front of your heart, enfolding whomever you have placed into the vortex into the abundance of Spirit. When we come to this part of the ritual, I will guide you through it. Before we do that we will open the four chambers of the heart.

Opening the Four Chambers of the Heart

Light the candle for each chamber as it is being read.

First Chamber

Leader: Now let us call upon the first chamber of the heart, Keeper of Compassion. We ask that compassion come forward in our lives for all those in need of healing and for ourselves, that compassion may guide us and nourish us with its strength and wisdom.

Second Chamber

Leader: We call upon the second chamber of the heart, Holder of Innate Harmony. We ask that the innate harmony that resides deep within each of us come forward within our healing circle that we may draw upon its peace and balance.

Third Chamber

Leader: We call upon the third chamber of the heart, Guardian of Healing Presence. We ask that the qualities of healing presence come forward into our circle and into ourselves this evening, that we may become a light and an anchor for each other.

Fourth Chamber

Leader: We call upon the fourth chamber of the heart, Source of Unconditional Love. We ask that the light of unconditional love come forward from deep within the wells of our being, from the sacredness of all that we are--that this might remind us of our wholeness, healing ourselves and all who are bathed in its light.

Pause

Naming the Recipient

Leader: Breathe deeply and bring to mind someone you would like to send healing to. Take one of the hearts scattered around the edge of the altar and imagine this person, letting their image or your sense of them become gradually clearer and clearer to you.

Pause

On the heart you may draw a symbol or picture of the person, or name the person you would like to send healing to.

Pause

Take another heart for yourself, and draw a symbol or write your name on that heart, describing or picturing what you would like healing for. When you are done you may sit quietly with your intention to send healing energy.

Healing Vortex and Meditation Practice

This is an active meditation in which the participant will be placing their hearts in the altar and doing the vortex practice with your guidance. It is helpful to hold this intention of meditation as you progress around the circle.

The script for the meditation is at the end of the ritual.

Remember to leave time at the end of the meditation for people to journal or just sit quietly. This provides a gentle and thoughtful transition into the next part of the ritual. It is also important for their integration of the meditation into current time.

Talking Stick

Leader: We will now pass the talking stick. Please share as you are moved. You may want to share something that came up during the ritual or whatever else is in your heart or on your mind. What is said here stays here in circle. It is all right to pass. Who would like to start?

Gift Giving

Leader: We invite you to take home a candle and light it every night for a week. As you light it think of this healing blessing

I call upon the healing energies of Spirit, Be with me.

Be with ____________(whomever you have named.)

Thank the Four Chambers of the Heart

Snuff each candle as you read each chamber of the heart.

First Chamber

Leader: We thank the first chamber of the heart, Keeper of Compassion, for your presence this evening.

Second Chamber

We thank the second chamber of the heart, Holder of Innate Harmony, for your presence this evening.

Third Chamber

We thank the third chamber of the heart, Guardian of Healing Presence, for your presence this evening.

Fourth Chamber

We thank the fourth chamber of the heart, Source of Unconditional Love, for your presence this evening.

Thanking and Releasing the Directions

Snuff each candle as you read each direction

SOUTH

Leader: We thank the spirits and archetypes of the South and bid you farewell.

WEST

Leader: We thank the spirits and archetypes of the West and bid you farewell.

NORTH

Leader: We thank the spirits and archetypes of the North and bid you farewell.

EAST

Leader: We thank the spirits and archetypes of the East and bid you farewell.

CENTER

Leader: We thank the spirits and archetypes of the center, the song of the stars, the tides of the moon, the help of Mother Earth and bid you farewell.

Meditation

Healing Heart

And so now, sitting comfortably in your chairs, call again on your breath.....noticing your breath as it moves in...filling your lungs....nourishing....and noticing again as your breath leaves.....clearing....sharing the nourishment.

And gently allow yourself to connect with Mother Earth.....imagining that you can move swiftly and surely to her....feeling the delicious, moist coolness of her soil........ smelling the dirt............the pools of water as you move deeper and deeper into her loving embrace.

There is a radiance that emanates from within..........that lights your path.....and you move deeper through stone passageways lit with crystals and sapphires..........feeling the steadiness and richness of her body...........and drinking up the vibrancy and strength of her healing powers.....as you move closer.....

You move steadily toward the radiant light...perhaps now hearing a gentle rhythm.....a beating...as if a living drumbeat...a heartbeat..........

As you draw near you realize that it is Her heart........beating........ beginning to hold you gently and compassionately in its rhythm..........And your heart beats with Hers...
Beating together.......you have found an inner sanctuary...a place of peace and compassion.

And She invites you to pause here......to be here.......for it is here.....guided by Her wisdom and love.....that we can further awaken these aspects, these qualities of the heart that reside in all of us.

And so we do. Inviting the archetype, the energy of compassion to grow and enlighten our hearts......
Inviting the holder of innate harmony to balance and enrich our hearts.......

Calling upon the guardian of healing presence to quiet and soothe our hearts.....
And inviting the energies of unconditional love to fill and nourish our being........

And hearing our call...they awaken even further........ Softly at first..... gently they grow and begin to warm our hearts.........golden embers of healing energy...ever stronger and more radiant...as they grow and fill our hearts with compassion.....with innate harmony......healing presence and unconditional love.

Pause. There is a slight shift in tone or pacing as the sense of a meditative state is preserved while guiding the participants through the vortex practice.

And it is from here that we will open the vortex......
And taking a deep breath...still held within the heartbeat of the Great Goddess...I invite us all to stand. We will do the healing vortex practice for yourself first, followed by the vortex for the person you have named on your heart. So, who would like to go first.

Please place the heart for yourself in one of the chambers of the inner heart, naming yourself and your healing if you like.

Guide them through the vortex practice. We found that a continued meditative voice and respectful open heart was essential to holding the space for this deep healing.

And now place the person you would like to send healing to and name this person and their need if you like.

You may go around the circle repeating the exercise as needed or desired. Some people have more than one person they seek healing energy for. This may be invited but is up to the leaders and the numbers attending.

When all are finished

And now...you may sit. As you become comfortable thank the Goddess...Mother Earth for her presence...and silently thank the energies of the heart for their presence ....

And now,..... bringing your attention back to your breathing…Making your way gently back up the pathways lit by crystals and sapphires…past the pools of water and the rich moist earth…and gradually to our circle. Pausing a moment here to notice your breath again…notice how it feels in your body...to breathe in…deeply…and to exhale …slowly and consciously….

SR 2008

Walking the Spiral Labyrinth

Theme

The labyrinth is an ancient form of healing, meditation, and worship that has its roots deep in the history of the world's peoples. The power of this spiral path comes to us down through the ages, from all those who have practiced its many mysteries. This labyrinth is a gift from Spirit.

Sources of Inspiration

Our labyrinth is an inspiration and melding of the spiritual life of the Quero of Peru and the spirituality of the spiral as it has come to us from Western Europe. From the Quero come the Archetypes of the South, two serpents Sachamama and Yacamama, both symbols of healing the self. Sachamama is serpent of the earth who sheds her skin when it is too tight so she may be born again and grow. Yacamama is the serpent-mother of the waters, which heal and replenish us. In the labyrinth they wind next to each other in a healing path to the center of our Earth Mother and to our own center, our heart and then out into the world anew. They assist us in our walk, as does the spirit of all labyrinths.

Altar

- *Altar cloth*
- *Candles for directions*
- *Lighting candle*
- *Snuffer*
- *Singing bowls*
- *Flowers*

Additional items for Sacred Space

- *Items to mark the labyrinth, i.e., plastic plant labels and ribbon.*
- *See diagram and instructions at the end of the ritual.*
- *Symbolic items for the four directions of the labyrinth*
- *Tables and bowls to put these objects on*

- *Bug spray if you are doing this in the evening*
- *Lighting if it is late evening or dark*
- *Objects for the center for participants to take*

Set Up

The diagram is at the end of the ritual. The labyrinth was created to be set up outside. We built it with plant labeling sticks and ribbon. You can use whatever is available to you that is easily set up and taken down. It took us about two hours alone, less with help. We started measuring the dimensions of each path from the center out, placing the small stakes as we went. We wound the ribbon around the stakes after they were all placed. We set up small altars for offerings to the four directions at the outer ring of the labyrinth. We set up a small altar in the center of the labyrinth for offerings. We also placed a variety of small objects on this altar that participants could take if they were inspired. Our group met first in the meeting room before going out to walk the labyrinth, so we set up an altar in the room.

Labyrinth Walking Paths

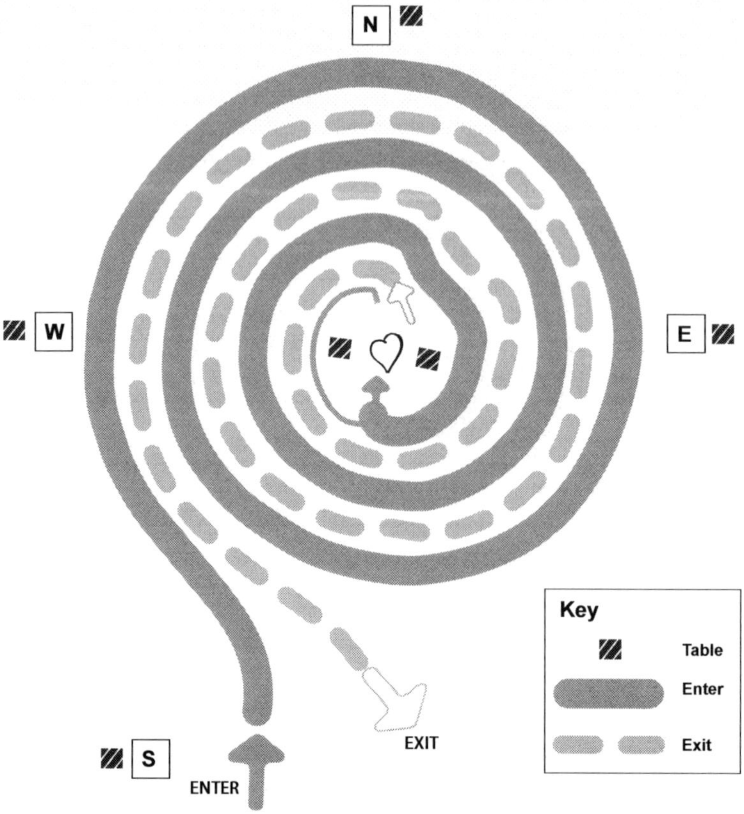

Smudge

Smudging outside the room allows each person a brief clearing and centering before walking into ritual space.

You may appoint a 'smudger', but do not forget to smudge yourself as leaders first. You may use whatever feels appropriate to you. Some suggestions are: sage, paulo santo, or mugwort. Have the participants enter the ritual room as they are finished being smudged

Calling the Directions

Once everyone has gathered in the room, open sacred space.

SOUTH

Leader: Spirit of the South, of love, compassion and healing, be here now to walk with us on our spiral path of life.

WEST

Leader: Spirit of the West, of patience, flexibility and constancy, be here now to walk with us on our spiral path of life.

NORTH

Leader: Spirit of the North, of inner strength, stillness and groundedness, be here now to walk with us on our spiral path of life.

EAST

Leader: Spirit of the East, of new vision, clarity and lightness, be here now to walk with us on our spiral path of life.

CENTER

Leader: Spirit of the Center, Above and Below, of wisdom and understanding, be here now to walk with us on our spiral path of life.

Labyrinth Ritual

Leader: Our lives are sacred journeys filled with change and transformation. Living challenges our vision of what is possible, stretching our soul, teaching us to see clearly and deeply, to listen to our intuition, and to take on challenges at every step along the way.

The labyrinth is a metaphor, an enactment of your path. At its most basic level it is a metaphor for the journey to the center of your deepest self and back out into the world with a broadened understanding of who you are.

The path of the labyrinth draws on the power of the spiral in an apparently meandering but very purposeful path. Our Labyrinth also calls on the guidance of The Dual Serpent Goddesses, Sachamama and Yacamama, from the tradition of the Quero in Peru. Sachamama is serpent of the earth who sheds her skin when it is too tight so she may be born again and grow. Yacamama is the serpent-mother of the waters that heal us and replenish us on our journey. In the labyrinth they wind next to each other in a spiraling, healing path to the center of our Earth Mother and to our own center and then out into the world anew. They assist us in our walk, as does the spirit of all labyrinths.

A labyrinth is an archetype with which you can have a direct experience. You can walk it. You can enter into its sacred energy, to learn, to heal, and to be held. As you walk towards the center you can release your attachment to whatever is holding you back. This is Sachamama.

As you abide in the center you may have new insights, clarity and focus. You can ask a question and pause for an answer. You can rest there in the center just to be, to be held, to connect with the Sacred, to receive healing or perhaps a message from Spirit.

When ready, you emerge from the center, gradually walking the spiral out. It is now the path of becoming, of being replenished, nourished and healed by what was received and continues to unfold. This is Yacamama.

The ritual will be done in silence. We will have a meditation to seek advice from the Wise Woman about our journey into and out of the labyrinth. In silence we will walk to the labyrinth and, one by one, we will walk the spiral seeking the answer to a question, an insight for a situation, or a healing of any sort.

Meditation

The script for the meditation is at the end of the ritual.

Remember to leave time at the end of the meditation for people to journal or just sit quietly. This provides a gentle and thoughtful transition into the next part of the ritual. It is also important for their integration of the meditation into current time.

Leader: And now we will walk the labyrinth. As you walk into the labyrinth, you may offer flower petals to each of the four directions, and the center, requesting their assistance on your walk. Gradually let yourself quiet and deepen as you near the center. Once there, stop, listen. You are at the center of the labyrinth, the center of you, and a vortex of sacred space. If you wish, you may take out of the arrangement in the center whatever is there that calls to you. Stop long enough to take a deep breath before you begin your journey out along Yacamama. Walk slowly, letting your experience gradually ground itself within you.

When you are done, you may return here to journal or draw your experience. When all have returned, we will pass the talking stick and you may speak—or not—as you are moved.

And now we will proceed outside in silence.

Walking the Labyrinth

We had one leader at the entrance of the labyrinth to help space the distance between people entering it. We gave each person quite a bit of space, as each one walks at a different pace, and some wanted to pause in the middle. The other leader was at the other side of the labyrinth, sounding the singing bowl. As leaders we walked last while one of the participants played the bowl for us.

Talking Stick

Leader: We invite you to share whatever of your journey you wish, or you may talk about whatever you wish, or you may pass the talking stick without talking. You are in control of the stick.

Thanking and Releasing the Directions

Snuff each candle as you read each direction

SOUTH

Leader: Spirit of the South, of love and compassion and healing, we thank you for walking with us on our spiral path.

WEST

Leader: Spirit of the West, of patience, flexibility and constancy, we thank you for walking with us on our spiral path.

NORTH

Leader: Spirit of the North, of inner strength, stillness and groundedness, we thank you for walking with us on our spiral path.

EAST

Leader: Spirit of the East, of new vision, clarity and lightness, we thank you for walking with us on our spiral path.

CENTER

Leader: Spirit of the Center, Above and Below, of wisdom and understanding, we thank you for walking with us on our spiral path of life.

The circle is open but unbroken. Blessed be.

Labyrinth Meditation

This is a meditation to meet your inner wise woman to ask for counsel on the coming labyrinth walk.

So settle into a comfortable position.............gradually bringing your attention to your breathing...........in a moment I will sound the bowl.......I invite you to follow the sound...............................letting the sound gradually begin to guide you inward...........to the beginning of an inner journey............connecting you to the earth and her wisdoms and mysteries..........you are Her child and so it is that the kernel of her knowing resides deep within you.........waiting to be called upon...............
and so you may begin the journey.....

sound the bowl

and gradually imagining yourself in a beautiful field.............green grasses splashed with a multitude of color from the wild flowers............the blue of the sky and buzzing of the bees blending deliciously with the warmth of the sun and coolness of the breeze.....there is a sense of gentle purpose and curiosity........

And so you set out to meet the wise crone...Walking down the path that unfolds in front of you.................walking lightly and with ease towards the growth of tall trees....................arriving at the edge of the forest......pausing briefly for a gentle breath...............

As you enter you may notice the coolness of the air here..........and you move forward down the path..........noticing any creatures that might come to greet you along the way...........

The path is leading you to a beautiful group of ancient oak trees..........
as you approach you notice an opening...........almost like an arched doorway of tall oaks.............. moving to the threshold you may notice the beams of sunlight as they

filter through portals in the green fluttering canope high above....... illuminating a circular clearing.....ringed by the majestic oaks who are guarding and protecting this space......

And you cross the threshold...........with eager anticipation..........there is a knowing of this place deep within you......it is familiar and embracing ....

A gentle, wise voice calls you.......welcomes you warmly...........Over here..I have been expecting you................How may I help you?......
You greet the wise crone respectfully...........
And you present your request for guidance.........explaining that you are about to walk the sachamama labyrinth........

> 'Wise crone, with what purpose shall I walk? What question or intent is most pressing to hold in my heart and mind as I walk. Walk with me.....let me open to your guidance.......and my heart's truth'

She may suggest a specific question that needs an insight.......or perhaps a healing walk........or a meditation that will unfold its purpose as you walk.............

pause

And she offers you this in farewell ....saying: "Most importantly.....walk this labyrinth with an open heart and mind....with love.........open to its subtle strength and depth.............I will be with you"

And so you thank her and leave the oak grove sanctuary........back through the green, shadowy forest and out onto the plain........ As you begin to return to present time and place....you feel assured that she will walk with you this evening, gently guiding you along your way.........
So taking a deep breath.....noticing the breath as you inhale......and then exhaling slowly begin to return to our space here tonight.......opening your eyes as you are ready.......

2010

Directions for Creating the Labyrinth

The following directions are how we set up the labyrinth. It takes about 2 hours, with two people working on the setup.

Needed:

- *sticks or plant labeling sticks, we used plastic ones from a garden shop*
- *ribbon, we used two different colors but that's optional*
- *tape measure that can measure up to 4 feet*
- *something for you to drink while working :)*
- *patience and several deep breaths*

Some basic information:

Center of circle is 3 feet in diameter

There are two separate paths, one into the center and the other out of the center, each path is 2 feet wide

The total diameter of the labyrinth is 25 feet

We constructed the labyrinth starting from the center, or the heart of the labyrinth, working out and around the many spirals to the entrance and exit of the labyrinth itself.

Creating the heart of the labyrinth

We started by finding the center of the circle.

1. We used a pendulum to help us with this process, along with what 'felt right' for the center. I placed one of the plant markers temporarily to mark the center. This is a more intuitive right-brained method.
2. For those who prefer a more left brained method, measure out the diameter of 25 feet from south to north, and then from east to west. Where the two lines intersect will be the center of the labyrinth.
3. Establish a 3 foot diameter for the heart of the Labyrinth.
4. From the center or heart of the labyrinth, determine the south direction. The entrance to the heart of the Labyrinth is from the South, the place of healing, change and growth.
5. Next find the north direction. The exit from the heart of the labyrinth is from the north, a place of stillness, inner strength and deep knowing.
6. Create an opening in the circumference of the heart of the labyrinth in the south that is 2 feet wide. This is the entrance into the heart of the labyrinth.
7. Create an opening in the circumference of the heart of the labyrinth in the north that is two feet wide. This is the exit out of the heart of the labyrinth.

The Paths

1. Stand at the south entrance to the heart of the labyrinth, facing north. Create a line of markers starting at the left hand side of the entrance (as you face north) straight out 2 feet toward the south. This is the side of the entrance path into the heart of the labyrinth.

   Now place one marker out at 4 feet from the side of the entrance.

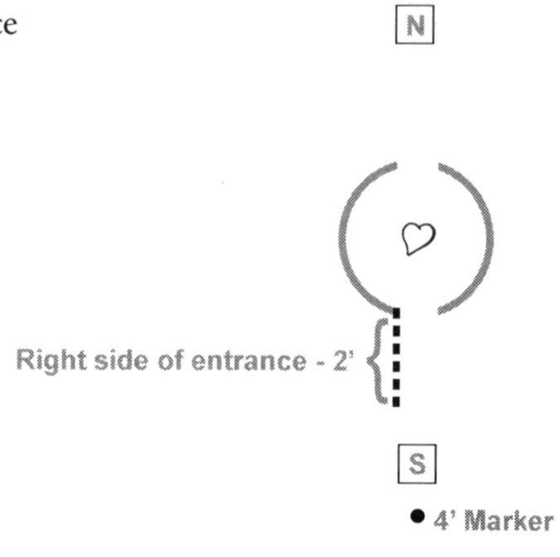

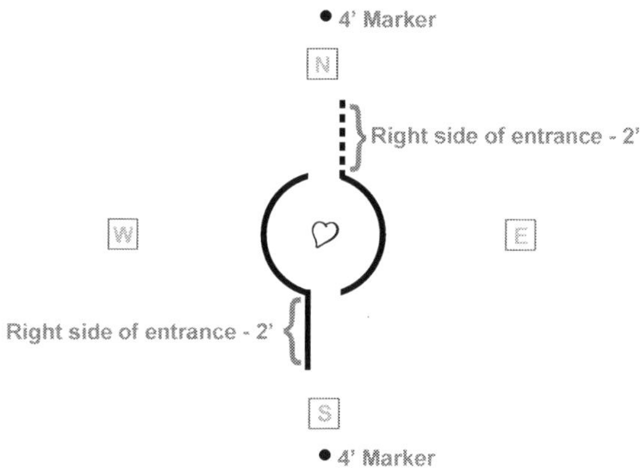

2. Stand at the north exit facing south. From the left hand side of the exit (as you face south) place markers continuously out from the heart to the 2 foot point. This is the side of the exit out of the heart of the labyrinth. Now place one marker at 4 feet out from the side of the exit.

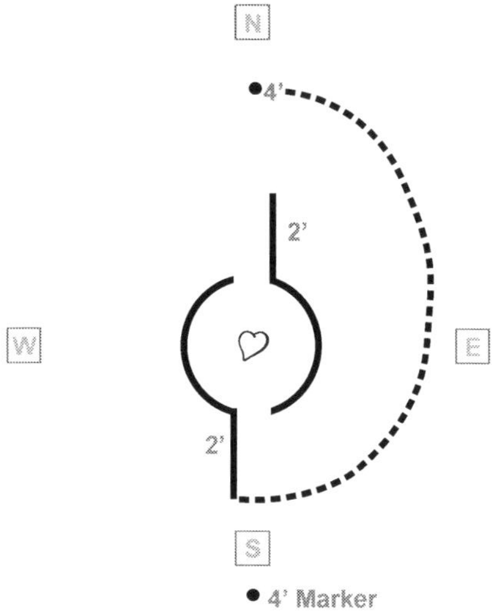

3. Return to the south entrance to the heart circle. Face east. Begin to establish a line of markers that starts at the left hand side of the entrance, moving around toward the north at 2 feet out from the boundary of the heart. This line of markers coming around from the south direction comes up to meet the 4 foot marker in the north direction.

4. From this point on we started measuring a 2 foot line of markers and a 4 foot line of markers. You are measuring two paths at once. This will save you a lot of time.

Continue measuring around the circumference, placing markers out at 2 feet and 4 feet. Go all the way around to the North direction again.

Note: The line of markers from the exit connects with the 4 foot marker in the south. From here continue to measure 2 feet and 4 feet from the outside circumference.

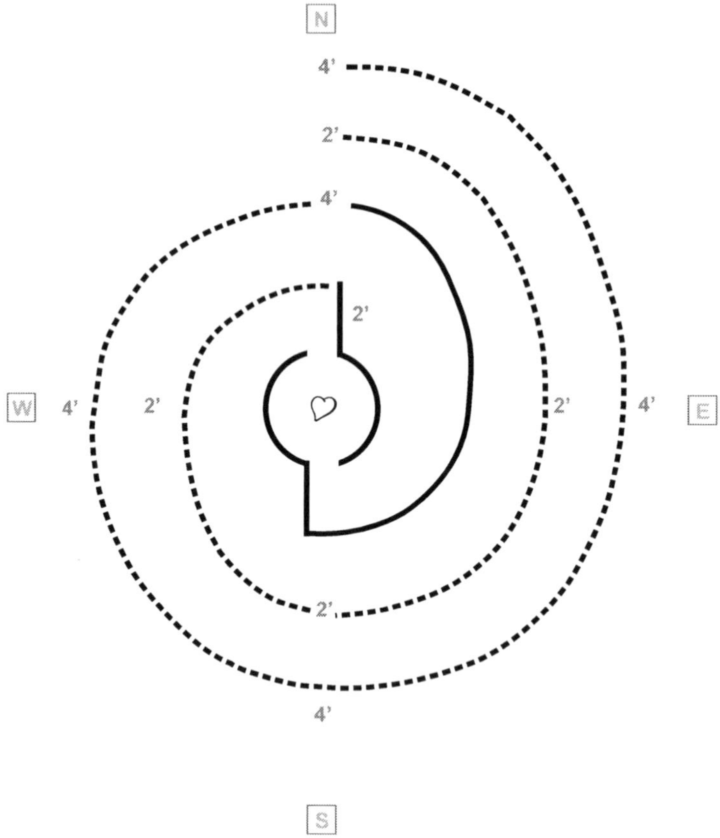

5. You are now at the North. From this position, go around the outside circumference one more time. Place the markers at 2 feet and 4 feet, about every 8 inches apart, until you get to the North again.

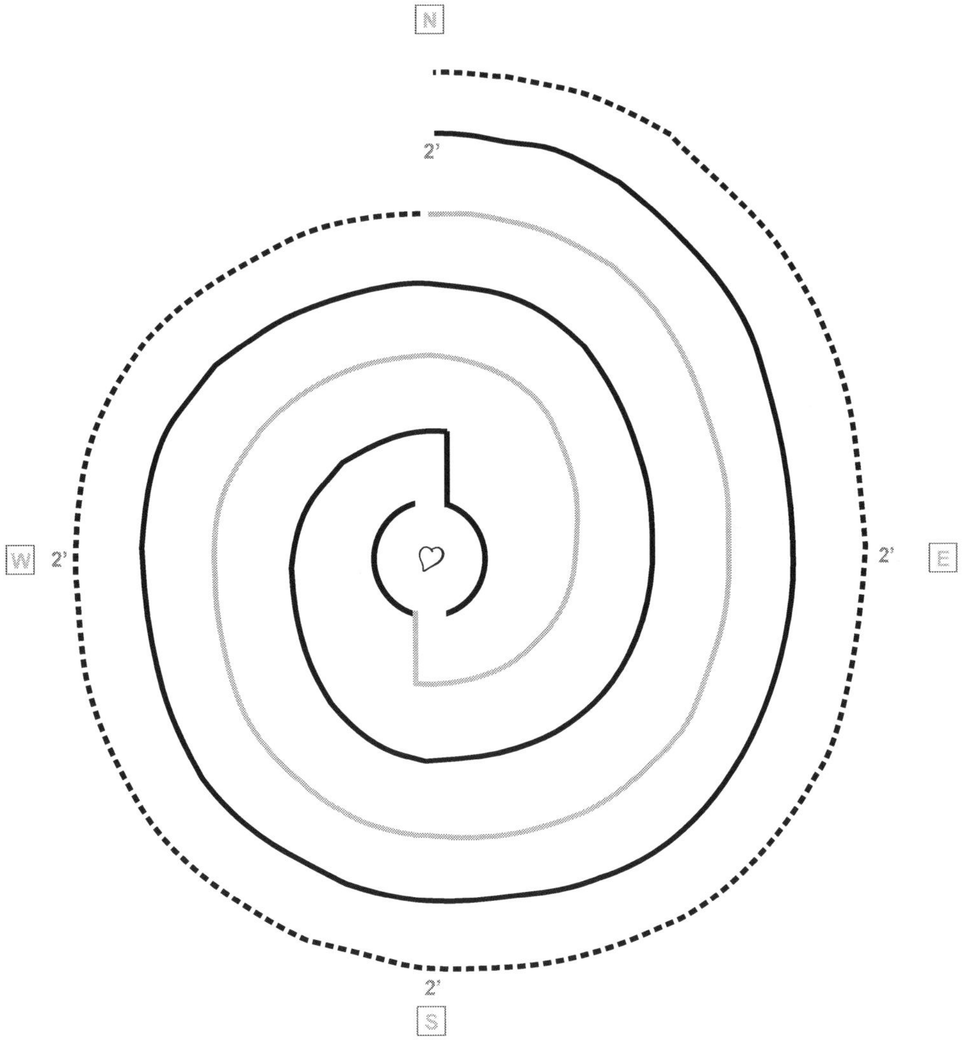

6. Now we started to create the entrance and exit of the labyrinth itself. Continue measuring out the 2 feet and 4 feet from the outermost ring. This time you will go only 1/2 way around, to the South direction. As you begin to reach the South, begin to flair the markers outward, as shown in the diagram. This creates a wider, more inviting entrance into and exit out of the Labyrinth.

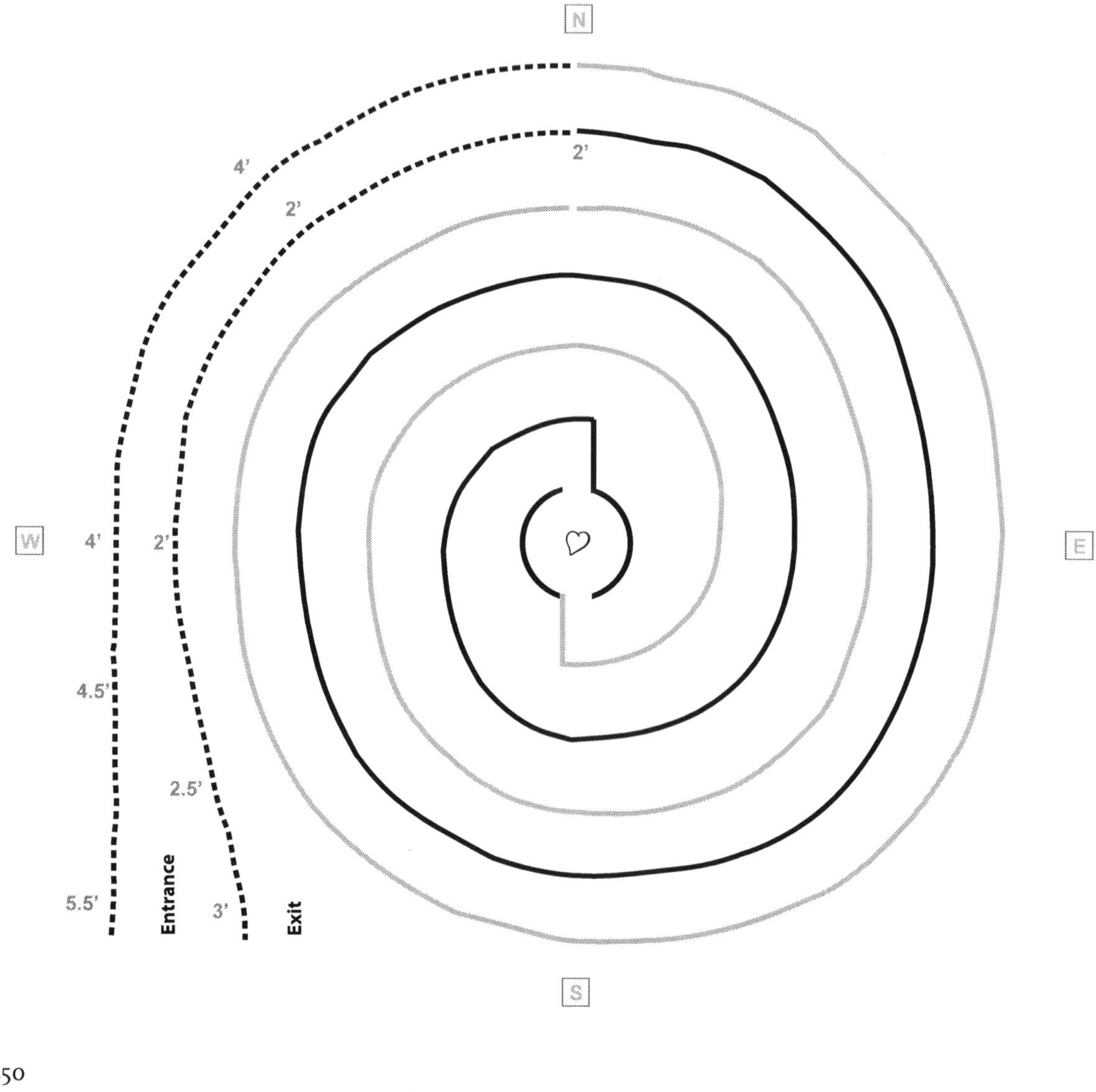

7. The last step is to wind the ribbons around the markers to completely outline the paths for the participants. We used different colored ribbons for the paths. The outermost ring should be one color. We used red. Follow the markers into the entrance. Do the same for the exit, we used blue ribbon and followed the markers out of the heart of the labyrinth to the exit.

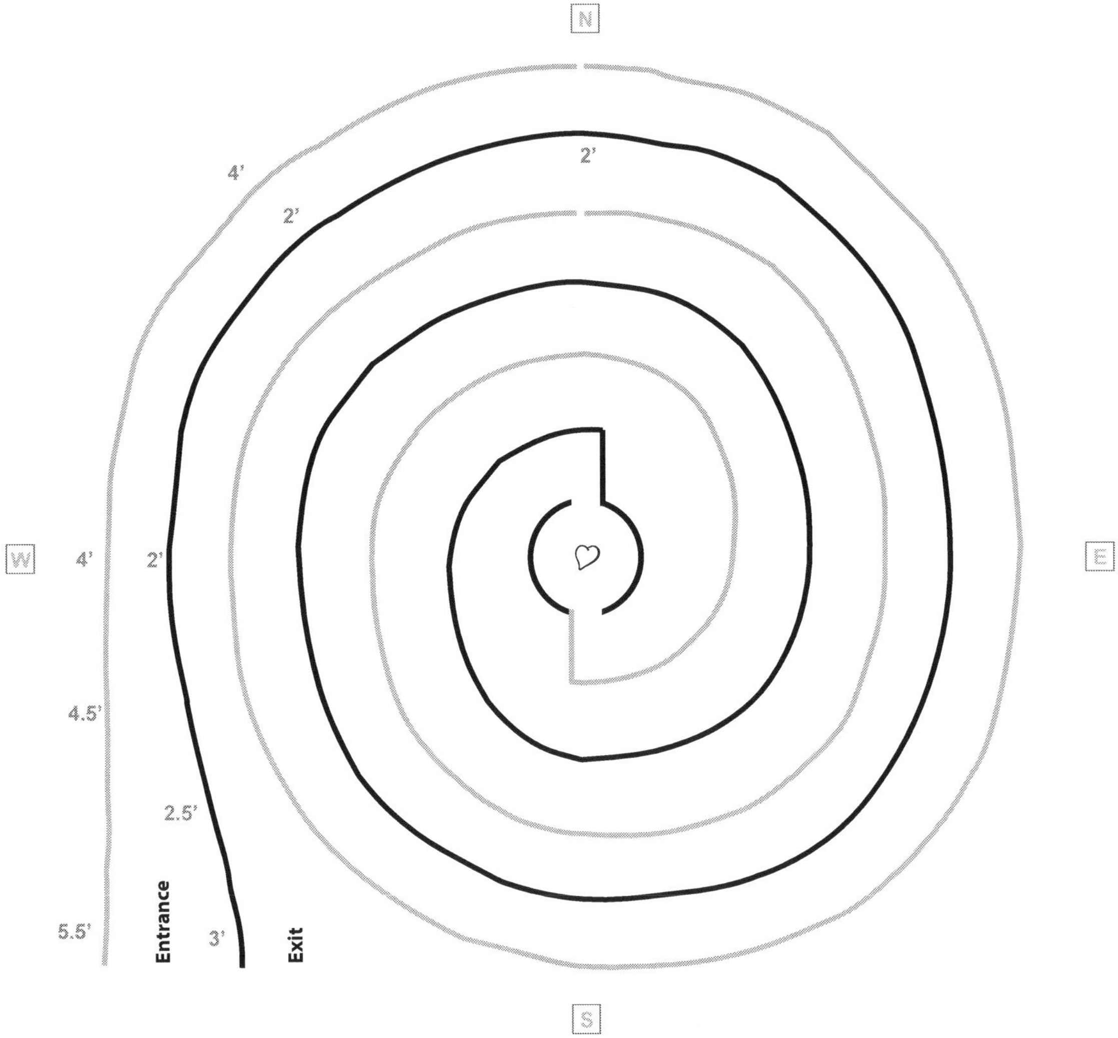

Peace Mandala

Note

For this ritual, everyone attending will help to create a mandala for peace, both inner peace and world peace. As the participants create the mandala in sacred space and with focused, prayerful hearts, the energetic for peace grows and is held in the mandala. For us, it was a beautiful and powerful moment. We brought the mandala to the vestry to share with the larger community on our Sunday morning service. Later, we dismantled it and offered it, with prayers, to Spirit. We chose a local place in nature where we could offer the mandala.

This ritual is also a wonderful opportunity to involve other groups in your community. We invited the peace initiative and the social action committee from our spiritual community to participate in the ritual. However, we are a small community, so an attendance of about 10 was good. In a larger community adaptions might need to be made.

This was one of the more complex rituals that we created and held. It was also one of the most meaningful and inspiring.

Theme

The theme of this ritual is to create a visible and tangible prayer for peace that everyone can actively participate in and thus provide them with a direct experience.

Sources of Inspiration

This ritual is based on the rich multi-cultural use of mandalas for worship, healing, and prayer. In Hindu and Buddhist practices, mandalas are created as prayers, a way of establishing sacred space, and aiding in meditation. Navajo mandalas called sand paintings are often used by the shamans for healing purposes. The word itself is a Sanskrit word meaning 'circle'. For our earth-based mandala we adapted an invocation from a workshop led by Brugh Joy, opening the four chambers of the heart as a way of focusing intention to create a prayer for peace and healing.

The calling of the directions blends several traditions. The Incan Shamanic traditions call upon the archetypes of serpent, jaguar, condor and eagle, and hummingbird and dragon. Using the Buddhist traditions we called upon the Chinese and Tibetan Goddesses of Tara and Quan Yin. We called upon the Native American Goddess White Buffalo Woman and the European goddesses of Gaia and Eirene.

Altar

- *Colored beans and seeds, sorted, at least 10 different kinds, preferably small*
- *We used a large box to offer a firm, flat surface and covered it with a cloth. An outlined design of the mandala was drawn on the cloth.*
- *Altar cloth, we used green felt for the prayers to stick to*
- *Cards with world peace prayers on them with velcro on the back*
- *Cards to write prayers on with velcro on the back*
- *Smudge kit*
- *Singing bowl*
- *Silver Heart-small to be placed on the seeds at the center of the mandala as it is being created.*

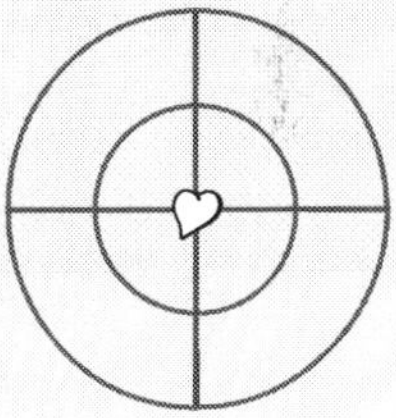

Additional items for Sacred Space

- *Basket of pens or colored markers for prayer writing*
- *Prayer flags, if available, hung around the room*
- *Candles for directions*
- *Matches, snuffer, lighting candle*

Set up

We used a round table that was low, so people could see the top of the table easily while sitting down. This was helpful as the work on the mandala progressed. The candles for the directions were around the periphery of the circle, so that they encircled both the participants and the altar. Cards, both blank and with prayers, were in baskets on the altar along with pens and markers.

When the altar was being set up, we outlined the inner circle of the Mandala with beans that represents the 4 chambers of the heart. We found that small beans worked easier. Having the center outlined ahead of time allowed us to fill in the quadrants when we called the 4 qualities of the heart. This proved to be a wonderful modeling for the participants for creating the rest of the mandala.

The platform for the mandala was set in the middle of the altar, on a felt cloth. The prayers could therefore be attached by Velcro to the cloth so they would stay in place. The different colored beans were placed in bowls around the edges of the mandala.

We also found it helpful to have more than one leader for this ritual. Leaders in the peace initiative and social action caucus at our church worked with us to create and lead the ritual.

Smudge

Demonstrating this breath is very helpful to the people present.

You may use a singing bowl with this centering. Sound the bowl. Do one AUM breath and pause. Sound the bowl a second time and do the second AUM breath. After a short pause, sound the bowl one last time, and do the third AUM breath.

Introduction to the Ritual

Leader: Tonight, we will create a peace mandala, a physical manifestation of our prayers and intentions for peace. We will place world peace prayers and our own written prayers on the cloth surrounding the mandala. To further deepen our intentions we will open the four chambers of our hearts, and the heart of the Mandala. Then we will create the mandala itself.

The peace mandala will be on display on Sunday, so that everyone may join their hopes and prayers for peace with ours. The mandala will then be offered to Spirit at a 'special' local site.

Centering -The Aum Breath

This is the centering exercise that helps people become more present and frees them from their day's events

Leader: We will use the AUM breath for a centering and coming together this evening. It is a three sound chant, Ahhh, Uhhhh, Mmmm, done in one exhaled breath.

The sound Ahhh is made when the breath is at the belly,
The Uhhh sound is made when the breath is at the chest, and
The Mmmm sound is made when the breath is exhaled mostly from the throat and head.
You can feel the different vibrations as you focus your awareness on the sound.

Demonstrating this breath is very helpful to the people present.

You may use a singing bowl with this centering.

Sound the bowl. Do one AUM breath and pause. Sound the bowl a second time and do the second AUM breath. After a short pause, sound the bowl one last time, and do the third AUM breath.

And now, let your breath flow naturally and take a moment to just be in this space.........and opening your eyes, perhaps looking around...taking another moment to just be here in our space together........

Sound the bowl to signal the end

Calling the Directions

Light each candle as you read the direction

EAST

Leader: We call upon the east, home of fresh spring breezes, of new beginnings and of hope for peace
We call upon Condor and Eagle.
Be with us as we soar above the mundane to see the many ways of living in harmony
We call upon Quan Yin, the Goddess of Mercy.
Teach us well.

SOUTH

Leader: We call upon the South, home of the life-giving force of the sun, of spiritual passion and sustenance that fills our spirits.
We call upon SachaMama, the serpent.
Help us to heal ourselves so that we may live in peace.
We call upon Tara, Goddess Protector of all humans as they cross the sea of life.
Guide us always towards compassion for all people.

WEST

Leader: We call upon the West, home of the healing waters that bathe us in peace and bless us when we drink.
We call upon Rainbow Jaguar.
Help us to stalk the ways of peace so that we walk in peace on the earth.
We call upon White Buffalo Woman.
May the age of peace and harmony that she foretells bring peace to all peoples.

NORTH

Leader: We call upon the North, Mother Earth, who grounds us and holds us in times of peace and difficulty.
We call upon Hummingbird and Dragon.
Teach us to drink up the nectar of life so that our sweetness brings peace to those around us.
We call upon Eirene, the Greek Goddess of Peace.
We ask you to bring peace to all parts of the world and to our inner selves.

CENTER

Leader: We call upon the Center, above and below, that nourishes our body-mind and spirit.
Be with us so that we may stand in the center of a peaceful life.
We call upon Star Brother and Star Sister, Sun and Moon.
Shine down on us that we may live in the light of loving kindness.
We call upon Gaia, Earth Mother, who sustains all people everywhere that we may learn to live in harmony with the earth and with those who live upon her.

About Mandalas

Leader: Mandalas are an ancient spiritual and healing practice. They appear in Islamic art, in the knot work of the Celts, in the sand paintings of the Tibetan and Navajo, and in the art of Christian mystics.

Mandala is the Sanskrit word for circle or center. The essential meaning of the mandala derives from the symbolism of these two aspects. The circle is a shape without a beginning or an end, representing wholeness and the cyclical nature of life. Within the circle lies the center that can be seen as the heart or the inner aspect of a person. The two aspects of the circle – the potential of its center and the totality of its circumference – are embodied in the mandala and remind us of the divine in the universe and in ourselves.

Creating a mandala is an artistic endeavor and an act of worship. The idea of impermanence, taken from Buddhist practice, is an important aspect of the life of a Mandala. After the mandala is created, it is always destroyed and offered in ceremony to Spirit. This ritual is performed as an act of healing for the world and for ourselves, with our intention being a prayer for peace.

Prayers for Peace

Leader: On the altar are prayers for peace from around the world. We will begin forming the foundation and ground of our mandala for peace as we read these prayers and attach them to the green cloth. In this way our mandala will be built upon and supported by these prayers from around the world, by our prayers and those of the larger congregation. When the mandala is offered to Spirit, it will be wrapped in all of these prayers.

As you are ready, we invite you to pick a prayer from the altar and read it to the circle and then attach it to the mandala cloth.

The prayers may be on the altar at the four directions, passed in a basket or however feels right to you. Let this be a relaxed and reflective process.

Leader: And now, let us take a few moments for quiet reflection. What is your prayer or hope for peace? Breathe and rest into your center……… inviting the prayer to flow genuinely and freely from your heart-mind. If it helps to sit quietly, eyes closed and hands on your heart, please feel free to do so. As you are ready, take a paper and pen and write your hope and prayer for peace.

Allow as long as they need. When the last person has stopped writing continue.

Leader: As you are ready, please read your prayer and attach it to the mandala cloth.

Allow time for the participants to read their prayers and attach them to the mandala cloth.

Creating the Mandala

Opening the Four Chambers of the Hearts
(the inner circle of the mandala)

Leader: At the center of our altar is our mandala, radiating out to the four directions and held by the wheel of life.

And now, as a reflection of our intent and prayers, let us open the heart of our mandala, as we open our hearts and pray for peace in the hearts of all people.

Leader: Hear our blessing.

At the center of our being is our heart.

At the center of the mandala is the heart.
May peace dwell strong within our hearts,
The heart of our mandala,
And the hearts of all people.

Outlined in beans ahead of time

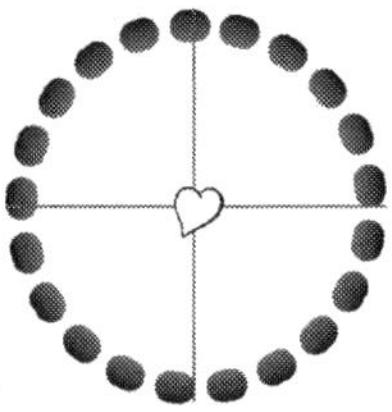

While one of the leaders is reading the blessing, another may place a small heart at the center of the inner circle representing the 4 chambers of the heart

Leader: And so we pray for Compassion. May the Keeper of Compassion awaken in us and all peoples.
May compassion guide us toward a benevolent and wise understanding of the other, towards strength and forgiveness, empathy and good deeds.
Help us all to offer Compassion to our own selves and to all people.

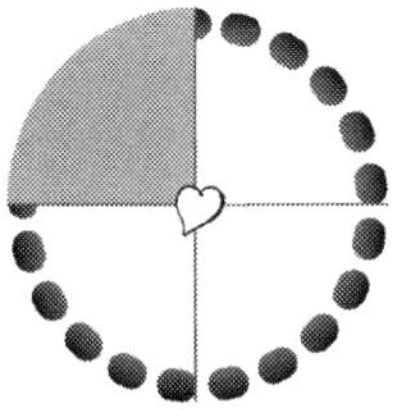

One of the leaders fills in this area of the inner circle while another reads. It may be filled in with any color of beans or seeds. We rotated reading and filling in, so that all leaders read a part and filled in a quadrant. Rotating the reading also helps to keep the ritual alive

Leader: We call upon Innate Harmony.
May the Keeper of Innate Harmony awaken in our hearts, watering the seeds of peace so that we may access our inner sources of balance, goodwill, and mutual respect.
Help us to dwell in our capacity for Innate Harmony, for as we dwell here, so we are able to share it with others.

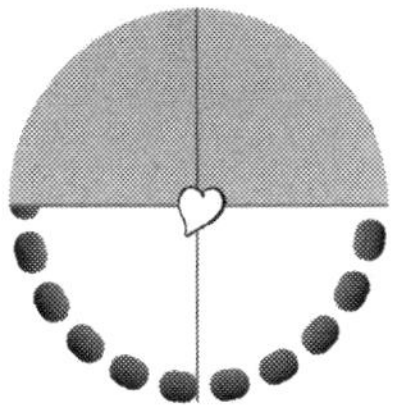

As one leader is reading, another is filling in a quadrant in the heart circle that will correspond to Innate Harmony.

Leader: We pray for Healing Presence.
May the Keeper of Healing Presence help us to cultivate a way of being with each other and all peoples that soothes wounds both old and new, and in their place fills us with the light of acceptance, caring and wholeness.

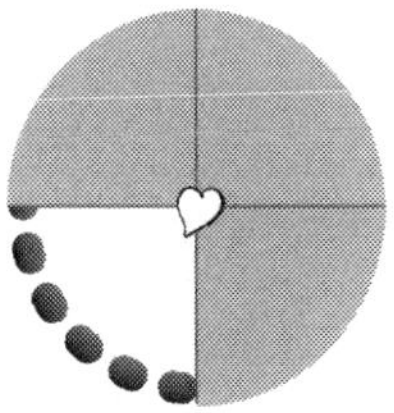

Help us to care for each other from the wisdom of our hearts.

Again, as one of the leaders reads, another is filling in a quadrant with a different colored bean or seed.

Leader: We call upon Unconditional Love. May the Keeper of Unconditional Love light the flame of Love in our hearts.
Guide us and teach us to walk in ways that create peace, that unite us through acceptance, tolerance, and brotherly love.
Help us to come from our heart's strength to all of life with equanimity, wisdom and hope.

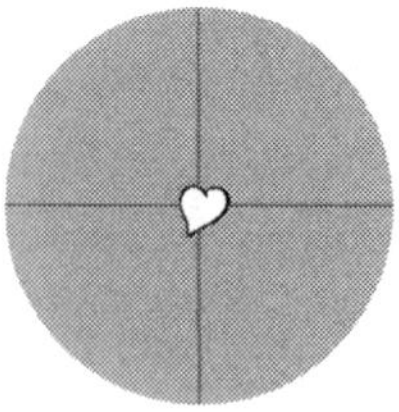

One leader reads, and the other fills in the last quadrant of the heart center.

Pause a moment here to let all of this settle and as a pause before beginning another aspect of building the mandala.

Leader: Our paths flow from our hearts outward to the four directions, to the Gods and Goddesses and the Archetypes and to each other. We manifest our prayers and intentions at the same time that we reach out and source ourselves in the Sacred that flows through all of life.

Prayers to the Directions of the Mandala

SOUTH

One reader reads the South direction. Using the beans, another leader forms the line from the center to the south direction in the mandala, and then around the outside to the west direction.

Leader: So, we move outward in our mandala to the South, to the peoples of the south.
May our capacity for mindful compassion move out to gently touch all beings with peace and harmony.
We pray for the strength of the South, the healing power of the sun to bring warmth and growth to all lands and all peoples.

We ask that our prayers are heard and strength is given to all peoples to work for peace, within themselves and for others.

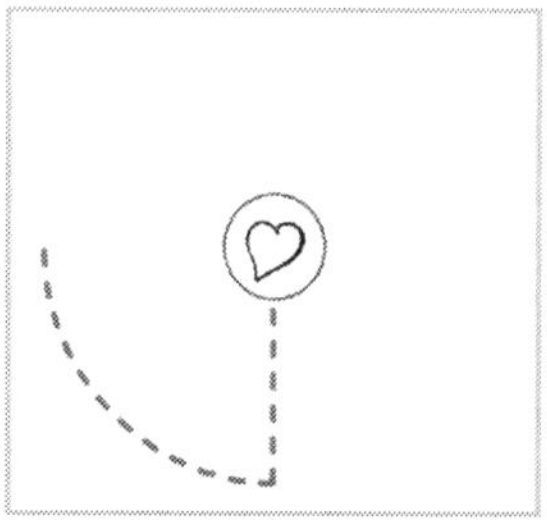

SOUTH

We call upon all Enlightened Beings, Angelic Hosts and Gods and Goddesses, hear us.

WEST

One person reads the West direction while another is drawing in the line from the center to the west and around to the north with the beans. This is a line of beans from the center to the west, and a quarter of the diameter filled in from the west up to the north direction.

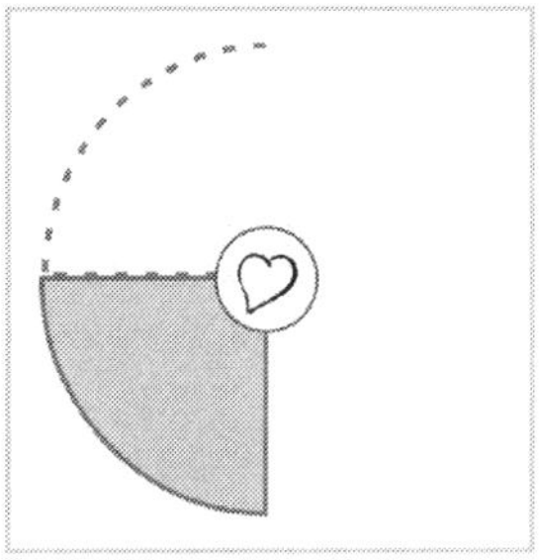

WEST

Leader: Our hearts move out to the West.
Sweet waters of Mother Earth, bathe our neighbors to the west and ourselves with your clear and replenishing elixir.
Bring meaning to our tears.
Unite us in our journey to understand and to be with the suffering of all peoples, that we might cradle them in our hearts of innate harmony, offering them shelter from the storms of life.

And in the West dwell the Gods and Goddesses, Angelic Beings and Enlightened Ones of all faiths. Bless us and hear our cravings for peace.

NORTH

Repeat the pattern of reading and laying out the beans for this direction also. The beans are formed from the center out to the north direction and around the outside to the east.

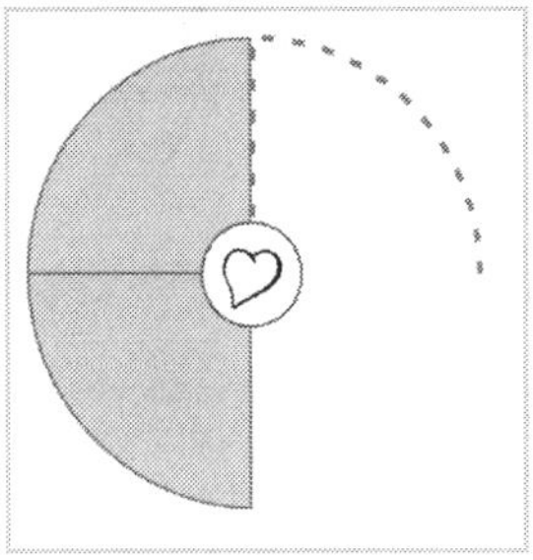

NORTH

Leader: Now we move out from our hearts of Unconditional Love to the North, bringing Healing Presence out into the world and to the peoples of the North.
Here in the North dwells the spirit of the mountains.
And deep within the mountain, as is deep within us, lays the heart of Healing Presence. This is our prayer of the North.
May Healing Presence become as strong and stable as the mountains, forming the foundation of our being and our relations with each other.
May all people be guided by a deep respect, tolerance, and reverence for all beings.
We ask the Gods and Goddesses, Enlightened Ones, and Angelic Beings of all faiths to bless and hear our prayers.
Inspire all people with the strength to be peace.

Again, repeat the pattern of reading and forming the outline of the mandala. This time the beans or seeds are formed from the center out to the east and around to join the south direction. The outside diameter of the mandala is outlined with beans and four lines of beans come from the center out to each direction.

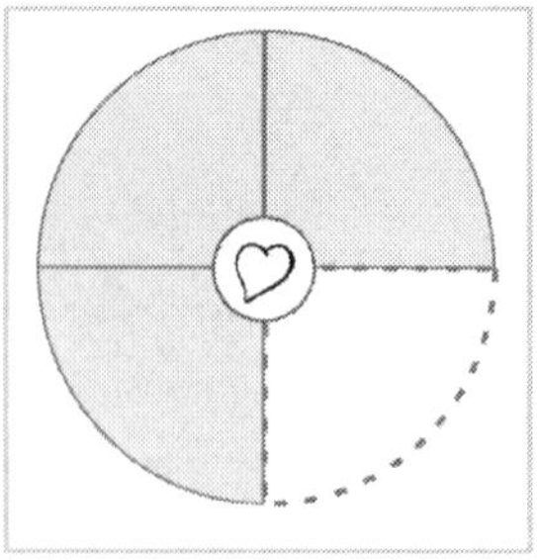

EAST

Leader: And also in our mandala we move to the East out from our hearts of Unconditional Love, to our brothers and sisters.
May we all be blessed with the sweetness of clean air, that we might nourish our bodies with this nectar.
Let us breathe in kindness, understanding and thoughtfulness and be nourished.
Let us breathe out benevolence, caring and empathy for all people and nourish them.
May Unconditional Love be as bountiful and free as the air around us and within us.

And in the East, Gods and Goddesses, Enlightened Ones, Angelic Beings, hear our hopes and requests.

Pause

Leader: Around the altar there are bowls of seeds and beans that you may use to finish creating our prayer for peace. We ask you to pick a direction and form a shape, design, or whatever you wish with some of the beans or seeds. Please feel free to come up and work as you are ready. We invite you all to come up, as the mandala is a reflection of all of our prayers and hopes. It is now a work in progress and will take form as we all work together.

Allow people to join in as they are ready, either solo or in a group. Our group needed some encouragement to begin and several shy participants needed extra support. We found that people came forward in clusters to work, and stepped back to look as others came forward. In the end, every inch of the mandala was filled with designs and patterns in different colored beans and seeds. It was very beautiful.

When everyone is finished and seated again, continue.

Leader: Our prayers are heard when we speak them and are received when they are offered. This is the custom with mandalas or sand paintings, to create and then to offer them to Spirit.

We ask you to take a few moments to release your attachment to the mandala that it might move sweetly to Spirit when it is time.

Give them a few minutes to silently release their attachment to the mandala, knowing that it will be destroyed as it is offered to Spirit in the near future.

Talking Stick

Leader: We will now pass the talking stick, please share, or not, what has come up for you here tonight as you feel ready.

Thanking and Releasing the Directions

Snuff each candle as you read each direction.

EAST

Leader: We face the East, Condor, Eagle, and the Goddess Quan Yin and bless you and thank you for being here with us

SOUTH

Leader: We face the South, Sachamama, and the Goddess Tara, and bless you and thank you for being here with us

WEST

Leader: We face the West, Rainbow Jaguar and White Buffalo Woman and bless you and thank you for being here with us

NORTH

Leader: We face the North, Hummingbird and Dragon and the Goddess Eirene, and bless you and thank you for being here with us

CENTER

Leader: We face the Center, above and below, Star Brother and Star Sister, the Sun and Moon and Gaia, Earth Mother, and bless you and thank you for being here with us

Making Room for Rebirth

Note

We suggest that it be done after Samhain, mid-November to mid-January. We offered this ritual late-November. In the Andes they do this ritual at the new year, January or February. It is a good ritual for the ending of one year and for the beginning of a new year.

In the fall the wheel turns to the harvest and a 'dying' of the growth of spring and summer. The harvest and dying allow for seeds to germinate, and for new growth in the following spring. We can follow this same cycle by taking up our own harvest and 'dying', or releasing our attachment to what has occurred during our past year, both positive and negative. The death rites are a 'sweet goodbye' to the year that clears the way so we can proceed unencumbered to germinate the seeds within.

Participants will be writing their own eulogies, which will be read to them as they 'die'. The eulogy focuses both on what to leave behind and also what your positive legacy is. The naming of one's positive legacy brings forward these gifts to nourish the new seeds that grow within, and to nourish the generations to come.

It is important that the person dying is firmly grounded and connected to someone during the ceremony by having the leader place their hands on the shoulders of the person 'dying' as their eulogy is read. People also need to be given a choice about whether to participate or not. This can be a very powerful ritual, with subtle but real energetic shifts. In our experience, people who participated found it very meaningful.

Please, do this ritual with impeccable intent and great love. It is a deep and beautiful way to affirm the cycle of life.

Theme

The theme for this ritual is a releasing, or symbolic dying to our attachments to the events of the past year, so that we can move unencumbered into the future. This allows us to be open to whatever may arise in the present. It is a way to affirm the cycle of birth, death and rebirth that occurs annually.

Sources of Inspiration

The ritual is adapted from an Andean ceremony we knew as the Death Rites in which a participant was given an opportunity to review their past year and release, or die to, the past in order to move forward with greater ease.

Altar

- Black cloth sprinkled with glitter or sparkles
- Black direction candles
- Lots of tea lights
- Herbs, such as: sage, lavender, mugwort,
- Paper, pens
- Matches
- Lighting candle
- Snuffer
- Special candle to honor the ancestors

Additional Items for Sacred Space

- *Black candles around the room,*
- *2 thin cloths to cover heads during death rites,*
- *Chairs, 1 or 2 for death rites, depending on the size of the group*
- *Smudge*
- *Food*
- *Cups, napkins*
- *Fire pit (grill) and cover*
- *Wood, small kindling*
- *Oil*
- *Paper*

- *Matches*
- *Printed words for the chant*

Set up

The room is lit mostly by candlelight. The altar is center stage. Off to one side there is a chair with a head cloth for the death rite ritual.

If you have a larger group, a second chair and cloth will be needed. It is best if the chairs are far enough apart from each other so there is a sense of privacy for each group. We were able to use separate rooms. A breakout group size of 4-5 is good, as the reading of the eulogies needs to be done slowly and with respect.

You will also need a leader for each group, who should be trained. The leader needs to place their hands firmly on the shoulders of the participant to be sure they stay grounded.

The Fire pit is set up outside, weather permitting. Otherwise, an alcohol and Epsom salts fire can be used inside. While you are setting up, please smudge the room, the altar and the chairs to clear the space of any disharmonious energy.

Smudge

Smudging outside the room allows each person a brief clearing and centering before walking into ritual space.

Set up the smudge outside the room. You may appoint a 'smudger', but do not forget to smudge yourself as leaders first. You may use whatever feels appropriate to you. Some suggestions are: sage, paulo santo, or mugwort.

Calling the Directions

Light the candle for each direction as you read it.

Leader: Please join us at the end of each direction by saying 'Be with us on our beauty walk.

EAST

Leader: Spirits of the East, of the morning of our lives, join us as we die to the past year
that we might embrace with joy the beauty of new mornings.
Hear us as we honor our ancestors.

Group: Be with us on our beauty walk.

SOUTH

Leader: Spirits of the South, of the joys and passions of our lives, join us as we release the past years events, that we might embrace with equanimity new joys and new passions.
Hear us as we honor our ancestors.

Group: Be with us on our beauty walk.

WEST

Leader: Spirits of the West, of the sorrows and challenges of our lives, join us as we die to the past year, so that we might embrace with courage the new challenges of our lives.
Hear us as we honor our ancestors.

Group: Be with us on our beauty walk.

NORTH

Leader: Spirits of the North, of the dreams of our becoming, join us as we release the past year so that we might savor the peace and beauty of what is to come. Hear us as we honor our ancestors.

Group: Be with us on our beauty walk.

CENTER

Leader: Spirits of the Center, the center of all things that are held in the Oneness, join us as we die to the past year so that we might embrace our oneness with all of life over and over again.
Hear us as we honor our ancestors.

Group: Be with us on our beauty walk.

Ritual

Honoring the Ancestors

Leader: Our altar tonight is a sea of tea lights. We invite you to honor as many of your beloved dead as you wish by lighting a candle for each one. Please speak the name of each person you wish to honor. We invite you to share their unique gifts and positive legacy that it might be brought forward and honored. In this way their positive legacy may become a part of your own inheritance and that of your children and their children. Who would like to go first?

This was a meaningful activity in the circle and brought people closer together. You may feel the ambiance of the room shift as you celebrate the gifts of the ancestors. Please be respectful.

Leader: We light this candle to provide a cradle of loving intention for our ancestors, that they may be held with our respect and gratitude.

Death Rites, Honoring Your Past Year

Leader: For us tonight, this time following Samhain is a celebration of our own personal harvest over the past year. We will honor and release the fruits of our labors through the death rites. It is customary in some traditions to die annually to the past year as a way of honoring and then letting go of the energy and attachment to what is now over. It is similar to de-cluttering one's house, only this time it is our inner selves so that we clear out to make room for the events of the coming year. These rites can help us to greet the coming year without any preconceived ideas or expectations about what is good or bad, desired or not. When we are this open to what "shows up" in our lives, we may be pleasantly surprised, or come upon new challenges that we may approach with creativity and new thinking.

During the meditation you will be asked to review the year in its fullness, and to consider these questions about the past in whatever way works for you. Then, in silence, we will all have a chance to write our eulogy's. In a few moments you will all be guided through this process, so please not to worry about remembering.

What would you like to die to, or to wish a sweet letting go to?

How would you like to be remembered?

What is your positive legacy, your gifts, to bestow on yourself and to future generations?

Pause a moment before you continue with the instructions to see if there are any questions.

Leader: I would like to describe what the death rites look like. Each group will have a leader to guide the group through the ritual.

After writing your eulogies, we will divide into two groups. One person at a time will sit in a chair already set up, your head will be covered with a thin cloth and you will have the opportunity to die to the old year to make room for the new. The person who has your eulogy will read it out loud. The other people in your small group will hold space for you. This is like surrounding you with a loving and compassionate energy, so that you might experience this sense of letting go gently and safely. To do this, one person will place their hands on the shoulders of the person in the chair. The rest of the group will form a circle around them, their palms open and facing toward the person in the chair. If it is possible to do so comfortably, please connect the circle with touch. When you are finished you will get your eulogy back.

A demonstration is very helpful, as the directions tend to be a bit complex. You can use one of the participants to model this with you. It helps if the leaders are trained before the ritual starts. We found that 4-5 in each group was a good size for this part of the ritual.

It is important that the leader keep her hands on the shoulders of the person sitting in the chair. It is also important to keep the circle around the person dying connected by holding hands lightly. The people next to the leader can gently touch the arms of the leader. This keeps the participant and the person dying well-grounded and present in the ritual.

Leader: When all have finished this part of the ritual, you can fill the paper your eulogy is written on with sweet smelling herbs and create a healing bundle. We will finish by going outside and offering the eulogies to our sacred fire as we chant. As the sweet smoke rises upward from the fire your bundle becomes a way of releasing to Spirit the energy tied up in your past year. At the same time, it is a way of honoring and giving thanks for your gifts and positive legacy. The ritual will be done in silence except for the chant.

The chant we will use is We All Come From the Goddess. We'll pass out the words, and sing it through once so you are all familiar with it.

See the appendix for chant.

Meditation

People remain seated around the altar for the meditation and the writing of their eulogies.

Have pens, nice paper and writing boards on the altar or pass them out before the meditation. We found that having music in the background for the writing is helpful for holding the space. We then had them fold their eulogies in half and write their name on the outside

Death Rite

This part of the ritual is done in as much silence as seems appropriate. Some participants may quietly comment on their experience while sitting in the chair but it is not a time for lengthy sharing of what has happened or especially for chatting. Occasional laughter is fine and can be an honest response. Please also be cognizant of other small groups if you have more than one. Your talking may be disruptive to others.

When everyone is done with their eulogies, divide into groups, and have each group go to one of the chairs that are set up. The chairs may be in different rooms or at least far enough apart so that people are not distracted.

The anchor/leader collects the eulogies. Then she asks for a volunteer to go first and hands out that person's eulogy to be read. The reader stands to the side of the one 'dying' and the anchor stands behind the person.

The anchor asks if the person sitting is ready to begin, places the cloth over their head, and places their hands firmly on the shoulders of the person in the chair. As best as possible, everyone forms a circle around the person in the chair connecting with the anchor and reader by touch. The reader reads the eulogy of the person sitting in the chair.

When finished, the anchor gently asks the person dying if they are ready to return. If so, remove the cloth and gently invite them to open their eyes and move. We offered this ritual several times and found that some participants needed a few minutes to fully return and move to standing. Be sure that everyone has a chance to die and to read.

Herb Bundles, Fire and Chant

As each group is finished, participants may make their herb bundles and stand by the fire. The first group out starts the chant. When all are gathered, light the fire and have people one by one place their bundles into the fire. People may smudge with the smoke of the fire if they wish.

The music and words for the chant are in the appendix. It is preferable to sing all the verses repeatedly as the concept of rebirth and the annual cycle of birth-death-rebirth is clear.

The chant we used is We all come from the Goddess.

When everyone had had an opportunity to offer their herb bundle to the sacred fire, we ended the chant and returned to the altar inside.

Talking Stick

Leader: We will now pass the talking stick. Please share as you are moved. You may want to share what came up during the meditation, what nourishes you through the dark of winter, or the gifts that you may have received during the meditation. Who would like to start?

Thanking and Releasing the Directions

Snuff each candle as direction is read.

EAST

Leader: Spirits of the East, we thank you for joining us as we died and were reborn to continue on our beauty walk

SOUTH

Leader: Spirits of the South, we thank you for joining us as we died and were reborn to continue on our beauty walk

WEST

Leader: Spirits of the West, we thank you for joining us as we died and were reborn to continue on our beauty walk

NORTH

Leader: Spirits of the North, we thank you for joining us as we died and were reborn to continue on our beauty walk

CENTER

Leader: Spirits of the Center, we thank you for joining us as we died and were reborn to continue on our beauty walk of the spiral of life

Leader: Blessed Be

We would suggest having food and drink as the ritual is intense and eating and talking help to ground everyone before they drive home.

Samhein: Honoring the Ancestors and the Dead

Samhain is a time to celebrate death as a part of the life cycle. Death is a powerful and emotionally intense transition into the unknown, perhaps to a new incarnation, the next phase, or even into nothingness. Death may be a departure from our earth-walk, but may also be seen metaphorically, as in the death of an idea, or project or phase of our lives. Celebrated in the fall, it is also a time of harvest, the 'death' of the plant beings, and the preparation for a time of withdrawal and reflection leading to rebirth.

Among Celtic earth-based practices, Samhain , October 31, is a major holiday in which the veil between the worlds of the living and the dead is thin and can be crossed easily. It is a time when people offer their ancestors respect and gratitude for the positive legacy that has been left them through ceremony, special foods, and other offerings. It is also a time that they may seek advice from their ancestors concerning any troubles and problems that may be plaguing them.

In Mexico, the day of the dead, November 1 & 2, is a major holiday in which spirits of the ancestors are honored with celebrations, creating of family altars, and foods left at gravesides. Its origins date back to the Aztec culture that once flourished in Mexico. Similar celebrations are held in Spain making 'ofrendas' to the dead. In Germany, Poland, Romania and the Scandinavian countries candles are lit at the graveside. In the Philippines it is called Todos los Santos and families have lively celebrations at the gravesides of deceased relatives, often camping out there for 1-2 nights. In Nepal, Gai Jatra is a holiday to honor deceased relatives with ceremony, prayers and festivities.

Sandy and I have adapted these celebrations to create earth-based rituals that honor our ancestors in ways that speak to current times and within our culture. As we honor the positive legacies that our ancestors have left us, we bring those energies forward to feed and nurture us now and for the generations to come.

Communicating Through the Veil

Theme

This is a ritual to celebrate and communicate with our ancestors. In order to do this with impeccability we set aside, through ceremony, a sacred place and time that is clear, open and filled with respect and sincerity.

Sources of Inspiration

We were inspired by the Celtic holiday of Samhain.

Altar

- *Picture or object to represent participant's loved one*
- *Sheets of lightweight paper*
- *Pens, crayons*
- *Books or magazines to write on*
- *Black candles for the directions*
- *Matches, lighting candle, snuffer*
- *Black altar cloth*
- *Dried fruit and nuts on a serving plate*
- *Bowl of water to sprinkle*
- *Bowl of flower petals*
- *Sage stick*
- *Bowl of loose sage*
- *Singing bowl*

Additional items for Sacred Space

- *Ceremonial cauldron (grill)*
- *Wood, paper, and matches for fire outside, weather permitting.*
- *If inside, use a cauldron (metal bowl) with epsom salt and rubbing alcohol for the fire.*

Set up

The main altar is set up inside and holds the flower petals, bowls of loose sage, water and dried fruits. Weather permitting the fire is set up outside. Otherwise the Epsom salt fire is set up off to one side of the altar or on the altar if possible. The indoor fire is made with Epsom salts and isopropyl alcohol poured directly into the cauldron in about equal amounts. This is a cool fire and may not burn the paper completely, so we used a thinner paper.

Smudge

Smudge outside the room. You can use palo santo or sage stick. Appoint a smudge mistress if appropriate. When smudged, people can go into the ritual room and be seated around the altar.

Sound the Singing Bowl

Sounding the singing bowl calls people into the circle and focuses their attention

Preparing the Altar

One person reads while another sprinkled and smudged the altar.

Leader: We are preparing to meet and celebrate our ancestors. As we prepare the circle we are creating space within our circle, and within hearts, to fill with the sincerity and respect of our intent.

Sprinkle water over the altar while saying.

Leader: We offer water as cleansing and releasing, symbol of the current of life that flows through the ages. We invite the gifts of our ancestors to come forward, that these may continue to inform the waters of life for our children and for us.

Sprinkle flower petals around the altar while saying.

Leader: We offer these flower petals as symbols of the beauty of our ancestors, beauty that is still fresh and living in our circle. We invite the beauty of our ancestors to enter.

Light sage and walk around the altar while saying.

Leader: We offer sage that our invitations and intentions to honor our ancestors may be taken swiftly and sweetly to Spirit on the rising smoke.

Chime the singing bowl. This helped to define the ending of the preparations of the altar.

Calling the Directions

Light each candle before calling the direction

WEST

Leader: Goddess of the West, Goddess of Water, of evening and autumn,
Be with us today.
Flow through us with a cooling, healing quietness and bring us the gifts of our ancestors.

NORTH

Leader: Goddess of the North, Goddess of Earth, of nighttime and winter,
Be here now.
Ground us in the wisdom of the changing seasons of our lives.

EAST

Leader: Goddess of the East, Goddess of Air, of morning and springtime,
Be here today.
Inspire us with a new perspective on our story that we may view afresh our memories.

SOUTH

Leader: Goddess of the South, Goddess of Fire, of noontime and summer,
Be with us today.
Warm us with strength and energy that we may use the gifts of our ancestors to benefit us and to benefit all beings.

CENTER

Leader: Old Crone,
Be with us today.
Lend us your knowledge of the unending wheel of cycles and the ebb and flow of life.
Be here with us in our ritual.
Blessed be.

Ritual

Leader: Samhain is a time when the worlds of the living and the dead become blurred and the veil between the worlds is thin. It is the time to honor those who have crossed over before us; to celebrate their joys and strengths; to honor their struggles and acknowledge their shortcomings. It is especially open to us to call forth the goodness and beauty of their lives, to call forth their strengths and gifts, so that we might bring this energy forward into our earth walk. It is the energy of their gifts and goodness that we seek to remember in our honoring.

We invite you to place the picture or object of your loved one on the altar, naming that person, your relationship to them and the positive legacy they have given you.

You may go around the circle in order or as people are ready to share their photo and ancestor. Allow this naming to be done slowly and thoughtfully.

Chime the singing bowl when everyone has spoken.

Leader: The Celts also believed that Samhain was a time when one could speak with the ancestors to receive messages or guidance in response to a question. We will now have a meditation that will bring you to a place of comfort and peace where you may talk with or ask questions of your ancestor.

Meditation

This is read in a slow, quiet voice. The dots indicate pauses. We have used more dots to suggest a longer pause. Please pause for a length that feels right to you. We have placed the meditation on its own page at the end of the ritual for ease of use during the ritual and to decrease shuffling papers.

Fire Ritual

If the weather does not permit going outside, this ceremony may be done in the same room. In this case, the fire can be made using a mixture of alcohol and Epsom salt in a cauldron or decorated fireproof bowl

Leader: We invite you to write or draw a message of whatever you would like to say to your ancestor. You may want to express gratitude for the gifts that your ancestor has given you. To send your letters we will burn them in the cauldron, for your message will rise on the smoke to the spirit of the person. You may fold into your message a leaf or two of sage to help it go on its way sweetly and powerfully. We will go outside, keeping silent, to offer our messages.

Allow people plenty of time to write or draw their messages. When the last person is ready, file out in silence to the fire.

Light the cauldron

Leader: One by one, you may burn your letter as we all chant.

Chants with music are in the appendix

We all come from the Goddess
And to Her we shall return
Like a drop of rain
Flowing to the ocean

After all have burned their letters, lead the group inside in silence back to the circle. Chime the singing bowl to signal the ending of this part of the ritual and silence.

Talking Stick

Leader: We invite you to share what it is that you would like to keep alive about your ancestor. What memories or energies would you like to cultivate? Of all your ancestors why this one? What was special about him or her? You may choose not to speak, this too will be honored. Who would like to start?

Pass the talking stick around the circle, allowing each person to speak as needed.

Afterwards, chime the singing bowl

Feasting

Leader: We eat fruits and nuts that we might grow from the harvest of our ancestor's earth walk, and the kernels of their light may be brought forward and tended in our lives.

Pass a plate of fruit and nuts around the circle for everyone to eat in memory of their ancestor's gifts

Thanking and Releasing the Directions

Snuff each candle as you read each direction

WEST

Leader: Goddess of the West, of water, of evening and autumn,
Thank you for being with us this evening.

NORTH

Leader: Goddess of the North, of Earth, of nighttime and winter,
Thank you for being with us this evening.

EAST

Leader: Goddess of the East, of Air, of morning and springtime,
Thank you for being with us this evening.

SOUTH

Leader: Goddess of the South, of fire, of noontime and summer,
Thank you for being with us this evening.

CENTER

Leader: Old Crone,

Thank you for being with us this evening.

Blessed Be

Meditation

Communicating Through the Veil

So now, moving and adjusting as you need to... find a position of comfort as we get ready for meditation. Gradually inviting your awareness to come to your breath............... breathing in and noticing where you feel your breath.........perhaps at the nostrils..... or your chest...or belly............and then letting the breath go......again noticing any sensations as you exhale gently and slowly. And again,......breathing in.........breathing out and just noticing.........

And gradually softening as you release the day.........gently moving into a kind of compassionate awareness....for here in our circle there is no right or wrong....better or worse.........there is only an open-hearted noticing.....and gentle acceptance of however this experience unfolds for you.......knowing that you are held in the safety and love of our circle....

And so, beginning to let a place arise in your minds eye.......a place that you may meet with your ancestor......this place is a special place.... filled with a peaceful radiance.... as the images begin to become more and more clear.............you may notice colors, shapes, or perhaps clear images as they begin to unfold....It is comforting and safe here....filled with compassion and understanding...

There may also be sounds in this special meeting place....let these arise gradually and softly into your awareness......

And using all the senses....noticing now any smells or fragrances that may arise for you..... sweet scents that affirm the joy and delight of your meeting....perhaps scents or fragrances that are especially reminiscent of your ancestor.....

And sensations....as you find your place to rest and reflect.....noticing any sensations that are here for you....perhaps the surface you rest on........either cool or warm....firm or soft.......the feel of warmth from the sun or a warm fire......

As you rest....you become aware of the presence of your ancestor or loved one that you have asked to meet.....they have come to greet you with great kindness and compassion in their hearts, for they have crossed over and have gained an awareness and perspective that we do not have ......

And so they come forward to meet you.....let yourself notice how this unfolds for you... with images...scents....sounds.....or perhaps a deep knowing of their presence.....

Pause.

You are free to embrace them as you are comfortable.....and as you are ready you may speak to them....taking a moment....moving at your own pace.....letting them know that you have come to honor them tonight...their earthwalk.....their strengths and gifts...... You are seeking to gather these gifts in your honoring so that they might continue to inform both you and those who will follow....your children and their children and so on....thus enriching all who walk on the earth.....

As you reflect on their earthwalk.....they share with you pieces of their story......in symbols, scents or thoughts.....you may gather these pieces....gathering the gifts of their wisdom....their insights.....listen with your inner knowing and hearing and vision..... and honor their story.....offer respect for the wisdom that they share...and gratitude for the gifts and positive qualities that you will bring more fully into your earthwalk......

Pause.

And you may also ask for their advice or guidance around a specific question or problem......or you may ask if they have a message or gift for you that they would like you to share........

Pause.

And now it is time to depart....you may share any last thoughts and messages....saying your goodbyes....letting them know that they will soon receive your gratitude and thoughts on the wings of the sage smoke......

And so returning.....gradually bringing your awareness to your breath....inviting a deep breath that fills the belly and chest.....and a slow, conscious releasing of your breath.... noticing now how it feels as you are sitting in your chair....noticing any prompting from your body to stretch and move....and doing so with enjoyment and pleasure.....Each movement.....each breath bringing you steadily and gently to our circle....becoming aware of the scents and sounds here in our circle.....

And gradually opening your eyes as you are ready......taking one last deep breath and returning to the present moment in our circle.

Feast of the Dead

Theme

This ritual is a feast to share with those who have passed on who we wish to remember and honor. It is an opportunity to bring forward their positive legacy so that we and future generations might benefit from their gifts.

Sources of Inspiration

A dumb supper is a traditional Celtic meal eaten in silence with the departed dead at the table. We included the writing of a eulogy to be planted with a spring bulb as a way of enhancing the idea of legacy and cycles. This was a very deep and meaningful ritual for all participants, and we repeated it with slight variations for several Samhain celebrations.

Altar

- *Cheese and cracker plate*
- *Crock-pot or tureen of squash soup*
- *Soup bowls*
- *Rolls and butter*
- *Halloween cookies*
- *Cider*
- *Water*
- *Seasonal decorations*
- *Candles for directions, black is commonly used*
- *Candle at place setting for ancestor*
- *Matches*
- *Snuffer*
- *Lighting candle*
- *Singing bowl*

Additional Items for Sacred Space

- *Decorate room as desired*
- *Bulbs in a bowl*
- *Spade*
- *Stationary and pens*

Set Up

The dining table is the altar for this ritual. We set two places for each participant, one for the participant and one for their honored dead. A candle is set at each ancestor's place. Directional candles are set in the middle of the table around the center candle. Black candles may be used. As the leaders, we served the food to the participants and to their honored dead. Have fun decorating and setting the table as if for a banquet.

Before the group arrives, find a place outside that feels peaceful. We used a flowerbed. You may prepare a space for burying the eulogies and bulbs ahead of time or have the participants dig their own space as a part of the ritual. Since the eulogies are buried, we used a lighter weight stationary that would fold and easily biodegrade. After the participants place their eulogy and bulb in the ground, they will cover it with earth themselves. To enhance the feeling of reverence and respect for the ancestors we had the participants come up to bury their eulogy one by one and in silence.

Smudge

Smudging outside the room allows each person a brief clearing and centering before walking into ritual space.

Set up the smudge outside the room. You may appoint a 'smudger', but do not forget to smudge yourself as leaders first. You may use whatever feels appropriate to you. Some suggestions are: sage, paulo santo, or mugwort.

Calling the Directions

Light each candle before calling the direction.

EAST

Leader: Spirits of the East, of the beginnings and sunrises of our lives, join us as we honor our ancestors.

SOUTH

Leader: Spirits of the South, of the warm and sunny days of our lives, join us as we honor our ancestors.

WEST

Leader: Spirits of the West, of the evenings and sunsets of our lives, join us as we honor our ancestors.

NORTH

Leader: Spirits of the North, of the endings and nights of our lives, join us as we honor our ancestors.

CENTER

Leader: Spirits of the Center, of the cycle of our lives, join us as we honor our ancestors.

Ritual

Leader: A Dumb Supper is a feast to share with those who have crossed over that we wish to remember. A plate is set to your right so that you may share food with your honored guest. We will eat the meal in complete silence as a sign of respect. In our process this evening, we will be writing a eulogy to honor the positive legacy of the ancestor we each are remembering. As we call forth their lives and name their positive legacy, we bring forward their strengths and gifts for ourselves and for generations to come. At the same time we are offering the dead an opportunity to send their strengths forward in time to benefit those they love. This is a deep honoring.

We encourage you to use this time of silence for reflecting and communing with your guest who has come to join you. How would they like to be remembered? How would you like to remember them? What are the qualities and gifts that this person has to pass on to you and the coming generations?

When the meal is over we will write and read a eulogy for our beloved guests telling what we have learned and thought about during the supper. Then we will go outside and offer our eulogy and a spring bulb to Mother Earth.

Before we begin our meal, we will go around the table and you may light the candle set at the place of the your ancestor and name the one you want to remember. Please describe your relation to them. When everyone has named their ancestor, we will ring the bowl and move into our time of silence. Who would like to go first?

Allow time for people to introduce their ancestor and speak a few words about them if desired.

Leader: Now that everyone has introduced their ancestor we will ring the bowl and move into our time of silence.

Ring the singing bowl.

What worked for us was one leader served the soup and another one carried the soup to each person and ancestor. That way no soup was spilled passing from one person to another. The other foods were passed around the table. After the meal, paper and writing materials were handed out so that people could write their eulogies. Give a lot of time for this exercise because the participants may need a lot of time to contemplate their ancestor.

When everyone had stopped writing we started the sharing time by ringing the bowl.

Leader: Who would like to share their eulogy?

If they seem reluctant, one of the leaders can start. After all who want to have shared their eulogy,we rang the singing bowl to signify a time of silence.

Leader: We will move into a time of silence for the offering of the eulogies to Mother Earth. Please take a moment and fold them in preparation for offering them.

Hold up the bowl of bulbs and a eulogy and say.

Leader: So that the goodness of their lives will grow in ours, we will go outside and offer the eulogies, the gifts of our ancestors, to Mother Earth.

We went outside with the bowl of spring bulbs, gathering around the chosen spot that had holes prepared in advance for planting the bulbs and eulogies.

Leader: Each person may come forward one by one and place their eulogy in the earth and cover it with a little dirt so that there is room for the bulbs to be planted with your eulogy.

You may pass the trowel if people need to use it to cover the eulogy with earth. When everyone was done offer the blessing of the eulogies

Leader: We offer these eulogies to Mother Earth, from whom we come and to whom we will return. May she receive them into her heart. May they grow and flourish also within our hearts.

Pass the bowl of bulbs.

Leader: I invite you to plant a bulb over your eulogy to encourage the growth and blossoming of your ancestor's positive legacy.

After all the bulbs were planted we blessed the bulbs.

Leader: As loving kindness and integrity manifested in our ancestors' lives, may it flourish and grow in our lives.

Return inside for the Talking Stick

Talking Stick

Leader: We will now pass the talking stick. Please share as you are moved. You may want to share what came up during the meditation, what nourishes you through the dark of winter, or the gifts that you may have received during the meditation. Who would like to start?

Thanking and Releasing the Directions

Snuff each candle as the direction is read.

EAST

Leader: Spirits of the East, of the beginnings and sunrises of our lives, thank you for joining us.

SOUTH

Leader: Spirits of the South, of the warm and sunny days of our lives, thank you for joining us.

WEST

Leader: Spirits of the West, of the evenings and sunsets of our lives, thank you for joining us.

NORTH

Leader: Spirits of the North, of the endings and nights of our lives, thank you for joining us.

CENTER

Leader: Spirits of the Center, of the cycle of our lives, thank you for joining us.

Honoring the Gifts of our Ancestors

Theme

The theme of this ritual is to honor the gifts of the ancestors on this night of Samhain, when the veil between the living and the dead is thin.

Sources of Inspiration

Our inspiration for this ritual was the traditional Celtic dumb supper. We included within it the Jewish tradition of eating cakes drizzled with honey to express the sweetness of life and of our honored dead.

Altar

- *Black altar cloth*
- *Many candles, tea lights or votives work well.*
- *Pumpkins, skeletons or seasonal decorations*
- *Honey or pumpkin cakes or other loaf cake cut into individual servings. You may drizzle them with honey if you like.*
- *Candles for the directions*
- *Matches*
- *Lighter candle*
- *Snuffer*
- *Bowl of lavender*
- *Bowl of sage*
- *Pencils, crayons and paper for writing or drawing*
- *Tibetan singing bowl or bells*

Death Altar

- *Black altar cloth*
- *Many unlit candles*
- *One lit candle*
- *Fall foods in small plates as desired,*

  We had apples and other seasonal fruits cut in slices and nuts
- *One place setting for the ancestor:*

  One chair, a plate, silverware, napkin, wine glass with flowers in it, and a lit white candle

Additional items for Sacred Space

- *Dark cloths*
- *Black candles*
- *Fall flowers like mums*
- *Crepe paper streamers for the door*
- *Do Not Enter signs*

Set up

This ritual has two altars, one for the gathering and one for the ancestors. Because the two altars were placed a distance apart, enough that participants would get up and walk to the altar of the ancestors, we went to extra measures to decorate all the surfaces in the room with dark cloths and black candles. The doorway was hung with black crepe paper streamers. We asked that people gather and enter as a group to dramatize the effect.

Calling the Directions

Light each candle as that direction is read

EAST

Leader: Hail to the East, to the powers of Air.
Samhain calls the winds of change,
And so tonight we celebrate.
So May It Be.

SOUTH

Leader: Hail to the South, powers of Fire.
Ignite the dark and warm our hearts
As we approach our ancestors.
So May It Be.

WEST

Leader: Hail to the West, powers of Water.
Wash us in the waters of Life
And Bless our ancestors.
So May It Be.

NORTH

Leader: Hail to the North, powers of Earth.
Guard the seeds of growth
So that we may be guided by the wisdom of our ancestors
So May It Be.

CENTER

Leader: I call the Goddess, Queen of the Night,
Who brings forth and nurtures life,
She of wisdom and mystery.
Be with us now and touch the sacred within us all.
Blessed Be.

Reading

We read and repeated one line at a time.

Leader: Please repeat after me:

I will love and harm none
I will live, love, die, and live again
I will meet, remember, know and embrace love once more
For the free will of all
And with harm to none
As I do will it, it is now done
So May It Be.

By Lady Bridget and Lady Terese, 1996

Allow a short pause before starting the explanation to clearly mark the shift in content and action.

Ritual

Leader: On this eve of Samhain we have come to honor those who have passed beyond the veil. The veil between the worlds is thin and this is the time to honor the dead and to commune with them. A dumb supper is a traditional Celtic ritual celebrated on Samhain eve and is a meal that is served and eaten in silence as a remembering of the ancestors. Tonight we will follow this traditional practice.

We are sitting around the Altar of the Living. On the other side of the room is the Altar of the Dead which is a feast table set with one place setting for your ancestor and one place for you.

Before visiting the Altar of the dead we will have a period of silent reflection on your ancestor and their legacy. The process of honoring is enhanced greatly by drawing or creating some representation of the positive legacy that this ancestor has left to you. You may take your drawing or writing up to the Altar of the Dead when you go to feast and share it with the dead person you are honoring. You may also partake of the foods and share some with your ancestor by placing the food on the plate while you are there.

Pause to allow a shift in activity.

I invite you now to sit in silence to reflect and write about your ancestor. Ask yourself what gifts or qualities do you admire in this ancestor? What about their life inspires you, nourishes you, or guides you in your life here and now?

When you are ready, you may go to the Altar of the Dead, light a candle for your ancestor and share your reflections and some food. As you honor your ancestor you are also acknowledging that these qualities are part of your inheritance. We will sit in silence while each one takes a turn at the Altar of the Dead. When all are finished, and have returned to the Altar of the Living, we will chime the Tibetan bowl.

Hand out writing materials. If your circle is large, you may want to let people go to the Altar of the Dead in two's or threes. The places can be set accordingly. The intent here is not to have the altar too crowded, so that each person has the space they need for their inner work.

Honey Cakes

After everyone has returned to the circle and the Tibetan bowl has been sounded and your sense of the moment is complete, stand and hold up the plate of cakes ceremoniously as you say the following words. Then pass the plate so that all may partake.

Leader: These honey cakes symbolize the sweetness of the cycle of life, both the living and the dying, that we each must encounter and that we each must do.

Talking Stick

Leader: Now we will pass the talking stick. We invite you to share with the group the ancestor you are remembering and their positive legacy or gifts. As you do this, you may take a bit of one of the herbs on the table. Rub them between your hands over the altar to release their essence. You may choose sage, for carrying your honoring quickly to Spirit. Or you may choose Lavender, for honoring the sweet memories.

Thanking and Releasing the Directions

Snuff each candle as you read each direction

EAST

Leader: Powers of the East.
We thank you for joining our Samhain celebration tonight.

SOUTH

Leader: Powers of the South.
We thank you for joining our Samhain celebration tonight.

WEST

Leader: Powers of the West.
We thank you for joining our Samhain celebration.

NORTH

Leader: Powers of the North.
We thank you for joining our Samhain celebration.

CENTER

Leader: Lord of the Shadows.
We thank you for being here this evening, for awakening the light of the sacred that resides in each of us.
Queen of the Night.
We thank you for being here this evening, for nourishing the light of the sacred that resides within each of us.

Blessed Be

You may close with the chant.
Music is in the appendix.

Leader: Stand and join hands,

May the Circle Be Open

But Unbroken

May the love of the Goddess

Be ever in your heart.

Merry meet

And merry part

And merry meet again.

Transitions and Rites of Passage

These are a group of rituals that are important rites of passage as we progress around the wheel of life from birth, the first rite of passage, to death, the last rite of passage. Rites of passage mark big transitions in our lives, ones that change our perspective, our status or our situation. There are elaborate ceremonies around the world in all cultures for Marriage, Birth, Death, and Coming of Age. In some cultures, as here in the US, some rites of passage such as menarche are not celebrated at all.

As pagans with a practice in earth based rituals, we have developed rituals for both birthdays and croning. The birthday ceremonies we have included here were ones that the individual felt marked a new beginning in her life, or were significant markers in age, as in Sandy's and Jean's birthday rituals. Sandy turned 70 and Jean turned 90.

Our group felt that croning, or the passage from menstruation, through menopause to post-menapause was a significant passage for all of us. It is the transitioning into the wisdom of the elders, the final phase of a woman's life that is rich and full and fertile in aspects that would have been previously unreachable. This is definitely worthy of celebration and proved to be an important and meaningful 'rite of passage' for all of us. This was especially true as we live in a culture that tends not to honor the wisdom, vitality and contributions of its elders.

Birthday Ritual for Jean's 90th

Note:

This was an especially fun and meaningful ritual for all involved. Jean loved the Memory Book and found the review of the decades of her life very moving. However, gathering the pages for the memory book ahead of time was necessary, but challenging. It required clear instructions for the size and format of each page and the date that the page was due so that the book was ready in time for the ritual.

The birthday rituals may be done in a circle that meets regularly or the birthday person may wish to have a private ritual with her own invitation list.

This ritual is suitable for any age, but we think this ritual is best suited for people over 50.

Theme

This is a birthday ritual to celebrate the decades of a life well lived.

Sources of Inspiration

Our sources were discussions among women we knew concerning the importance of decade changes in a woman's life.

Altar

- *Sparkling altar cloth*
- *Direction candles*
- *Snuffer*
- *Lighting candle*
- *Amethyst stone*
- *Wine glasses*
- *Wine- red and white, and sparkling water*
- *Pens*
- *Basket of paper petals*

- *Bowl of verses of poem*
- *Memory book*

Set Up

Ahead of time, each member of the group created a page to contribute to a memory book. The page could be a tribute, poem, memory, picture or lesson learned from Jean. They then sent this to the person in charge of compiling the book. The first page was reserved for the flower petal ritual page. That page had a small picture of Jean in the middle. The decade petals forming the flower were added during the ritual.

The feast of celebration was set up on another table. Bring whatever you want.

Calling the Directions

Light each candle as you read the direction

EAST

Leader: Leader:
Spirit of the East,
Be here with us.
Bless us with the beauty of new beginnings and clear vision in our lives.

SOUTH

Leader: Spirit of the South,
Be here with us.
Bless us all with the gifts of growth, passion and right action to propel and sustain us on our journeys.

WEST

Leader: Spirit of the West,
Be here with us.
Bless us with the gifts of gratitude and delight for the fruits of our labor.

NORTH

Leader: Spirit of the North,
Be here with us.
Bless us with the gift of your stillness, that we might know a deep inner peace.

CENTER

Leader: Great Goddess,
Be here with us.
Bless us with your wisdom and knowing that comes only with years and experience.

Ritual

Flower petal ritual

Leader: We will do a flower petal ritual to honor the decades of Jean's life.

Jean, we will ask you to look back on the decades of your life and share with us a memory or highpoint of each decade. We will go decade by decade, and after each one we will have a toast.

Everyone please pick a decade petal as the basket comes around. The person with the specified decade will write Jean's memories in a few words onto only one side of the petal because we will paste the petals in the book. As we pass around the petals, we also invite you to fill your glass with the wine on the altar.

Pass around the basket of petals and pens. Each petal was marked with a decade. As Jean spoke, the person with that decade petal wrote down a word or phrase that represented Jeans' memories. After the toast the writer handed the petal to the person in charge of the memory book. As leaders we guided the talking about each decade.

Leader: We start with the first decade of your life. Please share some of your memories of the first ten years of your life.

Jean talks about her memories while someone scribes on the petal.

Leader: Who has the first decade petal?
Will you please read what is on the petal?

Toast

Leader: We toast to the richness and uniqueness of your memories of this decade.

Everyone toasts and drinks.

Leader: Now we will go through the second decade. Jean please share some of your years from 11 to 20 years old.

Repeat this process through all the decades with the honored person speaking, the scribe reading the key ideas of that decade and ending with a toast. This was a really meaningful part of the ritual not only for the birthday person but also for the group. We took our time through this process as it needs to be savored sweetly.

Reading

We cut up the poem by stanza and passed it around, so that each person had a verse to read. We read it in random order.

Imagine a Woman *by Patricia Lynn Reilly*

Imagine a woman who believes it is right and good she is a woman.
A woman who honors her experience and tells her stories.
Who refuses to carry the sins of others within her body and life.

Imagine a woman who believes she is good.
A woman who trusts and respects herself.
Who listens to her needs and desires, and meets them with tenderness and grace.

Imagine a woman who has acknowledged the past's influence on the present.
A woman who has walked through her past.
Who has healed into the present.

Imagine a woman who authors her own life.
A woman who exerts, initiates, and moves on her own behalf.
Who refuses to surrender except to her truest self and to her wisest voice.

Imagine a woman who names her own gods.
A woman who imagines the divine in her image and likeness.
Who designs her own spirituality and allows it to inform her daily life.

Imagine a woman in love with her own body.
A woman who believes her body is enough, just as it is.
Who celebrates her body and its rhythms and cycles as an exquisite resource.

Imagine a woman who honors the face of the Goddess in her changing face.
A woman who celebrates the accumulation of her years and her wisdom.
Who refuses to use precious energy disguising the changes in her body and life.

Imagine a woman who values the women in her life.
A woman who sits in circles of women.
Who is reminded of the truth about herself when she forgets.

Gift Giving

Leader: Tonight we celebrate and honor Jean who symbolizes feminine wisdom. She has lived for nine decades and has grown in beauty and wisdom through all the years of her life. We gift Jean with the blessings of our circle. We will pass this beautiful amethyst around the circle so that each one may speak her blessing and blow it into the amethyst.

Everyone gave a one or two word blessing of a quality, such as joy, inner peace, etc. that they would like to bestow upon the honored guest. They spoke the gift and then blew it on to the amethyst to energize it. It was helpful for the leader to start this, to model it for the others.

Leader: We gift you with this amethyst filled with our blessings and gifts. And we present to you this memory book with its decades of your memories and our memories of our time together.

Talking Stick

Leader: We will now pass the talking stick. Please share as you are moved. You may want to share something that came up during the ritual or whatever else is in your heart or on your mind. What is said here stays here in circle. It is all right to pass. Who would like to start?

Thanking and Releasing the Directions

Snuff each candle as you read the direction.

EAST

Leader: Spirit of the East, we bid you farewell.
Thank you for joining us here tonight as we honor Jean.

SOUTH

Leader: Spirit of the South, we bid you farewell.
Thank you for joining us here tonight as we honor Jean.

WEST

Leader: Spirit of the West, we bid you farewell.
Thank you for joining us here tonight as we honor Jean.

NORTH

Leader: Spirit of Earth, we bid you farewell.
Thank you for joining us here tonight as we honor Jean.

CENTER

Leader: Spirit of the Center, Spirit of the Great Goddess, we bid you farewell.
Thank you for joining us here tonight as we honor Jean.

Birthday Ritual for New Beginnings

Note

We did this ritual for Deborah. We left her name in the ritual as it is easier to read. However, it is obvious that you can change the name to fit your celebration.

Theme

This is a birthday ritual especially suitable for someone setting out in new directions.

Sources of Inspiration

The symbolic and ceremonial use of fire to carry messages up to Spirit and as a cleansing or clearing ritual is as old as time.

Altar

- *Colorful altar cloth*
- *Direction candles*
- *Matches*
- *Snuffer*
- *Geode*
- *Cauldron with fire in middle the of the altar*

Additional items for Sacred Space

- *Epsom salts and alcohol for the fire in the cauldron*
- *Birthday cake and other goodies*
- *A bowl holding folded papers of what the birthday person no longer needs in her life*

We had asked the birthday person to write on slips of paper what she no longer needed in her life. There was one thing written on each slip of paper. These were for burning in the cauldron in a ceremony of releasing.

Calling the Directions

Light each candle as you read the direction

EAST

Leader: We call upon the Goddess of the East to blow away all that we no longer need and to open our hearts and minds to possibility.

SOUTH:

Leader: We call upon the Goddess of the South to burn brightly in our hearts with passion for what will be new in the year to come.

WEST:

Leader: We call upon the Goddess of the West to refresh us with the life-giving waters of the earth and heavens.

NORTH:

Leader: We call upon the Goddess of the North to keep us grounded in faith and hope and to give us strength to face the future.

CENTER:

Leader: We call upon the Great Goddess to help us attain balance in all things and to keep us aware of the light of the sun and the moon that blesses us each day and night.

Ritual

Fire Ritual

Leader: Deborah has written out that which she no longer needs in her life. She will speak them out loud and burn them in the cauldron of the Goddess for releasing.

Deborah read each one, one at a time and tossed it into the cauldron. Occasionally lavender or white sage was added to the cauldron to sweeten the request to Spirit for release.

Smudging

Leader: We will smudge Deborah so that in her 50th year she may walk her path, cleansed and pure, with happiness and joy in life. Then we will walk around the circle and smudge any one who wishes it.

You may use whatever feels appropriate to you to smudge with. Some suggestions are: sage or paulo santo. Please be cognizant of smoke alarms. We opened a window or door to allow for ventilation.

Gift Giving

Circle of Blessings

Leader: We will pass this geode that has within it hidden beauty now revealed. Each person may hold it while speaking a one or two word blessing or gift for Deborah. In this way the blessings are then held in the beauty of the geode.

We passed the geode around the circle with the leaders speaking first to model how the blessings were done.

Leader: Deborah, we present you with this geode filled with blessings and gifts. When you hold this in your hands at any time, it will help revive your spirit. Tonight we will transmit these blessings in a traditional manner.

We wrapped the geode in a beautiful cloth and sent those blessings into Deborah. This can be done by tapping the head gently with the wrapped geode and then rubbing it down each arm, the trunk and each leg. We preferred to have the person turn and did the same on the back.

Leader: Happy Birthday! We will now close the circle and celebrate with birthday cake and goodies.

Thanking and Releasing the Directions

Snuff each candle as you read the direction

EAST

Leader: We thank the Goddess of the East for gently opening our hearts and minds to possibility.

SOUTH

Leader: We thank the Goddess of the South for her pure flames that fill our hearts and minds with passion for new ways of looking at life.

WEST

Leader: We thank the Goddess of the West for her life-giving waters that help to heal us.

NORTH

Leader: We thank the Goddess of the North for her strength and spirit which helps us to face the future.

CENTER

Leader: We thank the Great Goddess for helping us walk the spiral of life with balance and blessings.

And now Celebrate!

Birthday Blessings

Note

We did this ritual as a birthday party. Participants were invited to come. It was well received by everyone. People who knew each other and those who were new seemed to mix easily and all contributed without difficulty.

Theme

The theme of this ritual is to celebrate the birthday of a friend and the richness, events and joys of her journey to this point.

Sources of Inspiration

This birthday was in the spring so we used flowers and the flower petals to hold the wishes and gifts of the participants. You might also consider something seasonal, such as colorful leaves in the fall or paper snowflakes in the winter.

Altar

- *Altar cloth, color appropriate for the season*
- *Direction candles*
- *Flower petals*
- *A small bowl for the birthday person to keep*
- *Blank decorative cards for writing gifts and blessings*
- *Three candles for the birthday person to light*
- *Birthday cake and refreshments*
- *A vase of flowers with enough for everyone to take one at the end of the ceremony*

Set Up

The altar is decorated with many colored flower petals. Be generous, as these petals are what the guests will use for the ceremony of the flower petals. The direction candles may be placed around the center so that people will not be reaching over the candles to pick up the petals. The birthday cake may be placed on the altar, used as the center, or placed on another side table with the rest of the refreshments.

Calling the Directions

Light each candle while reading the direction

SOUTH

Leader: Spirits of the South, be here with us as we celebrate the birth of our sister ________, _____ years ago.
Warm us, keep the fire of passion and creativity burning in us all, that we might continue to meet the challenges of our lives and grow.
Empower us.

WEST

Leader: Spirits of the West, be here with us as we honor ____________'s earthwalk over these years, the healing she has done and also offered others.
Bathe us in your sparkling, clear waters, refreshing us and reminding us of the fluidity of life.

NORTH

Leader: Spirits of the North, be here with us as we acknowledge the success of our sister ___________'s past accomplishments, the joy of skills learned.
Hold us gently in the quiet of reflection and introspection.

EAST

Leader: Spirits of the East, be here with us as we gather to rejoice with __________ in the lightness of being that comes with age and experience.
Show us the possibilities held in sunrises.

CENTER

Leader: Spirits of the Center, be here with us as we celebrate and give thanks for the richness of our lives, tasting the abundance of experience and embracing its rhythms and wholeness. Surround us with your light and wisdom.

Ritual

Lighting the three candles

The birthday person lights two candles to honor her life and relationships through the years. Using a thin decorated candle for lighting is advisable. She may light this from the direction candle closest to her

Birthday Person:

I light this candle to honor and celebrate the many events and memories, teachings and growth that have filled my life with joy, happiness and awe over the past _____ years.

Light candle after reading

Birthday Person:

I light this candle to give thanks for all the many relationships, mentors and everyday angels who have helped me along my path over the last _____ years,

Light candle after reading

Leader: And I light this candle to the joy of being ___________(age).

Birthday person's reading

This is an opportunity for the birthday person to share some aspect of her life or herself. She may choose a favorite poem or reading or a short slide show or write something herself.

Ceremony of the petals

Leader: And now I invite you to come up, one at a time, pick some petals from the altar and offer a wish, memory, blessing of celebration and joy for __________. After you have spoken your gift, blow it onto the petals and place it into the bowl.
It can be anything you wish, such as "I remember ___________"(event or saying).
or "I gift __________ with much joy and laughter in the coming years".

It is helpful if the leader goes first to model this for those who may be anxious about what to do. Doing this at a relaxed pace, allows the birthday person time to savor the moments. When everyone has spoken, the leader picks up the bowl and holds it.

Leader: This is your container of great joy and celebration----filled with the blessings of friends, and the abundance of ___ years. Keep it with you. Return to your bowl of petals whenever you need to be reminded of the joy and abundance that surrounds you and fills your life. Offer its contents freely and often to spirit in gratitude and thanks.

Hand the bowl to the birthday person

Leader: I will pass this bowl of flowers around so that each person can take a flower home as a remembrance of this party. You may scatter the petals out in nature when you feel like acknowledging the beauty that surrounds you.

Releasing the Directions

Snuff each candle as you say:

SOUTH

Leader: Spirits of the South, we thank you for being here

WEST

Leader: Spirits of the West, we thank you for being here.

NORTH

Leader: Spirits of the North, we thank you for being here.

EAST

Leader: Spirits of the East, we thank you for being here.

CENTER

Leader: Spirits of the Center, we thank you for being here.

Celebrate with the cake and refreshments.

Croning the New Crone

Theme

This is a rite of passage ritual to honor the newly arrived crone, who, for us, has stopped getting her menses for at least a year.

Sources of Inspiration

We were inspired by the Croning Ritual offered by Joanna Fink and others at the Unitarian Church in Lincoln, Nebraska.

Altar

- *Candles at the five directions*
- *Three special candles, one red, one white and one black*
- *A woven circle head wreath – Crown of Blessings*

  Weave a circle of whatever material appeals to you, such as ribbons, yarn, or suitable plant life in a size for the new crone to wear on her head during the blessing part of the ritual.

- *Bowl of ribbons cut 1½ feet long in various colors*
- *Matches*
- *Snuffer*
- *Ashtray*
- *Whatever decorations appeal to you*

Set Up

One of the chairs set in the circle around the altar may be decorated to be the throne for the new crone.

Smudge

Smudging outside the room allows each person a brief clearing and centering before walking into ritual space.

Set up the smudge outside the room. You may appoint a 'smudger', but do not forget to smudge yourself as leaders first. You may use whatever feels appropriate to you. Some suggestions are: sage, paulo santo, or mugwort.

Calling the Directions

Light each candle as you read the direction

EAST

Leader: Spirits of the East, of Air, the home of beginnings for all, maiden, mother, and crone.
Be here with us.
Bless us all with sweet Beginnings filled with the promise of growth, beauty and wisdom in all the phases of our lives.

SOUTH

Leader: Spirits of the South, of Fire, the home of passion and warmth.
Be here with us.
Bless us all with the gift of continued growth, filled with passion and right action to propel and sustain us on our journeys.

WEST

Leader: Spirits of the West, of Water, home of healing waters, forgiveness and maturity.
Be here with us.
Bless us all with joy and gratitude for the fruits of our labor and the generosity of your gifts.
May we be guided and nourished with these blessings.

NORTH

Leader: Spirits of the North, of Earth, the home of stillness and introspection, knowledge and insight.
Be here with us.
Bless us with the gift of your stillness and knowing, that we might live in harmony with all our relations and within our own being.

CENTER

Leader: Spirits of the Center, Triple Goddess, Maiden, Mother, Crone.
Be here with us for this ritual of transition.
Bless us all with your wisdom, your perspective and knowing that come only with years and experience.
May we listen carefully, openly and with great love in our hearts.

Ritual

Leader: What is a Crone?

She is the beauty of the dark moon and the dark earth beneath your feet. She is repose in the evening of your life. She is weathered by time. She is midwife to the dying, the promise of transition and rebirth. All acts of birthing and dying are her rituals.

She is the darkness you fear and welcome. She is the freedom to express your essence. She is the courage to cast aside the opinions of others as you live life in tune with your own truth.

She is the energy of the old, the knowledge of when to end, of when to cut the cord. She was with you at your birthing and will be with you to ease the transition of your dying.

Leader: We light the candles to honor the three phases of woman, the triple Goddess.
We light the white candle for the maiden.

The new crone lights the white candle.

Leader: We light the red candle for the mother.

The new crone lights the red candle.

Leader: We light the black candle for the crone.

The new crone lights the black candle.

Leader: Tonight we celebrate and honor the Crone, the final and the most sacred age of the Triple Goddess. It is She who is the keeper of wisdom, of the knowing that comes only with age and experience. This ritual of passage honors us as wise women.

Crown of Affirmations

The new crone may wear this crown or hold it, so that the group can come up one at a time and weave in a ribbon as each one blesses her. Place the crown on the new crone's head and say:

Leader: I give you this crown. It is the symbol of the life process. We will weave the ribbons of our blessings into your crown of emerging and celebration.

Please come up individually and tie a ribbon onto the crown. As you tie the ribbon speak your blessing. For example: "I give you this ribbon that symbolizes strength" and, then you may weave it into the crown.

We think it is helpful for the leader(s) to model the speaking and tying of the first ribbon.

Gift Giving

Leader: This gift is a symbol of your maturing and becoming as you transition into the role of crone. This gift holds the richness and the promise of the years to come as well as the memories and teachings of the years past.

The gift should suit the crone. We like to give an amethyst or semi-precious stone that the person will treasure, but a statue, some ritual object or art object is fine.

Reading

Imagine a Woman *by Patricia Lynn Reilly*

Imagine a woman who believes it is right and good she is a woman.
A woman who honors her experience and tells her stories.
Who refuses to carry the sins of others within her body and life.

Imagine a woman who believes she is good.
A woman who trusts and respects herself.
Who listens to her needs and desires, and meets them with tenderness and grace.

Imagine a woman who has acknowledged the past's influence on the present.
A woman who has walked through her past.
Who has healed into the present.

Imagine a woman who authors her own life.

A woman who exerts, initiates, and moves on her own behalf.
Who refuses to surrender except to her truest self and to her wisest voice.

Imagine a woman who names her own gods.
A woman who imagines the divine in her image and likeness.
Who designs her own spirituality and allows it to inform her daily life.

Imagine a woman in love with her own body.
A woman who believes her body is enough, just as it is.
Who celebrates her body and its rhythms and cycles as an exquisite resource.

Imagine a woman who honors the face of the Goddess in her changing face.
A woman who celebrates the accumulation of her years and her wisdom.
Who refuses to use precious energy disguising the changes in her body and life.

Imagine a woman who values the women in her life.
A woman who sits in circles of women.
Who is reminded of the truth about herself when she forgets.

Each section of the reading is given to a different person to read to the new crone. We numbered each section so that they could be read in order

Leader: (Name),....Imagine yourself as this woman, ever-growing, ever-changing and ever-emerging crone. You have been Maiden; you have been Mother; and now you are Crone. You are beautiful and you are strong.

Talking Stick

Leader: We will now pass the talking stick. Please share as you are moved. You may want to share something that came up during the ritual or whatever else is in your heart or on your mind. What is said here stays here in circle. It is all right to pass. Who would like to start?

Thanking and Releasing the Directions

Snuff each candle as you read the direction

EAST

Leader: Spirits of the East, of Air, we thank you for blessing us with the promise of growth, beauty and wisdom in all the phases of our lives.
Go in Peace.

SOUTH

Leader: Spirits of the South, of Fire, we thank you for blessing us with the gift of passion and right action to propel and sustain us on our journeys.
Go in Peace

WEST

Leader: Spirits of the West, of Water, we thank you for blessing us with joy and gratitude for the fruits of our labor and for your generosity.
Go in Peace

NORTH

Leader: Spirits of the North, of Earth, we thank you for blessing us with the gift of your stillness and knowing, that we might live in harmony with all our relations.
Go in Peace

CENTER

Leader: Triple Goddess, we thank you for blessing us with your wisdom, your perspective and knowing that come only with years and experience.
Go in Peace

Walking the Wheel of Life: Maiden, Mother, Crone

Note

Cronings are some of our favorite rituals as they are a concrete way in which to acknowledge and celebrate the phases of a woman's life, from maiden, to mother, and this transition, to crone and crone wisdom. It is a way to meaningfully and powerfully acknowledge the richness and potential of the last third of a woman's life. Our group usually established this transition to be at the end of menstruation, or anytime after as the woman wishes.

This ritual can be done for one or two women but we think it might be too cumbersome for more than that number. We did it originally for two, and have written it up this way for you to see what it was like, but the ritual could easily be adapted for one person. One word of caution: be aware of the length of the ritual as you go through with two crones, and structure it in ways that will keep the movement around the circle flowing.

Another suggestion concerns the poem at the end. Depending on the length of the ritual you may want to omit the responsive reading. You can gauge the reaction of your audience as you go. Hand the words out at the end if you decide to read it.

Theme

The theme of the croning ritual is to honor the transition from mother into crone and crone wisdom. We offer the new crone a chance to review her life in decades, honoring each one, as she transitions into this most wonderful and powerful of stages.

Sources of Inspiration

Most of us are familiar with the idea of seeing our lives in terms of decades, and speak often of what we did in our 20's or 30's. At the time of this ritual writing there was also quite a bit of literature available on the importance of decade changes. So we developed this natural tendency into a ritual where we could look consciously and deeply at the meaning and gifts of each decade of our lives.

Altar

- *Chairs in each direction reserved for the crones, each crone would have 4 chairs*
- *Five direction candles*
- *Pebbles*
- *Flower petals*
- *Fabric flower petals*
- *Fabric pens*
- *Bowl or goblet filled with water*
- *Bowl filled with flower petals*
- *One bowl for each person being croned that they can keep*
- *One votive or tea light for each person*

Additional items for Sacred Space

- *Four small tables draped*
- *Votives, one for each new crone*
- *Copies of the responsive reading*
- *Music*
- *Extra material for decorating the thrones*
- *Pens and paper for journaling after the meditation*

Set Up

As this is a deeply meaningful and celebratory ritual, decorating in a way that enhances the sense of reverential, spiritual space is important. It sets the tone of the ritual, which may include laughter but also may embrace the deep sense of honoring that this transition deserves.

Two chairs for the crones were set at each direction and draped elegantly to look like thrones. Between the two thrones we placed a small table, draped with a cloth, with the direction candle and two votives placed upon it. The votives are for the two crones to light when directed to honor the decades that they are reviewing. More than one decade can be honored at each direction, depending on the age of the crone.

The Center direction was a candle in the center of the altar. A bowl filled with water and another bowl filled with flower petals were also in the center. Each new crone had an empty bowl before her. We gave them the empty bowls to keep so they could take their flower petals home, dry them and keep them with the fabric petals they received.

The women to be croned sat initially in the south-the seat of healing and shedding of the old-in order to emerge into the new.

NOTE: If the crones are over 50, group the decades at the first three directions to accomodate their ages.

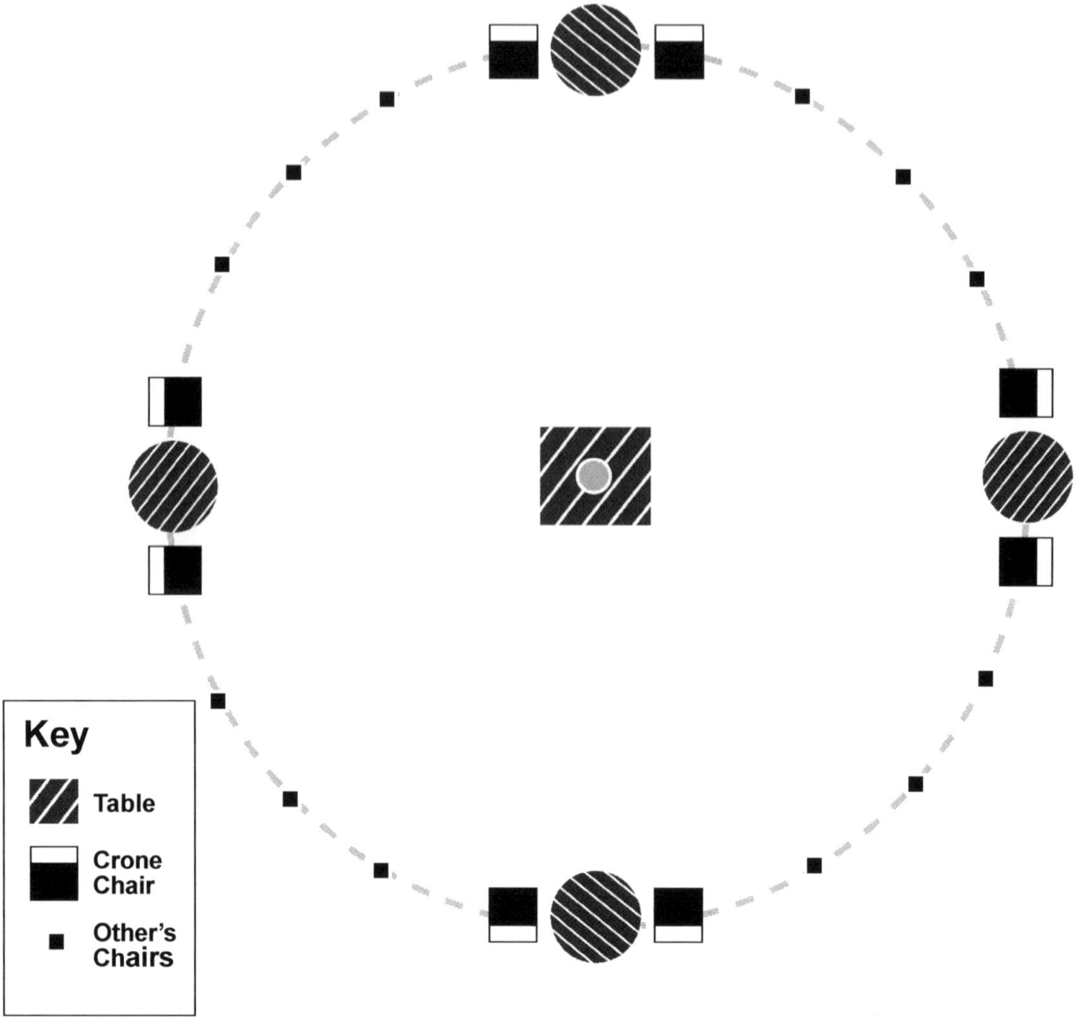

Calling the Directions

Light each direction candle as it is being read.

SOUTH:

Leader: Spirits of the South, Great Grandmother Serpent, be here with us tonight as we celebrate the transition of our sisters ________ and ________ from mother to crone.
Help them to shed the old that has become restricting and emerge into themselves as crones.

WEST

Leader: Spirits of the West, Mother-Sister Jaguar, be here with us tonight.
We celebrate the phases of all women, as maiden-to mother-to wise crone.
Tonight we ask you to be with us as we stalk the gifts of the wise elder.

NORTH

Leader: Spirits of the North, Brothers Condor and Eagle, be here with us tonight as we celebrate the croning of our sisters ________and ________.
Help us all to see the many facets of our lives, past and present, and how they have woven together.

EAST

Leader: Spirits of the East, Grandmother Hummingbird, Grandfather Dragon, be here with us tonight.
Guide our sisters that they may savor the gifts and the nectar of their lives and bring it forward into their crone-time to sustain and nourish them.
Help them to cherish their journey and the journey of all women.

CENTER

Leader: Sweet Mother, Earth Mother, we ask you to be here with us tonight as we crone your daughters ________ and ________.
Hold them gently in your embrace, be the ground upon which they can anchor their journey into wise crone.

Star Brothers and Star Sisters, Sun and Moon, Be here with us tonight as we celebrate change and growth.
Shine down upon our sisters and all of us.
Bless us with your love and compassion.
Guide us with your wisdom.

Meditation

Leader: It is good as we celebrate the croning of our sisters to also review our own journeys. In our meditation we will review each decade. Then, in silence, we will journal or draw. The meditation is twofold in focus. One is to reflect on those aspects of life and self that you want to leave behind as you enter crone-time. The second task at hand is to name what wisdoms and qualities you have learned in each stage that you want to bring forward into cronehood.

The meditation is at the end of the ritual. Pacing through the meditation is important. Please do not rush people through their reflections. It may help to count out each pause if you are unsure. Also, do not move into the ritual until everyone has stopped writing or drawing.

Ritual

Leader: There is a bowl of water in the middle of the altar and pebbles in front of you. As we call out the decades you may offer a pebble to the waters for all that you would like to release.

Also before you is a bowl of flower petals. We also have an individual bowl for each of you to gather your petals that represent all that you would like to carry forward into your crone-time, all that has nourished you and may continue to do so.

Blessing the Waters and Petals

Hold up the bowl with water.

Leader: May the waters cleanse and heal.

Replace the bowl onto the altar near the new crones.

Holdup the bowl with petals.

Leader: May this bowl of flower petals hold the treasures that guide you and keep you.

Replace the bowl onto the altar near the new crones.

Leader: You are sitting in the South, where we honor rebirth and healing. Serpent sheds her skin when it becomes restricting and limiting. She goes through a process of gathering her resources and strengths, her eyes become clouded and she is withdrawn and reflective. The old skin gradually falls off and she emerges, the same but new, a new presentation of herself. And so you, too, begin

Leader: __________ and __________ please light the candle before you to represent the first two decades of your lives. First Crone (name), what would you like to release from the decade of birth to 9 years old? You may gather some pebbles from the altar and as you place each one in the bowl of water, name what it is that you are shedding.

Pause while she names what she is releasing.

Leader: And collecting some flower petals, place some in your bowl to represent the treasures and gifts you would like to bring forward into your crone-time.

Pause while she names what she is bringing forward.

Leader: And again, with the pebbles, what would you like to release from the decade of 10 to 19 years old?

Pause

Leader: And with the flower petals, what would you like to bring forward to guide and sustain you?

We paused as we shifted everyone's attention to the other new crone to give space to a conscious shifting.

Repeat the sequence above for the second crone.

The goal is for each crone to have the opportunity to proceed at her own pace through each decade.

Leader: Now we ask you to move to the chairs in the West. You may light the candles to honor the decades of your 20's and 30's. Jaguar helps us stalk our medicine, our gifts and talents. She is fiercely protective of her young and a superb huntress. She gathers her resources and uses her skills to nourish and sustain herself and that which she has birthed. Now it is your turn to stalk the gifts that you gathered and cultivated during this time and to release all that you learned that is no longer helpful. Please light the candles before you to honor these two decades.

Leader: __________, gathering your pebbles, what would you like to release from the decade of your 20's?

Pause

Leader: And gathering your flower petals, what is it that you like to bring forward?

Pause

Leader: And again, gathering your pebbles, what would you like to release from the decade of your 30's?

Pause while she names what she is releasing.

Leader: Using the petals, what would you like to gather into your cronehood?

Pause while she names what she is bringing forward.

Then pause briefly as you shift your attention to the second crone. Repeat these decades for the second crone as shown above.

Pause

Leader: Now we would like you to move to the chairs in the North. Please light the candle next to you to honor the decades of 40's and 50's.

Pause

Leader: North is a time of reflection, a time when the old is reforming and the new is shaping. Condor and Eagle hold for us the ability to see from a different perspective, to have a vision of the larger whole and our place in it. They are able to soar to lofty heights, observe keenly, and swoop down to earth, to 'catch' what they have seen. It is your turn to revisit these decades with a fresh vision, catch what you would like to bring forward and leave behind whatever you please.

Leader: __________, gather your pebbles. What would you like to release from your 40's?

Pause while she names and releases

Leader: And gathering your flower petals, what would you like to bring forward to guide and sustain you?

Pause while she gathers the petals

Leader: What would you like to leave behind from your 50's?

Pause while she names and releases

Leader: And what would you like to bring forward?

Pause

Repeat these decades for the second crone as shown above.

Leader: And now we invite you to move to the thrones in the East. We all light our candles to honor and celebrate your transition into your crone-time.

Each participant lights the candle closest to her. The lighting candle may travel around the circle ceremoniously.

Leader: The East is a time of re-emerging and beginnings. Just as the spring emerges each year, you too now emerge as crone. Hummingbird and Dragon reside in the East. Hummingbird is blessed with many gifts. She can fly long hours and has an uncanny ability to seek out what nourishes her. She drinks with abandon to sustain herself on her long journey. Dragon walks with great courage, breathes fire, walks gently.

As you emerge as crone, a new presentation of yourself, you also travel as Hummingbird and Dragon. Walk with courage and gather the nectar around you to sustain you on your crone journey.

Leader: Sister crones, let us help ____________ and ____________ gather nectar and crone-wisdom. On the table you will see many silk flower petals. Please pick up one for each new crone and write upon it the gifts and blessings you wish to give to them.

Pause. Allow enough time for each participant to write and reflect if needed. We used fabric pens to write with.

Leader : And now, we will go around and gift __________. You may say something like "I bless you with ..." or "I gift you with ..."

Go around the circle as each person names the qualities that she is giving as crone wisdom.

And now we will go around and gift __________.

Go around the circle again as each person names the qualities she is giving as crone wisdom.

Leader: ____________ and ____________, newly born Crones, through the years you have taken many journeys. Now you are on an exciting new path, traveling to a new expression of self, one of strength and beauty. We are happy to be with you as you travel this new path on the spiral of life.

Pause for a brief moment.

Responsive Reading

Leader: We have a responsive reading to share. I will read the lower case words and all of you will read the upper case words for this responsive reading.

Leader: Friends let us hear the words of Wisdom from ancient times
Words that have come down to us from the wise old women:

All: THE CRONE
THE WITCH
THE GRANDMOTHER
THE GODDESS

Leader: Let us hear their words that have proved true by the experiences of all the peoples of the world:

All: LIVE IN PEACE
RESPECT NATURE
KNOW THYSELF
LOVE ONE ANOTHER

Leader: Wisdom is learned:

All: WISDOM MUST BE PASSED ON
GENERATION UNTO GENERATION.

Leader: Only those who are foolish ignore the Wisdom of the ages:

All: FORGET NOT THE LAWS OF THE CRONE GODDESS
FOR THEY WILL BRING PEACE AND SERENITY.

Leader: The ways of wisdom are the ways to happiness and all Her paths are peaceful:

All: A LONG LIFE
IS IN HER RIGHT HAND
IN HER LEFT HAND
ARE HEALTH AND WEALTH.

Leader: Wisdom is a wise old woman, and the ways of Wisdom are easy to understand:

All: CHOICES AND OPTIONS AND PATHS
PONDER EACH, AS YOU FIND YOUR WAY.

Leader: Wisdom is a wise old woman, and the value of Wisdom is far above rubies:

All: SHE WILL DO YOU GOOD, NOT EVIL
ALL THE DAYS OF YOUR LIFE.

Leader: Wisdom is a wise old woman, and strength and honor are Her clothing:

All: SHE OPENS HER MOUTH WITH LOVE
AND IN HER TONGUE IS THE LAW OF KINDNESS.

Leader: Wisdom is a wise old woman, and Her children rise up, and call Her blessed:

All: FOR SHE HEALS THE ILL,
TEACHES THE IGNORANT,
CARES FOR THE MOTHERLESS
AND HONORS PEACE.

Leader: So, as you seek your values, your morals, your goals
As you find your principles, your beliefs, and your truths:

All: HONOR WISDOM
OR YOU WILL FLOUNDER

Leader: For Wisdom is a wise old woman
Listen to Her words and be free:

All: BLESSED BE.

It is important to pause here for a moment so the reading may be held in silence and reflection.

Thanking and Releasing the Directions

Snuff each direction as it is being read.

SOUTH

Leader: We thank the Spirits of the South, and Great Grandmother Serpent for Her blessing us tonight

WEST

Leader: We thank the Spirits of the West and Mother-Sister Jaguar for Her blessing us tonight

NORTH

Leader: We thank the Spirits of the North and our Brothers Condor and Eagle for blessing us here tonight

EAST

Leader: We thank the Spirits of the East and Grandmother Hummingbird and Grandfather Dragon for blessing us here tonight.

CENTER

Leader: We thank the Spirits of the Center, Mother Earth, Our Star Brothers and Sisters and the Sun and Moon for blessing us here tonight.

Leader: Blessed Be

Meditation

Decades of Your Life

Begin to settle in and breathe, allowing your awareness to move to your breathing as it will..... noticing the inhale.......the exhale.......knowing that as you focus on your breath, you are gradually entering a place of great spaciousness and light.........a place where there is just noticing............noticing with openness and compassion your own process.

Pause. If the participants seem a bit restless you may guide them to focus on the breath again.

And, gradually a scene of a place outdoors begins to arise......it is night.....and the moon is full.....a path is before you, lighting your way............there is a sweet and pungent aroma in the air.......the night is warm and the air soft against your skin............and you come to a large tree..... silvery and soft in the moonlight..........it whispers on the breeze........it is safe daughter.....come and look....you are free to enter....you are of me and protected.....and so it is that you see a large hole in the tree...........you look in and see a ladder going down.......remembering the words of the tree, you climb down....... unafraid but curious.....At the bottom there is a door with a bright brass knob.......It shines and is cool to your touch......And so turning the knob.......the door opens easily.....and you are welcomed with a beautiful landscape of flowers, green fields and tall elegant trees..... There are birds singing and the smell of the grasses and flowers wafts gently on the breeze.....The sun is warm on your skin...... there is the hum of bees and crickets in the backround........

Pause

You walk along a path that takes you toward the water.....perhaps a lake or stream...... or the ocean.....let this arise for you in its own way...............There is a magical quality about this place.......... ....peaceful and safe..... a place for reflection and learning that is filled with the qualities of the heart.......compassion,.............and unconditional love..........and they bring a radiance and sparkle to all that is here........

As the place becomes more and more familiar...........you notice a figure sitting on a rock by the water.......it is an older woman....a crone......and she seems very familiar..... she is about your size......your coloring....and she is sitting in a position that you often take......

You approach her...eager and curious......and as she turns to you, you realize that you are looking at yourself as the crone you will be..........And she opens her arms to greet you.......warmly as an old friend would do........

Take a minute to notice her....how does she look.......dress.......what colors is she wearing.....notice her touch.....smell.....her speech....

She offers to sit with you as you review the decades of your life.........perhaps guiding or listening.....

She shows you pebbles scattered about and a bowl of water for the events or feelings you would like to release or to let go of your attachment to as they no longer serve you.......

and a bowl surrounded with brightly colored flower petals for the strengths and insights from each decade that you would like to bring forward into your cronehood....

And so you sit with your inner crone........ with your pebbles and flower petals

pause

And so, looking back to your early years.....0-9.........remembering.............. reflecting on what these were like for you.........what events or memories would you like to release with your pebbles....imagining you can gather as many pebbles as you need.

Short pause here so they may reflect a moment

and what qualities or insights you would like to bring forward into your cronehood ......again gathering flower petals for the qualities that you would like to bring forward..... ....

Short pause

Continue reviewing, now your teen years, from 10-19............reflect for a moment....... what would you like to release from these years......offering it to the sacred waters..............

Short pause

and what would you like to gather and bring with you into cronehood?

Pause

And now your twenties....again pausing to remember.......what were your twenties like? Your early twenties......... mid twenties, late twenties.....
What events or qualities from your twenties would you like to release.................

Short pause

and what qualities or insights would you like to bring forward........

pause

Moving into your thirties......what were these like.......again gathering your pebbles and noting what it is that you would like to release to the healing waters.

Short pause

and collecting your flower petals, what is it that you would like to bring forward.

Short pause

And now into your forties........what were you doing in your forties..........what would you release into the waters

short pause

And what is it that you would bring forward into your cronehood

pause

And your fifties.......gathering the pebbles, what from your fifties would you like to shed or let go of?

pause

And gathering flower petals, what wisdoms and insights would you like to bring forward into your crone wisdom?

pause

And for those of you that this applies....look back at your sixties..........remembering and reflecting on the events and times of your sixties......
What would you like to release?

And what would you like to bring forward?

And again, for your seventies,
And for your eighties and nineties.

Slightly longer pause here, to transition into a new phase of the meditation.

And so, gathering your pebbles and petals........it is time for you to thank your friend, your inner crone, for accompanying you......She asks you to take your thoughts and feelings with you, as they are needed and will help you in the coming ritual.......and so you say goodbye ....in whatever way feels right for you.......
and you return on the path.....through the field of flowers and the door........open and waiting for you.......you walk through and up the ladder and out of the hole in the tree trunk..........into the moonlit night....and here you may begin to gently bring your awareness to your breathing.......once again noticing the breath moving in.........and the breath moving out.........and now a big breath in........and a slow exhale out.........

beginning to be aware of the way you are sitting…….how this feels………noticing if any part of your body would like to stretch……and doing so ….. enjoying the motion……And as you are ready….you may open your eyes…..looking around the room gently……..and taking one more deep breath in…and out…..return to our circle……awake and relaxed.

And as you are ready you may journal or draw your experience.

SR 2009

Teaching Rituals

Offering rituals for people who are new to earth-based spirituality, or new to these types of rituals is something that Sandy and I enjoy very much. We feel it is important for newcomers to have a positive introduction to the concept of rituals that are experiential and earth-honoring. It is similar to introducing a kindergartner to school. The initial experiences of children will continue to color how they see school, just as a teaching ritual will influence how newcomers to earth based ritual feel about ritual.

We included two teaching rituals, one for children and one for adults. Both of them were given at our church and well received by the participants who were curious to learn.

The children were especially adept at connecting with their stone person and able to see all of life as filled with Spirit and a manifestation of the Sacred.

Facilitating and guiding newcomers to earth based rituals through a ritual that touches their spirits is important and necessary work.

The Basics of Earth-Based Ritual

Note

We were asked to offer a ritual for one of the regularly scheduled lay-led summer Sunday Services offered at our Unitarian Universalist Church. We used two leaders because there are two separate roles to be played. One is the Teacher and the other is the Ritualist. Although this ritual is organized around the UU Principles and Sources of Faith, that part of the teaching can be adapted to fit your needs.

Theme

This is an earth-centered ritual that honors and cultivates our connections with all of our brothers and sisters: the two leggeds, the four leggeds, winged beings, the creepy-crawlies, the sea creatures, the plant beings and the stone people, all who live on or within Mother Earth.

Sources of Inspiration

We caste the circle in a Wiccan manner calling the cardinal directions.The smudging or cleansing of each person was in the Native American tradition. The stone ritual was adapted from the traditions of the indigenous peoples of the Andes. The meditation was in the Buddhist tradition and is one of the core meditation practices of this path.

Altar

- *Altar cloth*
- *Candles for the directions*
- *Matches*
- *Snuffer*
- *Smudge stick or sweet grass braid in an ashtray or something suitable*
- *Votive candle for lighting the smudge stick*
- *Talking stick that may be a stone or a special stick such as a rain stick*
- *Bowl or basket of stones*

Additional items for Sacred Space

To make the room look more festive we put flowers and candles on windowsills and other places where appropriate.

Introduction

Teacher: It is an important part of the Unitarian Universalist principles to affirm and promote the inherent worth and dignity of every person and that includes our selves. Another important principle is to see ourselves as part of the interconnected web of life. We are drawing from the Sources of Faith, which are part of the Unitarian Universalist Principles, when we connect with the "Spiritual teachings of earth-centered traditions that celebrate the sacred circle of life and instruct us to live in harmony with the rhythms of nature." As UU's we also draw "on the wisdom of the world's religions which inspire us in our ethical and spiritual life". Our ritual today is a teaching ritual that draws on many sources of the world's religions. We present them to you in the form of an earth-centered ritual that honors and cultivates our connections with all of our brothers and sisters: the two leggeds, and also the four leggeds, the winged creatures, creepy-crawlies, sea creatures, the plant beings and the stone people, all who live on or within Mother Earth.

The customs of earth-centered traditions differ from country to country, from group to group. What they have in common is the concept that Spirit (or God or Goddess or whatever name suits you) resides within each person and within each thing in nature. Everything is an expression of Spirit and is Spirit. Each expression of Spirit carries qualities and gifts of its own. The Earth Herself is Spirit and in some traditions is seen as the body of the Goddess. So, Spirit is at once something within all things and outside all things. The Wiccan tradition and most traditions have customs and practices about how a ritual should be done. As Unitarians we respect these customs, but we feel that adapting practices without losing the intent of the practice is allowed.

Ritual creates a safe space, a sacred space, in which everyone and everything is respected. All of life is held as sacred. Ritual helps us to connect with this, through experiential practices, meditation, chanting or singing, and a variety of traditional activities. In the spirit of UU earth based ritual, we will caste a circle in a Wiccan manner calling the cardinal directions. The smudging or cleansing of each person is in the Native American tradition. The stone ritual is adapted from the tradition of the indigenous peoples of the Andes. The meditation is in the Buddhist tradition, and is one of the core meditation practices of this path. It helps us grow and nourish all those thoughts and feelings and actions that are compassionate, non-judgmental and loving of all of life and of ourselves.

Smudging

Ritualist: Smudging is an ancient tradition practiced around the world and found in many Native American traditions, in the use of incense in many Judeo-Christian practices, and in the work of shamans in most indigenous cultures. The substance used in indigenous cultures differs from group to group, but the intent is the same. The smoke from burning herbs is used to cleanse and clear the energy of a place or person. It is believed that the smoke can move through all the energies of creation, thus moving heavier, unwanted energies to Spirit. Today we will use Palo Santo, an herb from the wood of a tree in South America, and sweetgrass from North America that is used to draw in positive energies. We start with this as a preparation for the ceremony, to create a purity of intent to honor the sacred in a good way.

In deference to those who might be sensitive to smoke or scents, we will step outside to light the herbs. You will be smudged first with the palo santo to cleanse, then with the sweetgrass to bring in positive energies. Afterwards return to your seat. We ask you to do this in silence.

One leader will smudge with Palo Santo and the other with the sweetgrass.

Calling the Directions

Teacher: In most earth-based traditions, the earth and all her creatures are considered sacred. Everyday life is closely linked to the cycles and rhythms of the natural world. These cycles and rhythms are seen as circular and associated with the four directions, the archetypes, the seasons of the year, and the phases of life. Almost all of life can be seen as participating in this circle of ever-revolving cycles. So the altar forms a circle. Where one starts in the circle for casting depends on the tradition.

We will be starting in the East, which represents air, birth, spring, and the mind. In the traditions of the Andes the archetypes of Condor and Eagle represent clear vision.

As we move around the wheel, we come to the South which represents fire, summer and the growth of the new beginnings which start in the spring. Also in the South from the Andes, Great-grandmother Serpent represents change and healing.

Next we come to the West, representing water, maturity, the season of autumn and the harvest. In the Andes the West is given the archetype of Jaguar, who represents family and stalking our medicine.

And we continue around to the North, which represents earth, winter and the time of introspection and reflection. The archetypes of Hummingbird and Dragon are associated with courage and the sweetness and sustenance of life.

The Center is always addressed, and represents the center of being, the Great Goddess. In the Andean tradition the Center is represented by our Star Brothers and Sisters, by the sun and moon, and Mother Earth, Pachamama. This is the core that is all things.

Casting calls for the Spirits and blessings of the cardinal directions to come and hold sacred space for our ritual. Today, we call the directions in the Wiccan tradition.

Please stand.

Calling the Directions

Light each candle as you read the direction

EAST

Ritualist: Goddesses and Gods of the East, of beginnings and the spring, of air and flight, thoughts and musings, be here with us tonight.
Help us to soar and see with fresh eyes the shifting dualities of our existence and the core of our wholeness.

SOUTH

Ritualist: Goddesses and Gods of the South, of fire, warmth, growth and summer, of nurturing and moving towards fullness, of change and passion, be here with us tonight. Help us to tap the strength of your vitality.

WEST

Ritualist: Goddesses and Gods of the West, of water and autumn, of ripening wisdom, maturity and the pleasures of the harvest, be here with us tonight.
Cradle us and hold us in the richness of your bounty.

NORTH

Ritualist: Goddesses and Gods of the North, of the earth, of quiet and winter and the deep inner stillness that replenishes and nourishes our inner life, be here with us tonight.
Watch over us and help us to live from our inner spirit in the outer world, knowing wholeness and acceptance from within.

CENTER

Ritualist: Great Goddess and God of the Center, of above and below, of the circle that embraces and unifies our many rhythms and cycles, be here with us tonight.

Let Love and Compassion become the current that carries us forward and leads us into a knowing of our true essence, our true nature.

Ritual

Teacher: The stone ritual is adapted from the many indigenous cultures in which the stone spirit held the knowledge of the ancients. Stones are old, slow to change, and are seen by most cultures as grounded, centered sages of the earth. They are those that observe, take in, hold all that occurs, and offer this knowledge to those who come to receive in a good way. Stones are symbols of these qualities in cultures worldwide. We go to the mountains for a retreat. Mindfulness meditations use the mountain as a symbol of stability and centeredness. Indigenous cultures world-wide go to their respective "sacred mountains" on pilgrimages, vision quests, and to worship.

Ritualist: Today we will have a ritual of the stones. They have been gathered in ceremony and with great respect. We will pass this bowl of stone people around. As you receive this bowl, place your hand over the stones. Sense them for just a moment. They may offer you a memory or thought about a time in your life of peace or insight. Please share this with the group, if you would like. You may also remain silent. Please remain with your hand over the bowl as the energy of the moment will infuse the stone people. In deference to all who are here, we ask that you be brief.

Pass bowl. When it goes around the full circle hold it up and say:

Ritualist: This bowl is filled with the love and beauty of all those in our gathering today, and the love and wisdom of the ages. We will pass this around again and I invite you to share in the power of love and connection to all of life by taking a stone. You may see this as your connecting stone, and your loving kindness stone. I invite you to hold the stone as we do the meditation this morning.

Pass the bowl again.

Meditation

Teacher: In a moment, you will be guided verbally through the Loving Kindness Meditation.

The intent of this meditation is to send loving kindness to yourself, to someone you care about, to someone you may be annoyed or irritated with, and then to our entire community.
There are four phrases that are repeated silently during the meditation.

The first phrase will be: May I find safe haven. This refers to freedom from the torments of the external world such as violence, fear, or greed. It is a request of Spirit to be free from the things that bring hurt and harm to yourself or someone else.

The second phrase will be: May I have peaceful mind. This refers to freedom from the mental/emotional sufferings that plague most of us. We all have worries, thoughts, and patterns that keep us stuck and unhappy. It is a request to be free from this state of mind.

The third phrase will be: May I have harmony with my body. This is a prayer for physical well-being and peace with our physical state. It asks that we might act in ways that will help bring this about.

The fourth phrase will be: May Loving Kindness manifest throughout my life. This is an intention for balance and harmony in our everyday life. It asks that loving-kindness be a part of our relationships with friends, teachers, family, and weave through the daily-ness of our life.

Ritualist: And so making yourself ready for meditation, finding a comfortable position, either closing your eyes or leaving them open as is comfortable for you.
And bring to your awareness a time or event when you felt a great love and a deep sense of compassion or kindness. Imagine that this can flow from your heart like a beautiful stream of light that you can send out at will.

And first sending this beam of the light, of loving kindness to yourself, letting it fill and nourish you.
Repeating after me silently:

May I find safe haven
May I have peaceful mind
May I have harmony with my body
May Loving Kindness manifest throughout my life.

And now, bringing to your awareness a name or image of someone that you love and sending this beam of light to them, repeating after me silently:

May this person find safe haven
May this person have peaceful mind

May this person have harmony with their body

May Loving Kindness manifest throughout this person's life.

And now, bringing to your awareness someone that you may be annoyed or irritated with. It may be someone you know or a public figure, and send a stream of loving kindness to them.

Repeating after me silently:

May this person find safe haven

May this person have peaceful mind

May this person have harmony with their body

May Loving Kindness manifest throughout this person's life.

And now, beaming the light of Loving Kindness out to our Community.

May all of us find safe haven

May all of us find peaceful mind

May all of us have harmony with our bodies

May Loving Kindness manifest throughout all of our lives.

Pause here to allow people to rest in the energetic and intention that has been created during the meditation

Leader: And now, as you are ready, returning your awareness to this place. Breathing deeply and consciously, opening your eyes as you are ready, adjusting your position as needed.

Talking Stick

Ritualist: The talking stick is a Native American tradition, with a few simple rules. Whoever holds the stick may speak. No one else speaks unless they are given the stick. The rest of us offer the holder of the stick our attentive and compassionate listening. This is our gift to the stick-holder. Everything that is spoken in circle is confidential. You may share whatever joys and sorrows you wish or you may talk about what came up for you in the meditation or you can pass the stick without speaking.

Thanking and Releasing the Directions

Snuff each candle as you red the direction

Teacher: In all traditions, when the ceremony is over, the directions and archetypes are thanked.

EAST

Ritualist: We thank the Goddesses and Gods of the East and release them.

SOUTH

Ritualist: We thank the Goddesses and Gods of the South and release them.

WEST

Ritualist: We thank the Goddesses and Gods of the West and release them.

NORTH

Ritualist: We thank the Goddesses and Gods of the North and release them.

CENTER

Ritualist: We thank the Goddess and God of the Center and release them.

Blessed Be! The circle is open but unbroken.

Earth-based Ritual for Children

Note

Laurel Whitehouse, Religious Education Director at First Parish in Wayland, worked with us on developing and offering this ritual for the kids.

Theme

This ritual is to introduce children to earth based ritual and the shamanism of the Andes Mountains in Peru. In the Andes the mountains and the stones are important keepers of the spiritual energies and wisdoms. The kids loved this ritual and were intuitively attuned to seeing the sacred in all things and being able to listen to the teachings of their medicine stones.

Sources of Inspiration

Suzanne has been studying Andean Shamanism for many years, from Ginny Elsenhans, a shaman trained in the Andean traditions. Sandy has been studying for several years with Suzanne. We have borrowed from our knowledge and experiences in the practices that we first learned to structure this ritual. These practices have formed the foundation for our continued practice and growth. They are core practices in our spiritual lives and the lives of others.

Selecting the stone people was in itself a spiritual practice. Sandy and I went to a favorite beach nearby, opened sacred space by calling the directions, and called out to the stone people our need, asking who would like to come forward to teach the children. We gathered those that came forward, left an offering in thanks and closed space in a manner that expressed our gratitude to the spirits of the directions.

Altar

- *Book, If You Find a Rock, by Peggy Christian*
- *Direction Candles and snuffer*
- *Basket of stone people, enough for each participant*
- *Matches*

- *One larger stone person for children to put their wishes in*
- *Bowls of herbs*

Here are some suggestions

sage-carries prayers and thanks to Spirit, removes negative energies

lavender-calming, brings peaceful state, draws positive. energies to us

lemon balm-invigorating and refreshing, cleanses

sweetgrass-helps to shift negative emotions, calls positive influences forward

cedar-protection, shifts negative emotions, draws up earth energy, grounding

mugwart-moves energy, loosens and moves stuck energy, clears

tobacco-increases communication with Spirit and nature

- *small paper sack to place herbs in, one for each participant*

Additional items for Sacred Space

Paper

- *Crayons or pencils for drawing their special stone*

Set Up

We invite you to use any additional items to enhance the feeling of a quiet reverential space. You may want to turn over the soil in a special place outside so that the children can easily offer their herbs to earth by burying them. If this is not feasible fill a large bowl with earth and have them offer their bundles there.

Grounding

The goal here is to help the children settle down and move into a more quiet space. Explain to them that by stomping their feet on the ground they can send their itchiness into Mother Earth, who will take it away. One such exercise is to have them stand and stamp their feet three times, clap their hands on the earth three times, stamp their feet again three times. Then invite them to take a deep breath and be seated.

Calling the Directions

Light each candle as you read the direction

EAST

Leader: We welcome the Spirit of the East, of Air, that helps Mother Earth by spreading the seeds of flowers so that they can grow.

SOUTH

Leader: We welcome the Spirit of the South, of Fire, that warms us and helps the seeds grow.

WEST

Leader: We welcome the Spirit of the West, of Water, that nourishes all growing things.

NORTH

Leader: We welcome the Spirit of the North, of Stones, that hold our wishes and wisdom.

CENTER

Leader: We welcome the Spirit if the Center, who resides in our hearts to calm us when we need it and that fills us with love for all of life.

Story

We read the story <u>If You Find a Rock</u>, by Peggy Christian

Ritual

Leader: This stone person is a wishing rock. We will pass it around the circle and each one may make a silent wish and blow it onto the rock.

Pass the stone person around the group

Leader: Many cultures honor the earth and have ceremonies and celebrations to Mother Earth. They also go to Mother Earth for help, they honor how our food comes from her body-all our fruits, vegetables and grains grow in the earth.

The animals eat the plants that grow in Mother Earth and they grow.

We eat these plants and animals so that we can grow. So we grow from the foods and nourishment that Mother Earth gives us.

We grow from the beauty that she surrounds us with. A beautiful lake or river or the beauty of spring as the flowers begin to bloom and the trees begin to get green again, these things feed our spirits.

One of the most important ceremonies that we have for Mother Earth is one of thanking her for all that she provides for us. It is an important aspect or rule that we give back to those who give to us. And so we give back thanks and good deeds to Mother Earth who gives so much to us.

We have here a basket of special stones. We call these stone people because they hold knowledge and spirit. Please pick a stone person that will hold your thanks and gratitude. This is your medicine stone.

If you have a collection of stones that you have found on your travels, or that are special to you, you may bring them in and share them with the kids. Explain that these stone people have found their place with you because they have stories or favorite memories attached to them. We did not script this because it is best done personally.

Leader: The Seneca Indians here in North America also work with stones as keepers of great knowledge. They have a whole system of "reading the stones" to receive the messages that they hold for us.

In the spiritual traditions of the high mountains of Peru, stones are the keepers of the great wisdom of the ancestors. They are like the books and libraries that we have. The mountains are the libraries and the stones are like the books of knowledge.

A mesa is a medicine bundle of stones. The shaman would have a mesa that he or she would use during healings, ceremony and for seeking advice from Spirit and connecting with the energy places on Mother Earth. The stones in a mesa are called coya's. Coya's are used to connect a person and the shaman to places in nature that are special.
Your thankfulness stone person may be the start of your collection of medicine stones. Each stone person that you collect on your wanderings outside will connect you to the place where you found it, a place that reminds you how beautiful Mother Earth can be.

When you go to these places in your imagination with your medicine stone, you will find answers or new ways of thinking about things that may be bothering you.
You may keep your stone as a way of connecting to Mother Earth and a special place that you have outside in nature.

I will teach you how to bring this place into your stone. Imagine such a place for you...... a place that is beautiful and one of your favorite places.... You may see an image of your place in your imagination, or hear sounds of this place......or hold the name of this place in your mind.

Pause

Now blow this into your medicine stone. Hold your stone for a moment.
Now you can draw your stone--for it is now your medicine stone.

Pass out paper and pencils or crayons so that each child may draw his or her stone. The children loved this exercise. Pull the group back together when it seems like they are ready, and announce the next part of the ceremony/class.

Leader: Now we are going to make medicine bundles of herbs to offer to Mother Earth. These are to give our thanks for all the many ways that She helps us, such as giving us food to eat; trees, stone and materials for our homes; lakes and woods for us to play in, and all the other things that make us healthy and happy. There are bowls on the altar filled with different herbs that are used by the people from around the world to make such bundles.

Here are some of the herbs that you can use:

lavender-calming, brings peaceful state, draws positive energies to us

lemon balm-invigorating and refreshing, cleanses

sweetgrass-helps to shift negative emotions, calls positive influences forward

cedar-protection, shift negative emotions, draws up earth energy, grounding

mugwart-moves energy, loosens and moves stuck energy, clears

tobacco-increases communication with Spirit and nature

sage-carries prayers and thanks to Spirit, removes negative energies

Then demonstrate how to make a bundle by placing some herbs in the small paper bag, rolling it shut, and tying it or putting a sticker on it to keep it closed.

Leader: So I will make my bundle first. When you are done making your bundles we will all go outside and bury them in the earth in a place that we have prepared for this.

It is nice if you can go outside to bury them. We could not, so we got a big bowl or container, filled it with earth and had the children bury it in the room. We told them that we would take the bowl and offer it outside to Mother Earth that afternoon.

Thanking and Releasing the Directions

Snuff each candle as you read the direction

EAST

Leader: We thank the Spirit of the East, of Air, for being with us.

SOUTH

Leader: We thank the Spirit of the South, of Fire, for being with us.

WEST

Leader: We thank the Spirit of the West, of Water, for being with us.

NORTH

Leader: We thank the Spirit of the North, of Stones, for being with us

CENTER

Leader: We thank the Spirit of the Center for being with us.

Appendix

Meditations

Chants

Chant: Oh Great Spirit

Oh, Great Spirit,
Earth, Sun, Sea and Sky
You are inside,
and all around me

see utube: Oh Great Spirit

Rituals: Yin and Yang Ritual
Full Moon Ritual

Chant: adapted from Lord of the Dance

Dance, dance, wherever you may be
I am the Queen of the Dance, you see!
I live in you, and you live in me
And I lead you all in the Dance, said She!

see utube: Lord of the Dance (for the melody)

Ritual: Celebrating the Dance of Life

Chant: adapted from: I walk the Rainbow Trail by Lisa Theil

Chanter: I dance the turning wheel
Participants: Hey eh yeah, the beauty way
Hey eh yeah, the beauty way.
Chanter: Dark to Light and Light to Dark
Participants: Hey eh yeah, the beauty way
Hey eh yeah, the beauty way

Chanter: I dance the turning wheel
Participants: Hey eh yeah, the beauty way
Hey eh yeah, the beauty way
Chanter: Fall to spring and spring to fall
Participants: Hey eh yeah, the beauty way
Hey eh yeah the beauty way.

see utube: I walk the Rainbow Trail

Ritual: Honoring the Ancient Wisdoms

Chant: **Air Her Breath**
Air Her breath
Fire Her spirit
Water Her blood and
Earth Her body

see utube: Earth My Body, beginning refrain

Ritual: Yule Candle Ritual
Honoring the Darkness

Chant: **May the Circle Be Open**
May the circle be open
But unbroken
May the love of the Goddess
Be ever in your heart
Merry meet
And merry part
And merry meet again

see utube: May the Circle Be Open

Rituals: The Summer Goddess of Playfulness
Yule Candle Ritual
Rebirth
Celebrating the Gifts of the Season
The Promise of Peace
Honoring the Gifts or Our Ancestors

Chant: **Nitche Tie Tie**
Nitche Tie Tie
Ennui
Or-en-eka, Oreneka
Hey hey, Hey hey
Oo..Iii

Ritual: Full Moon Fire (music page 356)

Chant: **We All Come From the Goddess**
We all come from the Goddess
And to Her we shall return.
Like a drop of rain
Flowing to the ocean

Hoof and horn
Hoof and horn
All that dies
Will be reborn

Seed and grain
Seed and grain
All that falls
Will rise again

see utube: We all come from the Goddess/Hoof and Horn

Rituals: Making Room for Rebirth
Communicating Through the Veil

Chant: **Om Mane Padmi Hum**
Om Mane Padme Hum

see utube: Om Mani Padme Hume-Original Temple Mantra Version

Rituals: The Promise of Peace

Music

Musical notation by Margo Hennebach

Printed in Great Britain
by Amazon

66520754R00208